# Mabon and the Guardians of Celtic Britain

# Mabon and the Guardians of Celtic Britain

## Hero Myths in the *Mabinogion*

## Caitlín Matthews

Inner Traditions
Rochester, Vermont

Inner Traditions International
One Park Street
Rochester, Vermont 05767
www.InnerTraditions.com

Copyright © 2002 by Caitlín Matthews

**Library of Congress Cataloging-in-Publication Data**

Matthews, Caitlin, 1952–
  Mabon and the guardians of Celtic Britain : hero myths in the
Mabinogion / Caitlín Matthews.
      p. cm.
Rev. ed. of: Mabon and the mysteries of Britain. 1987.
Includes bibliographical references (p. ) and index.
  ISBN 0-89281-920-0
  1. Mabinogion. 2. Tales, Medieval—History and criticism. 3. Arthurian romances—
History and criticism. 4. Tales—Wales—History and criticism. 5. Mythology, Celtic, in
literature. 6. Great Britain—In literature. 7. Heroes in literature. I. Matthews, Caitlín,
1952- Mabon and the mysteries of Britain. II. Title.
  PB2273.M33 M37 2002
  891.6'631—dc21

                                                            2002007635

Printed and bound in the United States at Lake Book Manufacturing, Inc.

10  9  8  7  6  5  4  3 2  1

Text design and layout by Priscilla Baker
This book was typeset in Legacy, with Aon Cari used for initials

*Epona Reginae Sanctae*
*Brehines Nef a Daear ac Uffern*

*Is this the land where the sleeper sleeps, the sleeper who shall wake, is he in his island cave—does Briareus guard him yet, are the single standing stones divinities about him? In this charged land of under-myth and over-myth where lord rests on greater lord and by lesser names the greater named are called . . . What ageless Mabon re-collects . . . the axile line of the first of the sleepers?*

DAVID JONES,
THE ROMAN QUARRY

# Contents

# Preface to the Second Edition

$\mathfrak{M}$abon and the Guardians of Celtic Britain and King Arthur and the Goddess of the Land, the two volumes that make up the Myth Book of Britain, are a study and reader's guide to the myths, romances, and legendary histories of the collection of texts called the Mabinogion. First published in the late 1980s, these two volumes have been out of print for a number of years. I am therefore delighted to present them to a new readership, especially because these stories are the earliest literary source of the ancient British gods and beings that so inspire the cultural and spiritual resurgence of our times.

Whether we consider the archaeological and historical field, or the pagan spiritual traditions, or even the many fantasy novels which relate to this material, one thing is certain: Without reference to the source texts, we have little understanding of these stories. Returning to "the horse's mouth" of the source texts, rather than referring to retold and sometimes garbled accounts from tertiary research, we return most completely to the core meaning of the myths so that we can discuss them both relevantly and with respect.

Many visitors to the potent land of Britain come to these shores in order to encounter the mythic presences that still throng the Island of the Strong Door, as this land is called in the Welsh texts. Their search is for the landscapes of King Arthur, the healing of the Grail, the ancient mysteries of the gods who walked these hills when stories were sung, not written down. All these myths are part of the *Mabinogion*. These stories are interwoven with the subtextual myth of Mabon, son of Modron. "Son" or "Son of Mother" is a title as old as the hills, nameless and numinous in our memory. This preexistent divine child was stolen from his mother's side when he was only three nights old. We do not know why he was stolen, we do not know who stole him; we are not told. But as we read the stories of the *Mabinogion*, we can reconstruct that legend and suddenly an immensity of wonder clutches our heart as we realize that this being predates time.

Mabon's myth is a kind of story template that recurs throughout British tradition and which may be seen in a larger and more comprehensible way through the myth of Arthur, who is hidden as a child to be reared under the magical fosterage of Merlin or the Lady of the Lake, and who is later removed to Avalon in order to be healed. The ones who are hidden or imprisoned in this way are invariably in the same mold—heroic warriors and battlers for the light of truth who defend the land and its people from ravages and incursions. They are part of a mythic sequence that can be decoded with the help of Mabon.

Mabon is that primal innocence and integrity which is our birthright. He is our joy, wonder, delight, and power; he is our wisdom, surety, passion, imagination, whatever qualities are slowly but certainly leached out of us as we grow up. Mabon represents whatever is lost and his track can be discovered only through the oldest animals and through the dragon-path legends of the land.

Many of those who visit Britain know little of Wales, the ancient principality that lies to the west. It is a land of rivers and mountains, of poetry and song. This is the ancestral homeland of the Cymru, the native Brythonic, Welsh-speaking people whose legends and stories became so prominent in medieval times that even the Norman French courts knew them and adopted them as their own, for they are the people who brought us King Arthur. The Welsh are justly proud of the *Mabinogion* and remember its myths well. Some of these myths and stories have parallels in the traditions of their Celtic cousins, the Irish and Scots; though these cousins speak Gaelic, a very different language from Welsh, we can still discern a family likeness in the characters of the Welsh gods and legends. If you want to understand these stories completely, visit the magical land of Wales and enter the numinous regions where the gods still walk and the stories are still sung. Living here in Rhydychan (or Oxford, as the English call it), a city once considered to be the center of ancient Britain, according to the story of "Lludd and Llefelys," I am aware of the dragons of the Island of the Mighty, infusing the whole of Britain with their primordial power. The dragon-paths of story run beneath my feet still and I am hungry to walk them as far as wind dries and rain wets, as far as the sun rises and the sea stretches, as far as the earth extends. May the mysterious beauty and ancient wisdom of these myths re-enchant your vision of this sacred isle, and lead you to discover the hallows of your heart.

# Preface to the First Edition

## Into the *Mabinogion*

Since its first translation into English in 1849, the *Mabinogion* has sat rather unhappily on library bookshelves; not quite fiction, not quite mythology, almost folk story and almost history, it has puzzled readers who like their books clearly categorized.

There are those who read it for its stories alone, and others who find insights into the wider fields of Arthurian criticism. But while there are scholarly commentaries aplenty for the patient and resourceful student, there is nothing for the general reader in search of instant demystification. Some of its stories are so spare that what is not written becomes an overwhelming obsession for the reader. Why does Rhiannon do nothing when unjustly accused of eating her son? Who is the father of Arianrhod's twin children? Why is Bran's head cut off and how does it still give comfort to his men? Why does Efnissien cause so much trouble? These questions are not easily answered. Yet by reference to the subtext of each story and by comparative study of other well-known and accessible stories within Celtic tradition, we can gain a glimpse of an answer. If the reader is prepared to trust the characters to tell him or her the answers to these and other questions, rest assured that they stand ready with the information.

Like the cauldron of Ceridwen, this book has been brewing for a long time. It has come out of deep familiarity with the stories themselves and their parallel sources. It is a workbook, intended for in-depth study of the archetypal characters within the *Mabinogion*.

*Mabon and the Guardians of Celtic Britain* concentrates on the most ancient stories of the *Mabinogion*, known as the Four Branches: "Pwyll, Prince of Dyfed"; "Branwen, Daughter of Llyr"; "Manawyddan, Son of Llyr"; and "Math, Son of Mathonwy"; concluding with the pivotal tale of "Culhwch and Olwen" and the story of "Taliesin" which, though it is not from the same manuscript sources, was nevertheless included within Lady Charlotte Guest's first English translation of the *Mabinogion*. These stories bear a family likeness to each other because they represent a venerable tradition which I have identified as the Mysteries of Mabon and Modron. This volume deals with Mabon, just as *King Arthur and the Goddess of the Land* tracks the appearances of Modron in the rest of the stories covering the legendary tales and the Arthurian romances.

These two characters make their appearance within "Culhwch and Olwen" and are no more spoken of within the *Mabinogion* except as a glancing reference, yet they are mysteriously present throughout the other stories as identifiable archetypes of the Wondrous Youth and the Great Mother.

A word on the method I have adopted for this book. I have treated the texts of the *Mabinogion* with the respect that tradition has distilled in its complex and fragmentary stories. Where a parallel folk tradition of similar proto-Celtic source is extant, I have not hesitated to use it, setting it side by side with the original story for the sake of comparison, but I have respected the original story and added nothing to it.

I am not of the school of folklorists who uphold the distribution theory of oral tradition. It is evident that while certain folk themes arise spontaneously worldwide, these are not derivative from each other, in the main. I have drawn extensively from Irish and Scottish Gaelic sources where they are representative of a long oral tradition. Irish and Welsh mythologies show a marked similarity, especially when compared with the *Mabinogion:* This may indicate extensive borrowing between the traditions or it may show how both stem from a pre- or proto-Celtic source common to the British Isles.

Where stories are fragmentary or when episodes have been muddled or just plain lost, I have resorted to the closest corroborative sources— the Welsh Triads[5] and British mythic, poetic, and historical tradition. Such reconstructions as I have attempted are clearly indicated, so the cautious reader need not be afraid of stumbling into academically boggy patches. These reconstructions are in no way definitive; they are put forward only as aids to understanding.

Readers may be astonished that I have occasionally drawn upon classical mythology in some of the comparisons, particularly in relation to the Mabon theme. Since the cult of Mabon was closely associated with that of the Romano-British Maponus, which was in turn partially derived from the cult of Apollo, these myths lend corroborative detail to an otherwise meager file of data. However, most of the Mabon argument is derived from native sources; the classical themes are given for comparison's sake because they provide a familiar mythological model for most readers. The frequently cited, though seldom explained, association of Rhiannon with Epona has also required some classical backup in order to prove their closer acquaintance.

Although the *Mabinogion* was transcribed in the Middle Ages, I have taken for granted the fact that it sprang from a venerable oral tradition of storytelling beyond which lay an even more ancient tradition: that of the British mysteries. The word *mystery* is usually understood as "an enigma," but I intend the term to convey "a mythic tradition which infuses and inspires the spiritual life of a people."

The British mystery tradition was in no way the highly organized and deeply syncretic religion such as flourished in Greece or Alexandria, but a set of myths with common themes and localized manifestations. The essential symbols and stories which comprise the British mysteries were never lost but merely relabeled when tribal religion was later incorporated and synthesized by both druidism and Christianity. These common, archetypal patterns and deities remain stubbornly embedded within the *Mabinogion*. As the Myth Book of Britain, we can regard the *Mabinogion* as a treasure trove of such sources, the earliest literary evidences that we have of an ancient tradition.

Those who have spent their academic years painstakingly brushing the dust of centuries from these stories may be shocked that I have not only taken them down from the shelves but have attempted to view them in a practical context. The problem is that I have never cared for museum exhibits. I like to touch objects, to handle them and know what their makers knew. It pains me to see medieval triptychs tucked into gloomy corners knowing that once they would have glowed with the devotion of the faithful and been windows to heaven. I like to see household gods propped up by the herb rack among the pots and pans of a real kitchen, not lodged uneasily in a glass case with other "cult objects."

I feel the same about these stories, both for their own sakes and because they are the genuine lode-bearing mythic ore of our native European mysteries. To understand a tradition, one must enter it, I have discovered. After all, Arthur Pendragon did not enter Annwfn in order to arduously acquire some antique plate for his castle walls, but to find and wield the hallows, the sacred emblems which confer sovereignty.

My only wish is that the reader may enjoy these stories with better understanding, and with some warm appreciation for those nameless storytellers who once memorized and told these tales so that we might read them today.

# Acknowledgments

The author acknowledges a great indebtedness to all those scholars who have spent lifetimes studying original texts, without whose translations this book could not have been written.

Especial thanks and love to John Matthews, who supplied additional material from his own field of study—the Arthurian corpus over which long and heated discussions have raged. It was due to the *Mabinogion* that we met in the first place, and it seems appropriate to acknowledge its power in the shaping of our lives, for without it we might now be pursuing separate careers of engulfing boredom. Thanks to him and to Annie König, who got this edition on the road by arduously scanning the typescript into something readable by computers!

To Gareth Knight, R. J. Stewart, Wolfe van Brussel, and the by now fabled Company of Hawkwood who helped bring Mabon back from the Underworld in 1985 and who are as worthy and fitting companions as any who entertained the Noble Head: Grateful thanks for help, encouragement, and assistance. May the birds of Rhiannon escort you to the Otherworld in harmonious melody at the conclusion of your story! Thanks to Chesca Potter for her inspirational art.

To Kathleen Herbert, deepest thanks for her translation of the extract in chapter 9 from the *Gesta Regnum Brittaniae;* this helped anchor one of the crucial arguments of the book.

My deep gratitude to Jon Graham, Elaine Sanborn, and all at Inner Traditions who enabled the production of this fully revised edition. Many thanks also to my agent, Regula Noetzle.

# how to Use This Book

I have assumed that you have bought this book in order to understand the *Mabinogion* more completely. Accordingly, I have attempted to give as much cross-reference to parallel texts, traditions, and important themes as possible so that a full range of resources is available. This is a vast topic to explore and the serious student is presented with the same problems which beset the archaeologist who has to excavate an important site before the bulldozers move in, noting different strata, isolated finds, and other significant information before the soil covers it once more.

Chapters 2–7 are arranged so that you can read through each story, note interesting or puzzling features in context, and refer more specifically, if you require, to parallel sources. To this end, each of these chapters has a short synopsis of the story in which will be found parenthetical numbered references that correspond directly to the numbered commentary that follows. The synopsis should not be substituted for a full reading of the text, so it will be necessary to have at hand a copy of your favored translation of the *Mabinogion*. Within the commentary are references to other stories and major themes either preceding or following it. Each chapter concludes with a discussion of parallel sources and major thematic archetypes.

This explorative study is intended as a workbook to be used as an adjunct to your own reading and research. A full list of texts and other source works appears in the bibliography, which is indexed in numerical order. These numbers are cross-referenced with numerals in superscript found in each chapter's commentary to provide the reader with source information for quoted material or for text related to a particular point in our discussion. At the end of the bibliography appear useful works published since the original edition of this book was created.

# A Guide to
# Welsh and Gaelic Pronunciation

The following is a rough guide for those who do not speak Welsh. The Welsh language, called Cymraeg, is still spoken throughout Wales as an everyday language and is used in Welsh enclaves the world over from Patagonia to New Zealand. Wales has its own administrative assembly, where government issues are discussed in Welsh, and its own Welsh language television and radio networks. All public documents and road signs in Wales must by law appear in both Welsh and English. It is an everyday, not a dying, language of great vigor.

Welsh is pronounced as it is spelled and is therefore more logical than English. Once the reader is aware of these few rules, the seemingly impossible names of the *Mabinogion*'s characters will be quite pronounceable.

1. The vowels, both short and long, are roughly equivalent to Italian sung vowels, with the exceptions of:

   u      as in *ill* or French *tu* (e.g., Culhwch: Kil'hookh)

   w      as in *look* (e.g., Gwri: Goo'ree)

   y      as in *pin* (e.g., Glyn Cuch: Glin Kikh)

   y      the definite article *y* and in first syllables of multisyllabic words, such as the *u* in *bun* (e.g., Yspaddaden: Uspatha'den)

2. Diphthongs are logically pronounced:

   ae, ai, ei      as in *fire* (e.g., caer: kire)

| | |
|---|---|
| wy | as in French pronunciation of Louis: Loo-ee (e.g., Creirwy: Kryr'oo-ee) |
| aw | as in *out* (e.g., Llaw: Hlou) |
| oe, oi | as in *boil* (e.g., Goe'win: Goywin) |

3. Consonants are pronounced as in English with the following exceptions:

| | |
|---|---|
| c | is always hard as in *cake* (e.g., Custennin: Kusten'in) |
| ch | is aspirated *kh* as in Scottish *loch* or German Bach (e.g., Gwalchmai: Gwalkh'my) |
| dd | is voiced *th* as in *there*, not as in *thin* (e.g., Lludd: Hlith) |
| f | is voiced *v* as in *vet* (e.g., Efnissien: Evniss'ien) |
| ff | is *f* as in *fat* (e.g., Fflur: Fler) |
| g | is a hard *g* as in *get* (e.g., Gereint: Ger'ynt) |
| ll | is *hl*; if you raise the blade of the tongue to the roof of the mouth behind the tooth ridge and blow "huh," this roughly approximates the sound (e.g., Llew Llaw Gyffes: Hlew Hlou Guff'es |
| r | is slightly trilled |
| rh | is *hr*; the *r* is slightly trilled (e.g., Rhia'nnon: Hriannon) |
| th | is as in *thin* (e.g., Twrch Trwyth: Toorch Trooeeth) |

4. The stress falls on the penultimate syllable of a multisyllabic word or on the first syllable of a two-syllable word.

Irish and Scottish Gaelic share a common proto-Celtic root with Welsh, but are very different languages with complex rules of pronunciation which are too lengthy to reproduce here. Pronunciation equivalents of only the major names from the text are given below. Stress occurs on the syllable before the apostrophe, usually on the first syllable of Gaelic words.

| | |
|---|---|
| *Balor* | bay'lor |
| *cailleach* | kal'yech |
| *Cú Chulainn* | koo hull'an |
| *geis* (pl. *geasa*) | gesh, gyas'a |
| *Lugh* | Loo'h |
| *Manannán* | man'ann-awn |
| *Nuadu* | noo'ah-a |

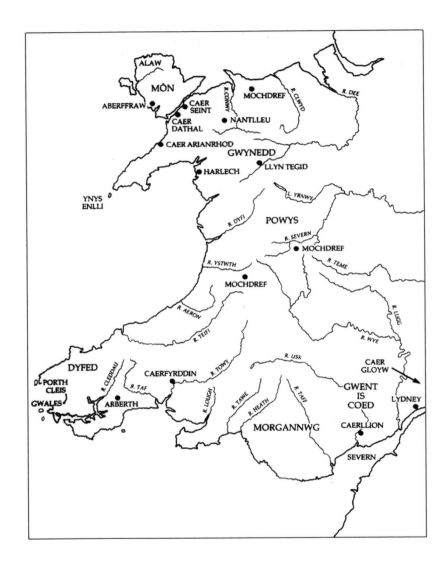

Figure 1. Wales and the *Mabinogion*

# 1

# The Realm of the *Mabinogion*

*For the Welsh to distinguish between myth and
history has always been a difficult exercise.*

EMYR HUMPHRIES

*Still lives on the ancient speech,
Still the ancient songs endure.*

JOHN CEIRIOG HUGHES

## The Welsh Storytelling Tradition

It is summer 1983, Caernarvon Castle, North Wales. Within the castle
grounds the timeless stories which form the Four Branches of the
*Mabinogion* are being presented by a bilingual team of actors, musicians, and storytellers. They are but the most recent in a long line of
storytellers who have helped transmit the *Mabinogion* from oral and
written tradition to the imagination of new generations. The audience
goes home in possession of a few fragments of a once mighty mystery
tradition in which men and women encounter the gods, animals talk,

leaves become gold, and the dead revive. A few may try to read the *Mabinogion* for themselves, puzzled, intrigued, and excited by the elusive hints which seem to dodge behind the main story just when revelation seems near. Many readers experience the same mixed emotions.

In order to untangle the complexity of the *Mabinogion*, it is necessary to understand that its stories arise directly from a lively oral tradition which, though it has parallels with the European chivalric cycles, ultimately derives from the folk traditions and mystery lore of Britain. It is the descendant of a venerable bardic tradition in which stories, poems, history, and ancestral lore were preserved in a professional though unwritten manner. We know from classical and Celtic sources that druids, poets, and storytellers taught their skills orally: They were never written down, although different forms of writing were in fact available.[71]

Why trouble to memorize the equivalent of a small library at all, it may be asked? To understand this we must realize that in the time of this tradition, one's word was one's honor; it still had the currency of authority, and learned and unlearned alike were equal under its wisdom. The oral education of Celtic society included all levels of learning: legal, genealogical, historical, prophetic, and religious—facets which are reflected in the *Mabinogion* itself and which put it outside modern categories of literature. But where once the druidic class had preserved the spiritual mysteries, in Christian times the ancient lore became the purview of the poet and storyteller. While this tradition was preserved freshly in many memories, as time wore on it began to lose touch with its roots. This is how we can distinguish traces of older belief within the stories which have come down to us.

The poet and the storyteller, who once shared professional status with the druid-kind (a class itself deriving from ancient shamanic tradition[71]) and preserved the old stories, slipped ever farther apart. The poet, or *pencerdd*, is represented in "The Dream of Rhonabwy" as chanting a eulogy which only another poet could understand; poetry had become technically arduous, its subtleties lost on the listener.

Noblemen in Wales retained such poets in their households well into late medieval times in order to eulogize their family and achievements and relate the complex genealogies by which the poet's lord might trace his bloodline to legendary kings. A pencerdd might not sing for common men; his fee was a high one, entitling him to honor and position. It is bards such as these—with an eye to the moneybags rather than their craft—that Taliesin satirizes so cruelly: "They sing vain and evanescent song."[2]

For ordinary mortals, a *teuluwr*, or household poet, might suffice, a bard who would sing in the lower hall while his superior, the pencerdd, sang to his lord and lady in the upper hall. Less honored even than teuluwr, the *clerwr*, or wandering minstrel, was musician and storyteller to outlying homesteads, something like the poor scholar in "Manawyddan, Son of Llyr," who comes from Lloegr, having begged his way: "I come from England, Lord, from song making," but whose fees amount to a mere pound.

The *cyfarwydd*, or storyteller, may not have retained the status of the pencerdd, yet he never lost his popularity, for his stories were always accessible to his listeners. Like the Irish *seanchai*, the cyfarwydd had a store of tales which were handed down from master to pupil orally. Through such an oral tradition we receive the *Mabinogion*—a collection of stories which had been current for centuries before they came to be written down. Although each story has been given different emphases by different storytellers, the results are often remarkably consistent, as tell the scattered manuscripts from which the diplomatic edition of the *Mabinogion* is derived. Interestingly, errors crept into the stories when copyists lost interest in their weary task. As is revealed below, from one such error the word *mabinogion* is derived.

Set against the formalism of court poetry, the mutations of the stories give a lively variety and colloquialism to an ancient oral tradition. Just as in the Welsh language, in which initial consonants mutate or *p* becomes *b*, *mh*, or even *ph*, so the stories of the *Mabinogion* shine with a changing iridescence of forgotten tradition, hinting at significant episodes yet simultaneously obscuring them. It is true that we have inherited a pied tradition from storytellers who had lost many of the inner keys, though memory may yet recall portions which are lost or hopelessly tangled.

The Welsh Triads, which have been collated by Rachel Bromwich from many manuscript sources,[5] give us a glimpse of the complex syllabus of bardic training and help enlighten many dark places in the *Mabinogion*. The triads are mnemonics for recalling stories; for example: three fearless men of the Island of Britain, three fortunate concealments of the Island of Britain, and so forth. They are training devices, keys to memory which, unfortunately for us, often merely serve to recall stories which tantalizingly hint at a deeper tradition but are now lost to us. The triads' terse style is due in part to professional bardic secrecy: The lines of each were a symbolic key evoking the story behind them. Their subject matter is reflected in the *Mabinogion*, where some of the stories are told and others hinted at.

"Three things that give amplitude to a poet: knowledge of histories, the poetic art, and old verse," says the *Llyfr Coch*, or *The Red Book of Hergest*—doubtless a triad which trainee poets imbibed at their first lesson.[5] The nature of many of the *Mabinogion*'s stories is historic, of national importance to the listener, but the triads constituted an index of oral tradition formed for the benefit of those whose professional duty it was to preserve and hand down the stories embodying the Britons' oldest traditions—stories concerning the national past alike of the people of Wales and of the lost northern territory, which was still remembered in the Middle Ages as a former home of the British race.[66]

When the storyteller parted company with the poet, the loss of many symbolic keys occurred and the mysteries implicit in the tales became more mysterious because they were removed from their common source. Of these mysteries we shall speak further.

The *Mabinogion* was formulated and eventually written down between about 1100 and 1250 C.E.—the very time in which the main Continental chivalric stories were likewise being recorded. Welsh storytellers were still practicing their skills when the Breton *conteurs* were influencing the course of European culture: The *lais* of Marie de France, the *minnesinger* cycles of Germany, and the romances of Chrétien de Troyes together with the *Mabinogion* are part of the European troubadour tradition, although we must not forget that the cyfarwydd drew on ancient bardic skills the function of which was educative, not merely entertaining.[140]

A partial text of the *Mabinogion* survives in the *White Book of Rhydderch* (c. 1300 C.E.), while the complete text appears in the *Red Book of Hergest* (c. 1400 C.E.). The story of "Taliesin" is contained in a seventeenth-century manuscript in the National Museum of Wales, itself a copy of a sixteenth-century manuscript. "Hanes Taliesin" is not considered part of the *Mabinogion* collection for reasons which will be discussed in chapter 7. These given dates do not preclude the stories occurring in earlier copies which are now lost to us, nor their derivation from the oral tradition in the manner described above. The Irish tales, which correspond in many particulars to those of the *Mabinogion,* began to be written down in about the ninth century. It is not known whether one or more hands were responsible for recording the stories, nor whether this person was a cyfarwydd. Certainly the *Mabinogion* may have been written while *cyfarwyddiadd* were actively practicing and even relating different versions of the recorded tales.

Storytelling did not cease with the introduction of books. It remains a lively tradition within many Celtic countries where impromptu assemblies of people inevitably conclude with mutual entertainment—stories, songs, and music. But at some point, the tales of the *Mabinogion* lapsed partially from memory, at least in the oral tradition. Until the first translation of the *Mabinogion* by Lady Charlotte Guest in the nineteenth century, even few Welsh people knew of its existence, although characters from the stories—Gwydion, Math, Arianrhod, Blodeuwedd, and Arthur—were remembered as individuals and recorded in poetry as examples of magicians, false wives, and famous kings. Inevitably, perhaps, memories grew shorter and tales grew more and more embellished with nonessential detail. Notably, in "The Dream of Rhonabwy" the writer concludes:

> This is the reason that no one knows the dream without a book, neither bard nor gifted seer [cyfarwydd]: because of the various colours that were upon the horses, and the many wondrous colours of the arms . . . the panoply . . . the precious scarfs, and of the virtue-bearing stones.

Lady Charlotte Guest's translation of the *Mabinogion* appeared in 1849. In W. J. Gruffydd's opinion, it was mostly the work of two scholars, Rev. John Jones and Rev. Thomas Price, who "devilled" for her.[46] It is to her that we owe the title of *Mabinogion*, which is a misnomer. Lady Charlotte concluded that *mabinogi* (the Four Branches were called *Pedeir Keinc y Mabinogi*) was a noun meaning "a story for children." *Mabinogion* appears once in "Pwyll, Prince of Dyfed" as a copyist's error; it is not a real word. Although purists may complain, the title *Mabinogion* is retained in this book as a matter of convenience. It is intended to include the full collection of stories: the Four Branches and other tales, and "Taliesin."

*Mabinogi* is more likely to parallel the Irish series of stories known as *macgnimartha*, the youthful or boyhood deeds of the hero. A fourteenth-century translation of an apocryphal gospel into Welsh, *De Infantia Jesu Christi*, was rendered as *Mabinogi Iesu Crist*.[25] Lady Charlotte's explanation of the term puts these tales in the same category as children's fairy stories—a far remove from their original purpose.

There is still much scholarly argument over the true meaning of the title, but we do not miss the mark if we consider the stories as part and parcel of the Celtic genres of story which have an authenticated history in Irish tradition: the stories of the conception, birth, adventures, cattle raids, elopements, courtships, and deaths of heroes.[87]

Many more translations of the stories have appeared since Lady Charlotte's attempt. A list of these can be found in the bibliography. Throughout this book a variety of editions and translations have been quoted.

## The Name of the Land

The *Mabinogion* is such an essentially Welsh cultural product that few consider it a source for British mythology. In most minds, Wales is virtually a foreign country with an alien, off-putting language. But to Welsh minds, Wales is the only remaining outpost of the Island of the Mighty, Ynys Prydein, the Island of Britain. Names are important in oral tradition, and the name of the land is of paramount importance. A fleeting glimpse at the early history of Wales will show even the most chauvinistic Englishman the rights of the matter of sovereignty. Wales is not an alien land generously taken under English patronage, but rather a kingdom whose legendary rulers once held sway over what is now English soil.

We say that when a monarch reigns wisely, he or she has the sovereignty of the land. This has come to mean that the monarch rules according to the laws which he or she imposes (from the French *sovrain*, "one who is supreme"). However, behind this notion is the personification of the land by a mythical female figure. The monarch holds the land by right of his union with her and by his championship of her freedoms and privileges over which he lawfully presides. Land and king must be in harmony, as husband and wife. (A female monarch embodies and personifies the figure of Sovereignty in her own person; the prince-consort polarizes and champions her power, but does not wield it himself.)

Throughout Celtic literature we read of many encounters with the Goddess of Sovereignty. She is alternatively beautiful or hideous, demands the achievement of arduous feats of endurance, and eventually gives herself only to the most worthy.[70] Throughout the *Mabinogion,* she is hinted at: in "Peredur" she is the empress of Constantinople, in "The Lady of the Fountain" she is Owain's countess, in "Gereint" she is the lady of the paradisal but deadly garden. Sovereignty is plainly represented by Elen in "Maxen Wledig's Dream"; she is also visible in the figures of Rhiannon, Branwen, and Goewin within the Four Branches. These stories will be dealt with in the second part of the Myth Book of Britain, *King Arthur and the Goddess of the Land,* but they reveal one of the underlying motifs of the *Mabinogion:* the Lady who personifies the land itself, who suffers when it is raped; the one whose favors are sought as fervently as the Grail.

The Romans, who recognized and understood the importance of the *genia,* or *juno locus,* named Britannia as the titulary spirit of Britain and gave her the attributes of Minerva: the spear and the shield. Caesar, following Pliny's hint, called these islands Britain, after the tribe of the Pretani, but this is one of many names.

Each country has its inner landscape, its inner name, its own lord or lady of the land. The British Isles have been through a succession of names. The *Mabinogion* and the triads speak of the Island of the Mighty, Ynys Prydein. It has been called Great Britain not for reasons of imperial grandeur, but to distinguish it from the Lesser Britain, Brittany, which was colonized by the British in the early centuries C.E., and with whom the Welsh still share a bond of blood and language. Today the countries of England, Wales, and Scotland are collectively called the United Kingdom, but somewhere within the early titles lie many others, hidden and forgotten, names which are applied only in a poetic way now, but which retain their own magic.

"The first name that this Island bore, before it was taken or settled: Myrddin's Precinct (Clas Merdin). And after it was taken and settled, the Island of honey. And after it was conquered by Prydein, son of Aedd the Great, it was called the Island of Prydein," say the triads.[5] This title, Clas Merdin, or Merlin's Enclosure, is linked with the lady of the land, Sovereignty, whom Kipling describes thus:

> *She is not any common Earth,*
> *Water or Wood or Air,*
> *But Merlin's Isle of Gramarye,*
> *Where you and I will fare.*[119]

*Gramarye* is the old form of *grammar,* meaning "magical lore," of which these tales of Ynys Prydein are redolent. Merlin makes no appearance in the *Mabinogion,* but there is no lack of enchanters to guard the land and reshape its destiny: Gwydion, Math, and the Otherworld kings who sleep fitfully beneath it. One of these, Poseidon's son, the giant Albion, gave his name to the land after arriving in what is now Britain. William Blake breathed new life into the titanic form of Albion in his prophetic poems.[16]

Geoffrey of Monmouth tells us that Brutus, the mythical Trojan leader and ancestor of the British race, had three sons—Locrinus, Kamber, and Albanactus—among whom his kingdom was divided. Their names remain the inner names of England, Wales, and Scotland: Loegres, Cambria, and Alban. Cambria and Alban have all but fallen out of use, but Lloegr is still the Welsh title for England,[37] while Logres is a title retained by the medieval Arthurian legends.

Every country has its inner resonance, a name which hints at a mythological hinterland where the ancestral values of tribe and familial cohesion are upheld, despite shifting boundaries and new appellations. C. S. Lewis's book *That Hideous Strength* is about this very antipathy of old and new identities:

> There has been a secret Logres in the very heart of Britain all these
> years; an unbroken succession of Pendragons . . . some of the
> Pendragons are well known to history, though not under that name. . .
> . But in every age they and the little Logres which gathered round them
> have been the fingers which gave the tiny shove or the almost imperceptible pull to prod England out of the drunken sleep or to draw her
> back from the final outrage into which Britain tempted her.[120]

For every separate kingdom within the United Kingdom, there is an inner home into which its people yearn longingly to enter. Many identify this as a politically achievable entity, while others perceive it as a spiritual homeland, a matching of outer and inner realities. This is not a book dedicated to the reestablishment of Celtic autonomy, but one which deals with the mythological patterns underlying the *Mabinogion*. Beneath the tribal squabbling which even yet breaks out into unbalanced nationalism and terrorism, the land awaits a

Pendragon—one who can wield the spirit of the people and tame the dragonish eruptions of violent factions. Within Merlin's Enclosure, numerous tribes are now sheltered: aboriginal British, Roman, Saxon, Norman, European, Asiatic, African, and many others, each newcomer bringing his or her native values and customs. Each individual is welcomed on his or her acceptance by the land and on personal willingness to agree to the rules which govern Merlin's Enclosure. These rules, which can be garnered by a close study of the underlying stories of Ynys Prydein, are exemplified most clearly by the rule of the Pendragon King Arthur, by the pattern of kings and kingly rule, and by the mysteries of the Goddess of the Land.

Neither the Britain of factional division, nor the submission of one kingdom to another, but instead the inner kingdoms of Ynys Prydein reveal to us the truth that every court is potentially Camelot, every leader a Pendragon, every subject a knight or lady within Clas Merdin. This book presents two challenges: the calling of the Pendragon and the naming of the land with the name of the mother, the Goddess of Sovereignty. Before these tasks can be undertaken, the reader must be able to distinguish between levels of reality, to travel the landscape of the *Mabinogion* without confusion. To do this we must define the boundaries clearly.

## World and Otherworld

A country is never composed of a single people living at one time with one purpose; it is a stratified society, informed by different levels of time, purpose, and inner resonance. The *Mabinogion* is no different; its main characters live within our everyday world, but they are motivated by internal conflict and personal encounter with otherworldly powers. The birth of our world from the Otherworld is not complete in these stories; the umbilical cord is still attached—it is possible to travel between the worlds and for the status of one world to affect another. Two-way traffic can pass through the portals and pathways that mark the thresholds of the worlds. These are used by the *Mabinogion*'s heroes and heroines, and are the authentic routes incorporated into Western shamanic practice.[142]

The Otherworld is the internal resonance of the everyday world. It exists out of time, simultaneously intersecting all time and thus accessible to visitation from any point of linear time. Within the Otherworld, spiritual beings are met and essential wisdom teachings are available to those who have the correct keys; it is the realm of quest and achievement, challenge and encounter, initiation and enlightenment. It is not illusory, a figment of imagination, or an anthropological invention. It is not heaven or hell or analogous to any drug-induced vision. The Otherworld is the mythological reality or symbolic continuum within which we can encounter the archetypal energies of the gods and their acts.

The Otherworld has its own valid reality which is not accessible to the five outer senses, though it is appreciable by the inner ones. It is often spoken of as a state of consciousness, though this definition uses psychological language to express its existence. The Otherworld exists in its own right, is consistent with its own rules, and is a reality which any can visit; it is not merely confined to those who have psychic abilities. The incredulous reader who is unwilling to attempt the paths personally may accept the reality of the Otherworld as a fictive one, but will have to come to terms with it on some level, for the majority of the stories within the *Mabinogion* weave between the worlds, often within the same sentence.

In the First Branch of the *Mabinogion,* Pwyll, Prince of Dyfed, sits on the mound of Arberth—a renowned magical place and a distinct gateway to the Otherworld—and his ordinary life starts to assimilate otherworldly elements very rapidly. In the Second Branch, Bran accepts an otherworldly cauldron which causes untold trouble. In "Peredur," the hero ignores the rules of the Otherworld and so prolongs his quest for years. In "Culhwch and Olwen," Culhwch can gain his bride only by the achievement of thirty-nine impossible tasks, which lead him and his companions through every level of the Otherworld. These and other examples will be discussed in their proper place, but important to realize is that what happens in otherworldly reality affects everyday reality, and vice versa.

It is clear that to ignore the Otherworld is to blur the definition of the *Mabinogion* totally. The stories may often be garbled in places, but the cyfarwydd is not inventing the magical episodes for the amusement of his audience; he is repeating lore which was commonly understood and accepted. Not one of his listeners would have dared sit on the mound of Arberth himself at night, for fear of the Tylwyth Teg—the household folk or faeries. Titans, giants, faeries, lake women, magical beasts, the Mamau or triplicity of mothers—all were known as inhabitants of the Otherworld and were likewise feared and respected. The elder gods were close at the time of half-light; they were associated with certain special landmarks denoting the entrance to their realm. They lived on in folk memory, often diminishing in stature but still portents of a larger world which was near at hand. The Otherworld remains inseparable from Celtic consciousness, existing as a borderland, "like boundaries between years and between seasons . . . lines along which the supernatural intrudes through the surface of existence."[87]

And yet at the same time we cannot but be aware of the everyday world within the *Mabinogion.* Many of the stories are onomastic—i.e., they are stories which name places. In "Math, Son of Mathonwy," Gwydion shelters his stolen swine at Mochtref and Mochnant (*moch* means "pig"), and the Llyn y Morynion (lake of maidens) is where Blodeuwedd's companions drown themselves. In "Branwen, Daughter of Llyr" Tal Ebolion is the place where Bran pays compensation to Matholwch, King of Ireland, for the mutilation of his horses (*ebol* means "colt"). The Irish *Dindshenchas* offer similar lists of stories that have given names to places.

Although Cornwall, London, Kent, France, Ireland, and Oxford are mentioned in the *Mabinogion,* the scenes, when they do not stray into the Otherworld, are firmly set in Wales. "Pwyll, Prince of Dyfed" and "Manawyddan, Son of Llyr" are set in South Wales, in Dyfed, while the stories of Branwen and Math are set in North Wales. (Figure 1, the map opening chapter 1, shows the various locations of the stories' actions.)

It is foolish to attempt any exact attachment of these stories to any particular era because they happen out of time, not within it. The stories themselves are dressed in clothes contemporary to early medieval Wales, but stray garments are clearly of an earlier date. Pagan and Christian customs overlie each other, as when in the Fourth Branch the spear destined to kill Llew can be forged only on Sunday when Mass is being said, yet Llew's threefold death is of a much earlier derivation related to the pagan kingly sacrifice. In the pseudo-histories, historical characters like Magnus Maximus appear, while a whole mixed bag of mythical, magical, fantastic, and heroic characters can be found in "Culhwch and Olwen." Harness and armor owe nothing to medieval chivalry, yet neither are they those of Celtic times.

The values of the Celtic world are still discernible: Honor, family pride, the laws of hospitality, the custom of fosterage, and tribal obligation are foremost in the realm of the *Mabinogion*. These were the currency of everyday life, laws, and customs surviving the early British era and coexisting fitfully beside those of Norman England, which sought to superimpose its weight on immemorial Welsh dignity.

Scholars can evidence internal clues and references to different Welsh noble houses existent at the time the *Mabinogion* was written down, but this is not of paramount importance to the general reader. The *Mabinogion* has won its own immortality among the stars. The Milky Way is known in Welsh as Caer Gwydion, Gwydion's Castle. The constellation of Cassiopeia is Llys Don—the Court of Don, mother of Gwydion and the rest of that turbulent family. The Corona Borealis is Caer Arianrhod, whose secret citadel is the tower of initiation. Ruler of the northern heavens and indicator of our true north is Arthur's Wain, or the Great Bear. And because no king can travel without his poet, Lyra is the Harp of Arthur, Telyn Arthur, and Taliesin, the supreme seer-poet, has his dwelling in "the region of the summer stars."[6]

The realm of the *Mabinogion* is a vast one, spanning the everyday and the otherworldly compartments of the Underworld, Annwfn, and the Overworld of the heavens. Its stories can likewise be enjoyed on many levels: as folktale, mythology, inner history, and, not least, as mystery drama.

## The Mysteries of Britain

The question must be asked: How far do the stories of the *Mabinogion* reflect the mysteries of Britain? By *mysteries* we mean core stories which act as personal or cosmic transformers, such as are used in the classical mysteries, those rites of divine revelation which devotées underwent in order to have communion with the gifts of specific deities. Those who engaged in these rites in Eleusis or who communed with Mithras, Cybele, or Isis emerged from these mysteries as initiates—literally, those who had "entered into" the unspeakable experience of divine union. It is clear that many such traditions can be found in the *Mabinogion* in partial form—the Grail quest and the possession of the sacred head and cauldron are all related themes which spill over into both the Matter of Britain cycle, that corpus of stories attached to King Arthur, and the esoteric heart of Christianity. Present too are the loss and finding of the Puer Eternus, the Wondrous Youth—Mabon, the quest for whom has power to transform evil custom and chaos.

The descent to the Underworld or the otherworldly journey undertaken by many of the heroes is paralleled by the personally transformative journey which the shamanic poet or initiate takes. This intercourse of the ancestral and the mythic with the everyday world is more clearly delineated and understood in the *Mabinogion* than it is in our own time in which the spiritual quest is more often restricted to the individual's search for meaning and inner refreshment. The heroes who plumb the mysteries of Britain do so on behalf of the whole land and its people rather than for personal merit or benefit.

Initiation into the mysteries of any tradition involves meeting its great archetypes face to face in the reality of the Otherworld. Within the *Mabinogion* this challenge often occurs in the course of a board game, in the combat between opponents, or through the aid of other-worldly, totemic beasts (see chapter 8).

In considering the British mysteries, we are looking squarely at a druidic tradition effaced by a diametrically different creed and set of training techniques. Certain original elements can be glimpsed embedded in the river of tradition, but mostly the stream is a muddy one. The mysteries that come down to us most authentically descend through the bardic traditions and through personal encounter with the spirits of the land and the beings of the Otherworld. The rites of the eighteenth- and nineteenth-century revival druidic sects have more to do with classical or Anglican scholarship than with the native mystery traditions under discussion here. Druidic revival was something of an antiquarian pastime whereby authentic genealogical and textual lore was "worked up" from the seventeenth century onward, with the aid of inspired archaeology and comparative religion, into nothing approaching the real thing. Its exponents merely cobbled together sundry pieces of druidic driftwood in order to make coracles which would not float. One of these, Iolo Morgannwg (Edward Williams, 1747–1826), was personally responsible for inventing or reinventing much of what passes for druidism today, thus presenting all manner of headaches:

> Since he knew more about Welsh classical literature than any man alive, he could do this with impunity, and over the years he invented so many medieval poems that the chief task of Welsh literary scholarship in the twentieth century has been the disentangling of Iolo's forgeries from the real thing.[74]

Iolo and his ilk gave rise to a morass of concepts including the lost tribes of Israel, pseudo-Kabalistic fable, and biblical aphorism—a substance as sticky and indigestible as Welsh toffee. At least twentieth- and twenty-first-century druidism resorts to the abiding traditions of the land and its sacred myths, and it is in these stories that poets and storytellers can find the clues to the original druidic mysteries.

Originally the professional bardic classes shared a high standard of

oral education, specializing in different subjects, considering themselves as fellow initiates of the inner corpus of mystery teachings. The
druids were the specialists, but their teaching did not come down
through written sources. Poets learned the complex meters, rhythms,
and stanza forms and thus formalized some facets of the mystery
teachings, as we can still perceive in the poetry of arch poet Taliesin,
who was himself initiate and Son of the Cauldron. Storytellers received
less formal training but dealt with the subject matter of the mysteries,
just as Homer and other Greek poets made the gods immortal to later
generations. Finally, it was not the praise songs of the poets which gave
us the insight we need, but the storyteller's skill.

> The old Welsh word for "story," *cyfarwyddyd*, means "guidance," "direc-
> tion," "instruction," "knowledge," "skill," "prescription." Its stem, *arwydd*,
> means "sign," "symbol," "manifestation," "men," "miracle," and derives
> from a root meaning "to see." The storyteller (cyfarwydd) was origi-
> nally a seer and a teacher who guided the souls of his hearers
> through the world of "mystery."[87]

The storyteller was an initiator—albeit unknowingly—because,
along with the poet, he became the sole guardian of the mystery teachings when the druidic role was taken over by the priest and monk. The
stories of the *Mabinogion* had power to communicate the underlying
mysteries to each and every listener, whether this was a family gathered
about a fireside to hear a wonder tale at the end of the day or a group
of initiates visualizing the scenes described by their leader. By the time
the *Mabinogion* was written down, these teachings were already being
forgotten or were obscure to their tellers, who substituted more plau-
sible explanations or tied a similar pair of stories together for the sake
of effect.

The storyteller's skill is quite a remarkable one. In the mind's eye
scenes come to life with vivid detail—and here lies one of the secrets of
traditional transmission: Inner knowledge of the mysteries does not
come down by means of written sources, but by means of symbols,

images, and music. This can be tested by each of us: Quite often, when listening to a story on the radio, a series of profoundly moving images or impressions will flash into our consciousness. These may seem unrelated, at least on the surface, to the material heard; yet if we meditate upon these deeply rooted images, a series of realizations will connect us to the true source of the material, re-creating it in an original way. Such moments of vision are gateways to the Otherworld.

In this way, singers, storytellers, and other performers work from the subtext of their song or script, their conscious minds recalling the words and music, their deep minds communing with the rhythms, images, and symbols which are the lode-bearing ore of their artistic quarry. Thus similarly awakening images, rhythms, and symbols are set up in the minds of listeners—and in this way, the performing arts are truly initiatory. However, no such transmission is possible if the artist is merely performing by rote, without communion with the sources and key images of his or her script. All audiences know this and, if the performer is making no such communion, subsequently register disquiet or boredom.

The symbolic keys of the triads and certain key passages within the *Mabinogion* work in the same way: They unlock doors to the Otherworld and allow us, the readers, to enter in search of mystery and knowledge. We literally enter the story, achieving a unique perspective. This method of mystery teaching is irrefutably authentic; great teachers such as Christ, Buddha, and Plato have taught by parable and analogous story. The classical mystery schools of Eleusis, Alexandria, and Epidaurus enacted their core stories, involving both initiates and candidates for initiation. This is why revival mystery rituals do not work: They do not evoke the frisson of creative response unless they are authentically part of the tradition.

The mysteries of Britain were not uniformly the same from north to south or from east to west. Names, cults, and stories were localized in a tribal way. Linking them together was a common understanding of certain key stories and symbolic tokens representing a formalization of otherworldly archetypes which could be universally understood among many different peoples. One such story underlies the texts of the *Mabinogion*. It has been called the lost Fifth Branch, but in fact it is rather more like the taproot of a mighty tree of traditional stories. It is the stories or mysteries of Mabon and Modron, wherein Mabon is stolen "from his mother and the wall" when he is scarcely three nights old. We can read, in "Culhwch and Olwen," how Arthur and his men search for, find, and liberate him from his prison so that he is able to find the hidden treasures of Annwfn.

The story of the lost child and the sorrowing mother is not merely a nationalistic story, but a universal theme cross-tracking both mythology and religion of all countries and times. The mysteries of Mabon and Modron are proper to the British Isles, just as the mysteries of Demeter and Kore are proper to Greece. All happen out of time, in the ever-present reality of the Otherworld. These mysteries have their own exponents and symbolic keys, which we will begin to perceive.

As we rehearse the stories of the Four Branches, "Culhwch and Olwen," and "Taliesin," we become aware that a subtle pattern of correspondences unfolds. If we read skillfully and imaginatively, we will begin to uncover the hidden story of Mabon and Modron from among a welter of other tales. And although we can draw on close Celtic parallels, the best evidence for our discovery is to be found within the *Mabinogion* itself.

The names Mabon and Modron are not personal appellations, but merely titles meaning "son" and "mother." This alerts us to the fact that their mysteries are very ancient; the absence of personal names for these protagonists indicates their otherworldly reality. Some characters within the *Mabinogion* wear these archetypal masks over their own personae so that the empty titles become inspirited with new life. If we look for the signs, we can spot the exponents of Mabon: a boy who is lost after birth or who is hidden away to be raised in secret—like Pryderi, in the First Branch, like Llew in the Fourth Branch, or like Goreu in "Culhwch and Olwen." We can perceive the mask of Modron worn over many features: a woman who loses her child or who must hide him from danger, like Rhiannon in the First Branch or the nameless wife of Custennin in "Culhwch and Olwen." These are but a few examples of how the mysteries of Mabon and Modron are manifested.

Always we must be sensitive to the way each character interacts with his or her totemic beast. The association of people with archetypal animals points to an interaction of this world with the Otherworld. One of the important symbolic keys to finding and releasing Mabon is the Initiation of the Totems (see chapter 8), by which his liberators descend the tree of tradition with the help of totemic animals, each of whom stands as guardian to a cyclic age going back to the beginning of the world where Mabon is imprisoned.

As the mysteries of Mabon and Modron unfold, we will begin to be aware of another pattern overlying them and revealed in the succession of the Pendragons, through which many of the mysteries of Britain are channeled. This pattern is radically interwoven with the ancient hope of the coming of Mab Darogan, the Son of Destiny, whose foretold coming will bring liberation to the people. In medieval times, this being was understood in a very political light, as the liberator who would release the Welsh from under the Norman yoke. Both anciently and in our own times, Mab Darogan has been associated with King Arthur, who is prophesied to come again.

But beyond the political aspirations of an oppressed people stands another, eternal harmonic of this mythic pattern. This core of our native tradition can be seen manifested through a set of inner guardians whose duty is to watch over the otherworldly life of the country. The duration of this guardianship varies, but when one guardian steps down, another takes his or her place as the former guardian succeeding to a new and different role.

There is a threefold cycle of this succession deriving from implicit mystery tradition stories that motivate our cultural heritage. Although the *Mabinogion* has been used as a source for these guardians in this book, the cycle revealed here is not the only one in operation. The three cyclic male roles are as follows:

**Mabon,** the Wondrous Youth, the Pendragon's champion, who succeeds to the place of . . .

**Pendragon,** the King, the arbiter and ruler, who succeeds to the place of . . .

**Pen Annwfn,** Lord of the Underworld, the judge and sage, who succeeds to the place of . . .

**Mabon** . . . and so the wheel turns once more in every generation.

The threefold female cycle, discussed in chapter 9 and more fully presented in *King Arthur and the Goddess of the Land,* corresponds to the male cycle and is associated closely with it.

It is possible to see many of the *Mabinogion*'s protagonists in these three roles. In the place of Mabon, for example, can be set Pryderi, Goreu, and Gwion; in the place of Pendragon stand Arthur, Math, and Taliesin; in the place of Pen Annwfn stand Pwyll, Bran, and Yspaddaden Pencawr. In turn, each role succeeds to the next in the guardianship of the mysteries. This pattern will become clearer as the stories unfold.

Mabon is everywhere and nowhere, a dream of the child Merlin, an echo of Apollo's lyre, a cry within a prison wall. Modron is visible and invisible, as woman and land, as giver of life and receiver of the dead, as Persephone the abducted and Persephone, queen of the Underworld. Whoever enters their story shares their story, becomes Orpheus to Eurydice, Demeter and Persephone, companion to Mabon, child to Modron, and they leave it singing, singing . . .

Mysteries are mighty stories and we are mortal stock seeking immortality. Our initiation into the *Mabinogion* re-creates these tales afresh. It cannot be told—not for lack of words, but because the real mystery must be experienced personally.

And now the First Branch is about to begin; the cyfarwydd is seated; the audience settles quietly to listen and share and enter the story of the boy who was lost and found, and of his mother's plan for her land.

# 2
# Pwyll, Prince of Dyfed

*And the penance that was imposed on her was*
*. . . that she should relate the story to all who*
*should come there.*

FROM "PWYLL, PRINCE OF DYFED"

*Ride a cock horse to Banbury Cross*
*To see a fine lady upon a white horse;*
*Rings on her fingers and bells on her toes,*
*She shall have music wherever she goes.*

TRADITIONAL NURSERY RHYME

## The Head of Annwfn

This First Branch concerns Pwyll, his otherworldly wife, Rhiannon, and their child, Pryderi, whose birth is "literally haunted by all manner of magical mixing-up."[86] Within it lie some of the most ancient and important themes linking it to the core story of Mabon and Modron, who are represented here as Pryderi and Rhiannon. The action of the story shifts continually between the everyday world and the

Otherworld, and it is this very interaction that gives the story pace and interest. If Pwyll had never gone hunting in Glyn Cuch or sat on the Mound of Arberth, the Four Branches of the *Mabinogion* would never have sprouted from the tree of tradition. We would be unable to account for the nature of Mabon's imprisonment and Modron's sorrowful captivity, and would be quite ignorant of the flavor of pork! Fortunately, both in the realm of the *Mabinogion* and in real life, there are those daring explorers who venture into uncharted worlds in order to make our own world a richer, more exciting place.

## Synopsis of "Pwyll, Prince of Dyfed"

(1) Pwyll, Prince of Dyfed, goes hunting in Glyn Cuch, where he encounters a rival hunting party which sets on a stag and bears it down. Driving off the other hounds, he sets his own dogs on the quarry. (2) A gray-clad huntsman arrives, rebukes him for discourtesy, and threatens to satirize Pwyll. He is Arawn, King of Annwfn. Pwyll can make amends by fighting with Arawn's enemy, (3) Hafgan, who is likewise a king in Annwfn. To effect this, Pwyll and Arawn exchange places, each taking the semblance of the other. At the end of a year and a day, Pwyll is to fight Hafgan, giving him a single blow.

(4) Having changed places with Arawn, Pwyll goes to Annwfn, where he is welcomed by the court as Arawn himself. He sleeps beside Arawn's wife, but never attempts to touch her. (5) He fights Hafgan at the appointed time and refuses him a second blow. Having defeated Arawn's enemies, Pwyll receives the homage of the lords of Annwfn on Arawn's behalf. (6) Upon Arawn's return, Pwyll and Arawn exchange places once more, each returning to his true form. Arawn finds his country has been well governed and makes love to his wife, who receives his unaccustomed embraces with surprise. Pwyll returns home to find none had missed him. He and Arawn remain firm friends, and because of the substitution (7) and because Pwyll has been successful in uniting the two kingdoms, Pwyll is henceforth known as the head or chief of Annwfn.

(8) While residing at his chief court, Arberth, Pwyll decides to sit on the Mound of Arberth, an act that causes any who engage in it either to receive blows or to experience a wonder. (9) After sitting on the mound, Pwyll sees a woman on a white horse pass by. On three occasions he sends men after her, but none of the horses is quick enough to catch up to her. Finally, Pwyll mounts his horse and gives chase. However fast he goes, though, she is quicker. (10) At length he asks her to stop. The woman reveals that she is Rhiannon, daughter of Hefaidd Hen (the Ancient). She has been promised to a man against her will when all the while she has loved Pwyll. He arranges to come to her father's hall a year and a day hence.

(11) With a hundred companions, Pwyll arrives to attend his wedding feast at Hefaidd's Hall. A supplicant arrives and Pwyll promises to grant whatever it is in his power to give. Rhiannon is displeased with this answer because the supplicant, Gwawl, son of Clud, is her former betrothed. Gwawl asks for her and for the feast. Because Rhiannon has offered the feast for the men of Dyfed, it is not in Pwyll's power to give it away. (12) Rhiannon gives Pwyll a bag and arranges a year and a day's delay before she can be given to Gwawl.

At the appointed time, the second feast begins, with Gwawl as guest of honor. In comes Pwyll, at Rhiannon's prior instruction, dressed as a supplicant. He asks a boon, which Gwawl promises to grant if it is reasonable. Pwyll asks that the bag be filled with food. Despite the fact that the bag is stuffed with food, it seems no more full than before. Pwyll tells Gwawl that only a noble can ensure its fullness by placing both feet in the bag and saying that it has had enough. Gwawl complies and at a horn blast from Pwyll, the men of Dyfed enter, fasten the bag, and each proceeds to strike it, (13) playing a game called Badger in the Bag. (14) Hefaidd objects to this treatment of Gwawl. Rhiannon ensures that Gwawl will extract no vengeance. (15) Rhiannon and Pwyll sleep together at last and return to Dyfed.

(16) They rule together for three years, but the people begin to mutter about Rhiannon's barrenness and charge Pwyll to put her away.

A year later, Rhiannon bears a son. The evening of his birth, the child disappears from the chamber and the nurses, in fear of punishment, kill a puppy, smear Rhiannon's face with its blood, and strew its bones about the floor. (17) Rhiannon is unjustly accused of eating her child, but Pwyll refuses to put her away, for she has at last given birth. Rather than dispute with the women, Rhiannon accepts her penance: (18) to sit at the mounting block outside the gate for seven years, to tell her story to all comers, and to offer to carry them into the hall on her back.

(19) In the meantime, in Gwent, Teyrnon Twrf Liant has a mare which, each May Eve, bears a foal that regularly disappears. Finally, he stands vigil and intercepts a monstrous claw that comes through the window to steal the foal. Returning from his pursuit of the monster, he finds in the stable a baby boy wrapped in rich swaddling clothes. (20) He and his wife pretend that the child is their own and call him Gwri Gwallt Euryn. The boy matures unnaturally fast and is so keen to be with the horses that the rescued colt is given to him.

(21) Teyrnon hears of Rhiannon's penance and perceives Pwyll's likeness in Gwri. He takes Gwri to Arberth where they both refuse to be carried into the hall by Rhiannon. Teyrnon tells the story of finding the boy and Rhiannon declares that she is released at last from anxiety (*pryder*). Pendaran Dyfed, Pwyll's foster father, says that a fitting name for the boy would be Pryderi. (22) Teyrnon is rewarded for his care and Pryderi is sent to be fostered by Pendaran Dyfed. (23) On the death of Pwyll, Pryderi rules Dyfed and marries Cigfa, daughter of Gwynon Gohoyw.

## Commentary

(1) The story begins with a hunt. The pursuit of a beast, often a stag, is frequently the prelude to a mortal entering the Otherworld. Although Pwyll seems to trespass across the boundary between the worlds, his presence in Annwfn is obviously required by Arawn. Pwyll's foolhardiness gives him no end of trouble: He pursues Arawn's stag, he ventures to sit on the Mound of Arberth, and he makes rash promises to Gwawl.

Ironically, Pwyll's name means "mind," and it is easy to see how his lack of thought may be due to his youthful inexperience.

(2) The King of the Underworld and his wild hunt are known by many names: As Arawn, he rides over Pembrokeshire; as Gwyn ap Nudd, he hunts between Glamorganshire and the West Country; while farther east he appears as Herne, the hunter. He is always accompanied by his white hounds, which have the telltale red-tipped ears of the Underworld. Annwfn is not analogous to a classical Hades or to a Christian Hell; it is not a place of purgatorial torment, but an abode of otherworldly dignity.[98] Annwfn translates as the "in world," meaning "the land beneath the earth."

"I will satirize you to the value of a hundred stags," threatens Arawn. The standard Celtic retaliation against insult was the exaction of a compensatory fine, called *sarhad* in Welsh, or "honor price." The higher the person's rank, the greater the sarhad; unfortunately for Pwyll, Arawn is a king. Nonpayment of the fine left the injured party in a position demanding satisfaction: He could employ the services of a poet to satirize his offender. Interestingly, Arawn offers this service himself. The links between poet-kind and the Otherworld were very strong, and it was not unusual for an otherworldly being to have "bird's knowledge," as inspired poetic colloquy was called. Pwyll is thus severely embarrassed and obligated to Arawn's future service.

(3) Evidently Hafgan cannot be defeated by a fellow king of Annwfn, but only by a mortal. Pwyll is Arawn's destined champion. Hafgan's name means "summer song," a hint which enables us to view this otherworldly combat by means of a parallel tradition: the *Gawain* cycle of stories.[47] In "Sir Gawain and Dame Ragnell," an Otherworld giant called Sir Gromer Somer Joure (lord of summer's day) places Arthur under severe restriction which can be countered only by Gawain—who substitutes himself for Arthur. Hafgan and Gromer have common roots, without doubt; it has long been established that Gawain and the

stories associated with him stem directly from Irish tradition in that Arthur's champion is shown to derive directly from the Ulster hero Cú Chulainn.[17] Further parallels are apparent from a reading of the medieval English text "Sir Gawain and the Green Knight," in which the Green Knight can be beheaded by one blow. Here Pwyll is instructed to give just one blow because the second will only revive Hafgan. How a blow can revive anyone seems a mystery, but it may refer to the way in which the *first death* is magically considered only the death of the body, whereas the *second death* is the term for initiation into the mysteries. We will see how in "Branwen, Daughter of Llyr" soldiers die by mortal blows but are revived by being put into the Cauldron of Rebirth, itself a reference to the poetic initiation.

(4) If we look again at "Sir Gawain and the Green Knight," we can recall that Sir Bertilak gives hospitality to Gawain in a way that's similar to Arawn leaving his kingdom in Pwyll's charge: "Treat what is mine as your own" is the implied invitation and trap. As Gawain is tempted by Lady Bertilak, so Pwyll suffers the blandishments of Arawn's wife. Pwyll, scrupulous to the letter of his bond, resists sleeping with Arawn's wife (see note 6, below). In Irish and probably in preliterate British tradition, it was a basic requirement of hospitality for a guest to share the bed of the woman of the house. Numerous instances of this occur in the Irish mythological and kingly sagas, in which the king's privileges extend to spending a night with every woman in his domain.

(5) The combat between Pwyll and Hafgan is paralleled in "Culhwch and Olwen" by the combat between Gwyn ap Nudd and Gwythyr ap Greidawl for the hand of Creiddylad in the eternal combat between summer and winter for the Queen of the Year (see chapter 6). In this instance, Pwyll has come to claim Annwfn on behalf of Arawn, yet there may be more than this at stake. Throughout his visit to Annwfn, Pwyll is not once referred to by name but is called "the man who was in

Arawn's shape," or merely "he," which makes for confusion when reading this passage. This uncertainty is further reinforced by the statement "by noon of the next day the two realms were in his power." The fact is that mortals can often perform deeds that immortals cannot achieve.

(6) It has been suggested by more than one commentator that Arawn's wife may be none other than Rhiannon.[46] Both women wear the same gold brocade gown. This is not so unlikely as it might seem if we consider the subsequent outcome of the story and see it in the wider context of the otherworldly woman as fay or goddess who loves a champion, yet first wishes to test his worthiness (see chapter 9). The combat of Pwyll and Hafgan, or that of the Green Knight and Gawain, becomes understandable in this context. Further such combats can be inferred from "The Lady of the Fountain" and "Gereint and Enid." A discussion of Rhiannon as a type of Sovereignty follows.

(7) Although he has only acted as champion of Arawn, Pwyll is nevertheless accorded the title of Head of Annwfn. We are told that because of his bravery in bringing the two kingdoms together, his old name falls out of use and Pen Annwfn is what he is always called afterwards. Pwyll acts as a bridge between the everyday and otherworldly realms. All of Pwyll's—and his family's—subsequent actions are influenced by this very otherworldly contact. Those who venture into Annwfn in order to effect a change there—whether it be through a redemptive act such as the harrowing of the Underworld by Mabon or Arthur or through the sacrificial action of Bran (see chapter 3)—always suffer a substitution: Each hero takes on the attributes of his combatant or of the Underworld king. The effect of this action is clearly seen in the Grail knights of later Arthurian legend; both Perceval and Galahad, as Grail winners, succeed to the role of Grail guardian. This substitution of champions is a clear motif in the succession of inner Pendragons,

those beings who govern the otherworldly realm bordering the Island of Britain. In this way, Clas Merdin (Merlin's Enclosure) is the very tower of his imprisonment—a willing service on another level of existence (see chapters 3 and 9). Pwyll is Arawn's substitute and his successor, if we read this story rightly.

(8) The Mound of Arberth can be seen from several standpoints: It is a place of assembly for the people of Dyfed, on which only the tribal officials would sit and arbitrate in times of war or festival; a place where judgments were given and disputes resolved; and, from the evidences of the First and Third Branches, a gateway between the worlds where strange things happen—which give it an ill-omened reputation. Pwyll's experience is similar to the Highland custom of *dreuchainn*: To foretell whom he or she would marry, a person climbed a hill that no four-footed beast could climb; the first creature seen on descending would show the nature of the intended.[100] The Scottish/Scandinavian story "The Black Bull of Norroway" is connected to this theme. The seven-year penance of the heroine (who must climb a hill of glass in order to gain her husband) is closely paralleled by Rhiannon's story.[24] The Mound is also Sovereignty's Chair—an inaugural mound where kings are installed.

(9) The veiled woman on horseback is none other than Rhiannon—an otherworldly woman whose antecedents are of great antiquity, as we will see shortly. Her connections with Epona, the Celtic horse goddess; the Black Demeter of Phygalia; the king-making rituals of Indo-European culture; and the Irish goddess Macha make her a compelling archetype whose legends give us the substance of Modron herself.

(10) No one is able to catch Rhiannon except Pwyll, but he succeeds only when he requests her to stop. She has evidently already chosen him as her consort, which reinforces the suggestion that she has already tested him as a suitable champion. Pwyll has proved himself worthy of the title of Pen Annwfn—and as such is a suitable husband

for Rhiannon, who is herself from the Underworld. Her father, Hefaidd the Ancient, plays a negligible part in the story.

(11) The order of precedence at feasts and assemblies of the Celtic peoples was always scrupulously determined by stewards. Pwyll's prowess has been tested once in the Underworld, but this next test he fails badly. Rhiannon's former suitor, Gwawl ap Clud (radiance, son of light), sounds remarkably akin to Hafgan (summer song); this whole episode seems like a continuation of Pwyll's combat. The first combat entailed that no second reviving blow be given to Hafgan. This second combat shows Pwyll less than prepared—he gives an answer from which a number of severe blows can be inflicted upon himself by Gwawl.

(12) Fortunately Rhiannon is wiser than her betrothed. Her bag, like the many cauldrons and wonder-working bags of Celtic legend, has wonders of its own. It may be akin to Epona's plentiful basket, which she is shown carrying on her lap in numerous bas-reliefs,[68] or her manger at which two foals feed. Pwyll here substitutes for Gwawl, entering as a beggar. This is one of the most famous themes in folk story: the man who disguises himself as a poor harper and sings for his bride in the Underworld. From Orpheus in classical times to King Orpheo in Scandinavian/Scottish story, the retrieving of the bride from Hades has been an important folk motif in world myth.[26] Here Gwawl falls into the trap and is placed under Pwyll's authority. The way he is enticed into the bag is similar to the way Mollie Whuppie in Highland folk story, by exclaiming, "Oh, if you could see the wonders I can see!" induces a giant and his family to enter a totally empty bag in which she herself has previously been trapped.[24] Because the salient features of the Mound of Arberth are either blows or wonders, the gifts of Rhiannon seem to be either great misfortune or great happiness, a factor which is borne out in the subsequent story.

(13) The game of Badger in the Bag is the ultimate insult for a Celtic

nobleman. Because they play such an important part in the tripartite story, this First Branch might well be entitled "The Mabinogi of the Three Blows": the blow upon Hafgan, the blows upon Gwawl, and, last, the blow upon Pwyll of the loss of his son and disgrace of his wife. Truly, Pwyll has blows and wonders in equal measure. Interestingly, a similar parallel is found in modern sexual warfare: the Badger Game in which a woman seduces a man then cries rape, at which point her husband appears on the scene to blackmail the victim.

(14) Gwawl cannot claim sarhad here, but Rhiannon exacts no such sureties from Gwawl's family, as we see in the Third Branch. It is apparent in subtext that Hefaidd approves of Gwawl and Rhiannon's marriage, for he objects to Gwawl's treatment. Hefaidd can be seen in the light of those giants and otherworldly kings who are destined to lose their position on the marriage of their daughters and who subsequently place all manner of restrictions upon them (see chapters 5 and 6). Rhiannon and Pwyll make their quick getaway and do not accede to his suggested delay in the Underworld.

(15) Rhiannon and Pwyll sleep together without ceremony. Indeed, the only marriage ceremony in the *Mabinogion* occurs in "The Lady of the Fountain." In early times, the assembly of the tribal family at a wedding feast was sufficiently effective in publicizing the union of a couple. "And the wedding feast lasted a year and a day" is the frequent conclusion of a folk story. But Pwyll does not linger, wisely abducting his bride before Hefaidd can trick him into staying away long enough so that he can offer his daughter to another suitor.

(16) The barrenness and subsequent unpopularity of Rhiannon, who goes out of her way to smooth enmity through the giving of gifts, parallels Branwen's disgrace (see chapter 3). While the people of Dyfed are keen to applaud Pwyll's prowess in becoming Pen Annwfn, they are less excited at the prospect of an otherworldly bride.

(17) The abduction of the child and the sorrow of the mother are familiar to us as far back as the story of Demeter and Persephone. The distinct parallels between Rhiannon and Pryderi and Modron and Mabon are further pointed out in chapters 8 and 9.

(18) The seven-year penance of Rhiannon is the first of her imprisonments. She and Pryderi both suffer two captivities in the course of their careers, as we will see in the Third Branch.

(19) Teyrnon Twrf Liant (of the raging sea) has parallels with the god Manawyddan. In chapter 4 we will see further connections between the queen of the Underworld and the king of the sea. The fates of the child and the foal and their twinned destinies are discussed in the section The Adventures of the Mare and the Boy, below. The Otherworld malignancy manifests as a claw on May Eve, Beltane, one of the Celtic fire festivals and a day on which the way between the worlds is open. These "fording places" between worlds—the most feared being Samhain or October 31, All Hallows Eve—were marked by games and festivals. The claw is reminiscent of Grendel, whom Beowulf fights, and is even more closely related to an incident in the Irish Fionn cycle "Feis Tighe Chonain." These interrelated themes are also discussed in the following section.

(20) According to the archetypal *mabinogi* of the hero, Pryderi is fostered in a place of obscurity and security. He is given a childhood name, Gwri Gwallt Euryn, or Gwri Golden Hair, which protects him against both Otherworld malice and worldly anxiety. His interest in horses is not unnatural in the son of a horse goddess.

(21) In Celtic custom the mother gave the child a name and was responsible for arming him at manhood. Names could be acquired at different times for different uses in Celtic society; there was the childhood name, usually dropped at weapon-taking, followed by the manly name, often

with the addition of an epithet coined from some daring exploit or peculiar feature. (A number of men bearing these names appear in Arthur's company; see chapter 6.) Rhiannon inadvertently gifts her son with the name "trouble" or "anxiety," a hard destiny for a young child. Because his father's name, Pwyll, means "mind," Pryderi is really Anxiety, son of Mind. The Son of the Mother can have many names.

(22) The custom of fosterage was almost universal among the Celts: A child was raised by a noble family where he was taught household customs and given a general education. Fosterage wrought ties of mutual dependency and trust between different clans, thus blocking possible avenues to clan warfare. Pendaran Dyfed appears in Triad 26 as Pwyll's foster father; he is the one to whom Pwyll gives the swine which come from Annwfn. Pryderi is said to have tended them during his fostering.[5] There is an anachronism between this branch and "Branwen, Daughter of Llyr," in which Pendaran is described as a young pageboy left with Bran's son to govern Britain in Bran's absence. Yet among those seven who return from Ireland is Pryderi himself!

(23) The end of this story and the conclusion of the Second Branch merge to give us the Third Branch, which continues the story of Pryderi's exploits in "Manawyddan, Son of Llyr."

## The Adventures of the Mare and the Boy

This First Branch establishes Pwyll as an Underworld champion, Rhiannon as a representative of the Celtic horse goddess, and Pryderi as one in a long line of heroes whose destinies are interwoven with a totem animal. Pryderi is the only character in the *Mabinogion* to appear in every one of the Four Branches, and as such, his destiny is most clearly discernible. He goes to Ireland with Bran in the Second Branch, suffers an otherworldly imprisonment in the Third Branch, and is finally slain by Gwydion in the Fourth Branch. We know from the triads that he is a herdsman, keeping his father's Underworld swine (a gift from Arawn); and that he is called "the Powerful Swineherd because no one is able either to deceive or to force him."[5] He is also a huntsman, like his father. These twin pursuits, herding and hunting, are Mabon's as well, who also suffers a mysterious and long-term captivity. When he is grown, Pryderi follows the pattern laid down by his father, yet in his youth he is the son of Rhiannon, whose captivity he shares and whose nature he most reflects. He is the son of his mother, just as Mabon is the son of Modron. While a fuller discussion of this association can be found in chapters 3 and 9, it is possible to show from Celtic tradition how Pryderi and the foal relate to the conception of the hero and the fate of the land.

In parallel Irish tradition we see how the story of Cú Chulainn's conception, from the Ulster cycle, is dependent upon an early story, "The Debility of the Ulstermen," in which Crunnchu mac Agnoman is without a wife. An unknown woman called Macha comes to his house and tends it without speaking, to Crunnchu's satisfaction. One day, before he goes to an assembly, Macha warns him not to speak of her to anyone. At the assembly the king's horses are paraded, with everyone's agreement that they are the swiftest steeds in the land.

Disregarding Macha's warning, Crunnchu boasts that his wife is swifter still. He is immediately imprisoned and his wife is summoned before the king. Great with child and near her time, Macha is forced to compete against the horses, which she easily beats, but upon giving birth to twins, a girl and a boy, she expires. Before dying, however, she reveals her identity at last as Macha, daughter of Sainreth mac Imbaith (strange one, son of ocean), and prophesies that whenever Ulster is oppressed and in greatest need, all Ulstermen should suffer the weakness of a confined woman.[148]

Here Macha is in the place of Rhiannon: an otherworldly woman forced by her husband's foolish boasting to give birth to her children in public. The difference here is that Ulster shares her penance. Macha is silent regarding her origins, as many otherworldly brides are; she demands absolute secrecy concerning her otherworldly abilities and attributes—the infringement of which usually causes the bride to return to her home. Macha and Rhiannon clearly share horsely qualities, the speed at which they both run and ride, in particular.

Beneath these two stories is the folk-story theme of the faery bride whose life among mortals is dependent upon her earthly husband not inflicting blows upon her. Blows make a nag of a loved wife who has no other option than to return to her former state.

The birth of twins, or of a child and a foal, is a frequently occurring motif in the related stories of Rhiannon and Pryderi. In "Cú Chulainn's Conception," the king of Ireland, Conchobor, and his sister Deichtine are in pursuit of a flight of birds yoked with silver. They come to a newly built house where a woman is giving birth, and Deichtine helps deliver the baby. Simultaneously, a mare gives birth to two foals. In the morning the baby dies. Deichtine laments her foster son's death but dreams that the god Lugh comes to her, telling her she will conceive the same child of her own body, and that the twin foals are to be raised as the boy's.[101] The boy is Cú Chulainn—the only non-Ulsterman able to aid the land when the curse of Macha falls upon its men. The twin foals, Dubh Sainghleann and Liath Macha, later yoke his chariot.

Here the story begins with the hunting of otherworldly birds. The hunt often leads protagonists into the Otherworld, but here these birds may be relevant in another important way. The birds of Rhiannon, which first appear in "Branwen, Daughter of Llyr," are famed for their ability to cause forgetfulness and induce paradisal bliss in their listeners. These companion birds make Rhiannon a queen of Annwfn—not a classical Persephone giving the waters of Lethe to the dead, but a Celtic Persephone whose musical birds give passage to paradise. The foster son of Deichtine is instantly lost, but will be born of her and will come again in the shape of Cú Chulainn, who, with his bravely yoked chariot, will defend the stricken Ulstermen cursed by the horse goddess. As with Pryderi, the foal becomes the companion of the child.

A final variant clinches the heroic Pryderi archetype: the story of "Feis Tighe Chonain," an oral tale from Irish tradition. In this, a giant comes to a woman's house and steals her newborn children by putting an arm through the smoke hole in the roof. At her next confinement, the hero Fionn keeps watch with his eleven companions. A bitch whelps two puppies as the woman gives birth. The giant returns, is beaten off, and is tracked by the companions to a cliff top, where six children and the two puppies are found. The giant is killed, the children are restored, and Fionn keeps the puppies, which become his fabled hounds, Bran and Sceolang.[53]

The connection between the destiny of the hero and that of the animal is here confirmed: Cú Chulainn takes the foals as his chariot horses, Fionn takes the puppies to be his hounds. We are not told in "Pwyll, Prince of Dyfed" who is the possessor of the monstrous arm, only that Teyrnon is able to beat it off and rescue both foal and boy. The implication seems to be that Gwawl's cousin, Llwyd of Cil Coed, likewise the predator of Pwyll's family in the Third Branch, means to abduct Pryderi as well as Teyrnon's foal. It would not do to leave one half of the hero's destiny alive, after all. We have no parallel stories telling of the rescue of the hero by his companion animal—at least, not in relation to the hero's birth—but we frequently come across the helping animals in folk tradition. A fuller discussion of totemic beasts is found in chapter 8.

Yet, we may argue, there are no stories in which Pryderi and his foal ride to daring adventures. This is because Pryderi is the foal, just as his mother is the mare whose otherworldly nature is endangered by his mortal birth. The totemic association of people and animals is a subtle one, operating on more than one level. Rhiannon and Pryderi operate as human beings, yet their otherworldly personae are those of mare and colt. In order to comprehend this mystery, we must examine just who Rhiannon really is.

## The Mare of Sovereignty

Why is Rhiannon associated with horses and what role does the horse play within the symbolism of the native mysteries of Britain? The people of Britain and Ireland are unique in Europe in their refusal to eat horse meat. Hindus revere the cow and will not eat it, and the British and Irish revere the horse in a similar way. In the Second Branch, we will see how horse mutilation is greeted as a most unnatural and abhorrent act.

In Indo-European culture the horse or mare has always played a prominent part in king-making rituals. We have Giraldus Cambrensis's shocked medieval account of an Irish kingship rite in twelfth-century Donegal in which the king symbolized his union with the land by mating with a mare and bathing in the broth of her flesh. A similar ritual, the *asvamedha,* involving a queen and a stallion in a tantric horse sacrifice,[78] occurs in Vedic tradition. The distance between Donegal and the Indus valley may seem great, yet we cannot discount the evidence of parallel customs in Ireland and India.[87] Part of the asvamedha ritual involves a kingly claimant sending out a horse to wander at will. Whatever lands it traverses become kingly territory. Similarly, in Ireland, kingly claimants let loose their horses onto disputed land, thus making the universal gesture of the conqueror. The horse or mare seems to have had a central function within rites of sovereignty.

We have already seen that when the representative of the land's sovereignty is violated—as in the case of Macha—the land suffers as well. Both Rhiannon and Macha are sovereignty-giving women who resort to their totemic mare shape when needed; both women are simultaneously revered and disgraced, denoting a duality of function or else a devalued origin. Scholars have universally agreed on the derivation of Rhiannon's name from the proto-Celtic title Rigantona, or "great queen," yet we can also connect her with Rhiain (maiden) Annwfn (Underworld), a title also appropriate to Rhiannon, and one which equates both these titles with those of Demeter and Persephone.

The cult of the Black Demeter, as attested by Pausanius, is also associated with a wider mare-cult across Europe, as we shall see. We are told that Demeter is searching for the abducted Persephone when Poseidon attempts to rape Demeter. She hides herself among the mares of King Onkios, but Poseidon, in the form of a stallion, finds her and couples with her. Demeter assumes her dark form and flees to a cave in Phygalia where she bears twins, a boy named Anon and a daughter called Despoina (mistress). She is depicted in a nearby temple as Demeter Erinys (angry Demeter) and is shown with a mare's head. Demeter's daughter is therefore both Maiden (Kore) and Mistress (Despoina) of the Dead. The priests of this cult were called *pouloi,* or "colts," a name that uncannily replicates Pwyll.

We are still not free from the association of the mare with death. The goddess of bad dreams is called Nightmare. Superstitiously we still refer to a white horse as "gray"—a euphemism that perhaps arises from a long-forgotten respect for the Goddess of the Land. In South Wales to this day the folk custom of the Mari Lwyd, Holy or Grey Mary, is continued. Every year, between Christmas and Twelfth Night, a company goes from house to house with a beribboned hobbyhorse made from a mare's skull. They attempt to gain entry with Mari by means of a riddling contest which, if the residents cannot answer, causes the door to be opened to the company of the gray mare:

> *Mari Lwyd, Lwyd Mari,*
> *A sacred thing through the night they carry.*[127]

A legend has it that Grey Mary was summarily ejected from the Bethlehem stable to allow for the birth of a more prestigious child, and that ever after, she roams for a place to birth her colt. The Underworld queen of the dead is present in both Mari Lwyd and Rhiannon: Both are outcasts and burden bearers; both welcome the dead.

One of the strongest associations of Rhiannon is with Epona, a European Celtic horse goddess. The textual evidence for Epona is thin on the grounds that she has no legend and her cult can be deduced only from inscriptions which turn up all over Atun, Metz, and Worms district—those places where the Roman legions which spread her cult were stationed. Of Epona we have this fragmentary statement: "A certain Phoulonios Stellos who hated women had intercourse with a mare. In time, she brought forth a beautiful maiden whom she named Epona, a goddess of horses."[78]

It seems she was a goddess of abundance, the newborn, and the dead; of horsemen, fertility, and animals. Her feast day, incorporated into the Roman state calendar, was December 18, fixed at midwinter between the Consualia (December 15) and the Opalia (December 19). Consus was the god of seed sowing and was connected with horses, asses, and mules. His altar was cleared of earth twice a year on feast days; races were held in his honor; and horses, mules, and asses were rested on this day and given garlands. Consus was further associated with Poseidon Hippios. Ops was the goddess of harvest; she inherited the attributes of Rhea. Thus, it will be seen, Rhiannon and Epona really do have connections: Rhiannon and Manawyddan, as deities of Underworld and sea, respectively, equate well with Consus and Ops, but also with Demeter Erinys and Poseidon.[2]

Epona's image appeared in stables from Gaul to Thessaly. Ostlers offered her roses and the legions in Germany dedicated many plaques to her on which she is shown with a foal following her progress, or with a foal or pair of foals eating from the manger of her lap.[68] Two of Epona's symbols, the key and the dog, also mark her as a goddess of the Underworld.[4] The custom of honoring Epona with rose garlands and her association with asses and horses may also give us new insight into the predicament of Lucius Apuleius, who, in "The Golden Ass," is turned into an ass by mistake and is destined to remain in this shape until he can consume roses. While in the stable he notices a little shrine of the mare-headed mother, the goddess Epona, standing in a niche in the post that supports the main beam of the stable. It is wreathed with freshly garlanded roses, but, unfortunately, before he is able to eat them, thieves break in and he begins a long series of adventures in his new shape. It is not until he encounters a mystery procession in honor of Isis, at which he succeeds at eating a garland of roses, that he becomes a man once more. But this is not before he is vouchsafed a vision of the goddess and is taken under her protection:

> When at the destined end of your life you descend to the land of ghosts, there too in the subterrene hemisphere you shall have frequent occasion to adore me. From the Elysian fields you will see me as queen of the profound Stygian realm, shining through the darkness of Acheron with a light as kindly and tender as I show you now.[9]

Such is the promise of the queen of the Underworld, whether she be Isis, Epona, or Rhiannon: She who lost her own child, or who has had to hide him from danger, welcomes the confused initiate into her mysteries with the love of Modron, the Great Mother.

The Celtic mania for horses has not lessened, as a trip to any racecourse in the world will show. Yet the respect given the horse was not due only to its speed and faithfulness, but also to a remembrance of the lady of the horses herself, the Mare of Sovereignty who bore the burdens of others and who lost her own foal. Such resonances strike us deeply still. After all, is not Pryderi found in a stable, just as Christ was found in a manger on Epiphany, surrounded by newly dropped lambs? Pryderi's totem is the foal, then, just as Christ's is the lamb.

If we look at a depiction of Epona, certain iconographical features are quite startling. She is seated on the right side of the horse (not the more customary left). She does not ride astride, but sits as a woman sits on an ass. Of course the image is familiar: Epona travels into exile with her endangered foal, just as Mary flees into Egypt, and always, iconographically precise to the last feature, travels from left to right.

In a tangled web of stories, Rhiannon and Pryderi are but one pair of protagonists. Other parallels, Christian and pagan, Celtic and classical, have still to emerge. If we are to arrive at a complete mosaic of Mabon and Modron, other pieces are still to be found and put in the right place. Rhiannon and Pryderi have shown us the way into the Otherworld, where we shall travel again.

# 3
# Branwen, Daughter of Llyr

*O Land!—O Bran lie under.*

DAVID JONES, *IN PARENTHESIS*

*"Do you want to hear my story?" said the*
*head.*
*"I've already said so more than once," I said.*
*"My story," said the head. "You must pay for*
*it, there is a price if I tell it."*
*"What's the price?" I said.*

*"The price is that if I tell it, you'll know it,"*
*said the head. "You won't be able to get it out*
*of your mind, it doesn't stop, it just goes on*
*happening with whoever falls into it, maybe*
*you."*

RUSSELL HOBAN, *A CONVERSATION*
*WITH THE HEAD OF ORPHEUS*

## Entertaining the Noble Head

"Branwen, Daughter of Llyr" is one of the most poetic and cohesive of the Four Branches, in which it is possible to perceive distinct parallels between Irish and Welsh traditions. Branwen herself suffers a similar fate to that of Rhiannon, being yet another "foreign" wife of whom the people disapprove, while her brother, Bran, has a long-established role of guardianship. Together they manifest the archetypes of Sovereignty and her champion. Efnissien, the jealous brother, is one player in the long tradition of "disruptive elements at the feast." Central to the story is the Cauldron of Rebirth originally brought from Ireland, which returns there to effect the devastating finale of the story.

The fetching, gifting, or theft of the cauldron is related to an early Welsh poem, "Preiddeu Annwfn" (The Spoils of Annwfn), which we shall be discussing in chapter 6. This theme gives us the proto-Grail story which developed in such profusion in medieval literature. The guardianship of the Grail or cauldron by the Fisher King is also Bran's function, for the holy vessel is a symbol of the sovereignty of the land. It is for this reason that Bran is always known by his epithet Bendigeid (the blessed): He who guards the hallows of sovereignty guards the kingship of the land, and is thus in the place of a priest or holy man. As we shall see later, Bran is an example of the inner guardian, one who is to be encountered by the kingly candidate to the seat of the Pendragon.

## Synopsis of "Branwen, Daughter of Llyr"

(1) Bran the Blessed is crowned King of the Island of Britain. Seated one day with his brother, Manawyddan, and their half brothers, (2) Nissien and Efnissien, he sees thirteen ships sailing from Ireland into the bay at Harlech. (3) It is Matholwch, King of Ireland, come to ask for an alliance with Bran through marriage to Branwen, his sister. Negotiations are concluded and the marriage takes place at Aberffraw, (4) where tents are pitched—for Bran, because of his titanic size, cannot be accommodated within a house.

(5) Efnissien, Branwen's half brother, arrives to find his sister already married. (6) In retaliation he mutilates Matholwch's horses. Bran offers a generous honor price and replacement horses, but Matholwch is not appeased; so Bran gifts him with the Cauldron of Rebirth, into which dead men can be placed to emerge revived, though they remain forever speechless. (7) Matholwch knew the cauldron's original owners, who came from a lake in Ireland: The woman gave birth every six weeks to a fully armed warrior and was a titan, like her husband. Their behavior had so offended everyone that Matholwch had ordered their deaths in a specially built house of iron, which was then heated from without. Both man and woman escaped. Bran has received them hospitably, divided their number, and set them to work fortifying each place in which they stayed.

(8) Although Branwen bears a son, Gwern, to the king of Ireland, after two years the Irish talk Matholwch into putting her away. She is sent to the kitchens where each day the butcher strikes her on the ear after he has finished slaughtering animals. The king places an embargo on travel to or from Wales. At the end of three years Branwen has taught a starling to speak. She binds a letter to its wing and sends it to Bran at Caer Seint, who reads the missive and knows Branwen's disgrace.

(9) Bran musters the men of Britain, leaving seven men in charge in his absence, with his son, Caradawg, as chieftain. The British men sail for Ireland, but Bran strides through the waters, carrying the musicians on his shoulders. (10) Matholwch's swineherds report an amazing sight: a forest moving through the sea with a mountain. Branwen is summoned to solve the mystery, and she identifies the wonder as Bran and his men come to rescue her. (11) Matholwch and his men withdraw beyond the river Shannon, destroying its bridge and hoping that the magnetic stones in the river will prevent ships from crossing it. Bran makes himself a bridge for his men. Matholwch sends conciliatory messages to Bran, offering to abdicate in favor of his son, Gwern. (12) Because Bran receives this offer coolly, the Irish ask Branwen what will please her brother. (13) The Irish then build a house to contain Bran, but on every one of its hundred pillars are hung two bags, each

holding an armed man. Efnissien inspects the house and, when told that the bags contain only flour, crushes the skulls of each warrior.

(14) At the feast to acclaim Gwern as king of Ireland, the boy is passed round to each uncle until he comes to Efnissien, who seizes the boy and (15) thrusts him into the fire. Bran first prevents Branwen from joining her son, and then leaps up amid the uproar and bids the dogs of Gwern to beware of (16) Morddwyd Tyllion. (17) The Irish kindle the Cauldron of Rebirth and thrust in the corpses of their dead. (18) Efnissien is struck with shame and remorse and, hiding himself among the Irish dead, he is thrown into the cauldron. He, a living man, stretches himself out and so breaks the cauldron too. (19) Only seven men escape from the ensuing rout, along with Bran himself, who is wounded in his heel by a poisoned spear. He bids his men cut off his head and bear it to the White Tower in London, with his face turned towards France. He then promises that he will be a good companion to his men on their journey, that they will stay in two places for many years in great blessedness, but that they must beware of opening the door towards Cornwall. (20) Returning to Wales with Bran's head, they disembark at Aber Alaw, where Branwen despairs over the destruction wrought because of her. She dies and is buried there.

(21) The company hears that in their absence, the island has fallen to Caswallawn, a kinsman of Bran. They learn that Bran's son is dead, and that only Pendaran Dyfed has escaped. (22) They pass to Harlech, where they feast for seven years while the birds of Rhiannon sing to them, making them forget their sorrow. They then go to Gwales and feast in a hall with three doors—two open and the third closed. For eighty years they remain there—recounted in an episode called "The Assembly of the Noble Head." (23) Then Heilyn opens the door towards Cornwall. They remember all that has befallen them and feel their sorrow more bitterly than before. (24) They inter Bran's head at the White Tower, which is called one of the three fortunate concealments and is afterwards called one of the three unfortunate disclosures because Arthur digs up the head.

(25) Only five pregnant women are left to populate devastated Ireland. These five have five sons who mate with each other's mothers, and so they divide the land into five districts. (26) This branch is comprised of the stories "Branwen's Blow," "The Men Who Set Out from Ireland," "The Assembly of the Noble Head," "The Feasting in Harlech," and "The Singing of the Birds of Rhiannon."

## Commentary

(1) The name Beli appears as the ancestor at the head of many British genealogies, often coupled with Anna (see figure 2). Although they do not appear in this story, it is significant that they have been identified with the deities Belinus and Anu,[5] the grand ancestors of the Celtic pantheons. Caswallawn, the shadowy conqueror of Britain, is Bran's uncle; he appears in the next branch.

(2) The names Nissien and Efnissien translate as "peaceful" and "not so peaceful." The brothers are polarized to no purpose in this story because Nissien contributes nothing to the action. Efnissien's role as disrupter is readily paralleled throughout mythology and folk story. Like the goddess Eris, who throws the apple of discord at Peleus and Thetis's wedding in Greek myth,[40] or like Loki, who sows dissension at Aegir's feast in Norse myth, [29, 79] or the Irish Bricrui Poison-Tongue,[28] Efnissien is fated to wreak havoc on both family and nation.

(3) Branwen is named here as one of the three chief ancestresses of the Island of Britain. This is clearly from a lost triad, but we are unable to make much of this puzzling statement without the names of the other two ancestresses. Branwen has no descendants who live to have children, for her only child, Gwern, dies as a boy. Perhaps this lost triad becomes comprehensible if Branwen is seen as one of the many women who represent the Lady of Sovereignty. This is almost the only reason that makes Efnissien's subsequent behavior understandable (see note 5, below).

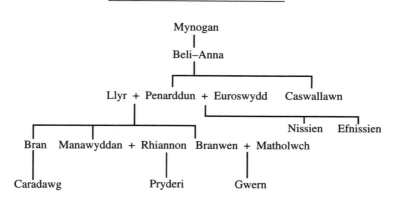

Figure 2. The family tree of Bran

(4) Bran is of titanic stature, one of the lost giants of the former races, yet his brothers and sister are of normal size. (For further discussion of this, see the section Cronos and the Sleeping Lord, later in this chapter.)

(5) Efnissien is not consulted about his sister's marriage. His reaction is that of the jealous brother John of traditional folk ballad[26] whose sister is courted by a man who asks consent of all her kin except him. John then ambushes the newlyweds and slays them in an incestuous revenge. If we consider Branwen as a type of Sovereignty—the royal woman whose blood confers sovereignty on her husband and children—Efnissien's seemingly anarchic reaction is seen in a more honorable light, as that of a defender of Sovereignty. Efnissien's reasoning is that if Branwen marries the Irish king, the Island of Britain loses its royal line. He is, then, the champion of both Sovereignty and the land of Britain.

(6) The mutilation of Matholwch's horses is a gross insult to the laws of Celtic hospitality. In light of the fact that the major totem of British sovereignty is the horse, this action takes on deeper significance. The crime of horse mutilation seems to recur when national identity is threatened, both in myth as well as within living memory, several cases being recently documented. Bran's generous sarhad is not acceptable

until the Cauldron of Rebirth is also thrown in, but like many otherworldly gifts that are wrongly used, it subsequently devastates Ireland
and disempowers Britain.

(7) The man and woman with the cauldron are called Llassar Llaes
Gyfnewid and Cymeidei Cymeinfoll. They are clearly Underworld
beings and their prototypes appear in the Irish story "The Destruction
of Da Derga's Hostel" as Fer Caille and Cichuil, who are likewise unwel-
come guests. [148] Llassar and his wife and children are grudgingly
received by Matholwch but more hospitably welcomed by Bran, who
finds them so cooperative that he leaves behind one of their children,
Llashar, to help govern Britain in his absence. Both giants come from
a lake, and just as the cauldron gives birth to armed warriors, so too
does Cymeidei give birth to a fully armed warrior every six weeks. The
preparation of the iron house by Matholwch is the same ruse which the
Irish king Labriad Loingsech employs to kill his troublesome uncle,
though at the cost of burning alive his mother and his jester also.[32] Of
all the parallel Irish themes, this is the strongest in the story of
Branwen. The iron house also encloses the drunken Ulstermen in "The
Intoxication of the Ulstermen."[28] After all, what is an iron house that
cooks things but an inverted cauldron? A full study of the major Irish
borrowings and parallels can be found in *Branwen, Daughter of Llyr* by
Proinsias MacCana.[65] The fact that Bran is able to control the cauldron
folk is significant, for he himself becomes the guardian of the hallows
and an otherworldly king of power.

(8) As Rhiannon's reception is pleasant when she is first married, so is
Branwen's, but she is soon disowned because of the shame her brother
has brought on the Irish people. During their punishment, both women
resort to their totemic beasts: Rhiannon to the mare, and Branwen to the
starling (see chapter 8). Triad 53 records this blow as one of the three
harmful blows to the Island of Britain, one of the others being the striking of Gwenhwyfar, Arthur's queen. This triad clearly references the

shamefulness of blows to Lady Sovereignty—which also dishonor the land—further strengthening Branwen's identification with Sovereignty.

It will be recalled that in legend each of King Lear's daughters is questioned by her father as to how much she loves him so that he might decide who should have the sovereignty of Britain. Branwen is the daughter of Llyr, and although an analogous episode is absent from our story, it brings out many interesting resonances for consideration. In the folk story "Cap o' Rushes," which is derived from the legend of Lear and his daughters, the king asks his question and receives fulsome answers from his first two daughters, but the third daughter replies, "As much as meat loves salt," thus causing her father to reject her. She then weaves a cloak or cap of rushes and, like Branwen, becomes a kitchen maid whose gentle ways are mocked by the scullions. Cap o' Rushes is rescued from her predicament only by sending to her appointed prince a ring baked in a pie. He recognizes it as the jewel of the girl with whom he danced the night before. They are subsequently married and she is reconciled to her father who recognizes her true love by granting her sovereignty.

Unfortunately, we have no such parallel solution in Branwen's story. Reduced from her duties as queen of Ireland to kitchen drudge, she nevertheless shows herself resourceful and skilled in the riddling patterns of understanding which grace this story (see note 10, below).

(9) We learn from the text that the sea passage is shallow between Ireland and Wales, and that the Irish Sea has inundated many lands since then. Both landmasses were once joined, but at a time some thousands of years before the writing of this story, though this tale still remembers an earlier time. Parts of the Irish and Welsh coastlines are still subject to the sea's incursions to this day, and drowned lands and villages beneath the sea are the stuff of living folk memory. The influence of Llyr is with us yet.[76]

(10) Bran strides through the waves with his musicians on his shoulder—

he is so disproportionately huge that the Irish swineherd's perception is baffled. Their reportage reads like the riddling of poets. Just as Macbeth cannot believe that Birnham Wood has come to Dunsinane, neither can Matholwch fathom the riddling message of his swineherds. Only Branwen can interpret the riddle of the forest as the British fleet and the moving mountain with two lakes as the nose and eyes of her brother, Bran.

(11) Ancient Celtic kingship continually revolves around the words of Bran: "He who would be chief, let him also be a bridge." To whom more is given, from him more is required. A king cannot stand aside and let his ministers or warriors act for him; he alone must stand in the place of mediation or sacrifice, hazarding his own person. This understanding is an important key to Bran and to the succession of the Pendragons. Inherent in this phrase is the kingly sacrifice which Bran is willing to undergo for the good of his people.

(12) Just as Matholwch was not satisfied with the mere replacement of his horses, neither is Bran satisfied with seeing his nephew made king: Why should he not be king himself? Just as he once trapped the guardians of the cauldron, so Matholwch plans to destroy Bran in the iron house. This killing of guests violated hospitality in a way we find hard to grasp now; for the British, as for the Greeks and many other people in traditional society, the guest was holy, sent by God. Once anyone had eaten and slept in the host's house, that guest was henceforth a "guest-friend." Murder was unlawful—but to kill a guest deeply dishonored the tribe. Welsh listeners to this story would have been reminded of the massacre at Ambrius: Each Saxon was seated next to an unarmed Briton at a feast when, on a given signal, each stabbed his neighbor with a knife concealed in his long sleeve. Thus perished most of Britain's nobility[37] as also happens here in this story.

(13) The grisly humor of this episode disguises some more poetic rid-

dling. Efnissien is told that the bags contain flour, but in crushing to death the warriors hidden within, he merely supplies the cauldron with invincible fodder against his own countrymen. The Irish dead literally rise again, like kneaded dough that is baked in the oven. The grim ingredients of the cauldron raise up dead men by the score. This theme of grain which dies and yet rises again is the subject of one of Taliesin's poems (see chapter 7).

(14) According to various translators, before he casts Gwern into the fire, Efnissien exclaims either "No one here realizes what I am about to do," implying that his kindred are guiltless of his intentions, or "Everyone here assembled will be outraged by my actions." This patched peace cannot remain stitched for long, and Efnissien ensures that hostilities quickly resume.

(15) Why does Efnissien cast his nephew into the fire? The myths of both Isis and Demeter tell of their sojourn in a household in which they nurse a young baby and attempt to make the boy immortal by holding him in the fire—until so prevented by the boy's mother.[40]

A similar story is told of Achilles, whose mother bathes him in fire, rendering him immortal and invulnerable except for the heel by which she holds him. Such a theory might gain strength from Bran's following remark (see note 16, below). If Efnissien is motivated solely by malice, then we need look no further. If a happy ending were possible for this story, this feast would be the point at which to conclude it, with the Irish and British reconciled at the celebration of Gwern's succession to the kingship. But if Efnissien is, as we have postulated, the defender of Britain's sovereignty, then the death of Gwern would render the Irish succession void and Branwen free to marry a British noble, and would leave sufficient British troops on Irish soil to effect a conquest. Efnissien finally reveals his noble nature in breaking the power of the cauldron by entering it as a living man, thereby saving the British host at the cost his own death.

(16) Bran shouts: "Dogs of Gwern, beware of the pierced or wounded thigh!" He has not, at this point, been wounded, so unless he is prophesying, what does this signify? First, he is addressing the dead Gwern's troops. Second, he is speaking of himself as though Pierced or Wounded Thigh was a rightful title, like his epithet of Blessed. As we shall establish below, Bran is a prototype of the Fisher King or Grail guardian, who is likewise wounded through the thigh.

(17) The scene is now one of utter horror and devastation. The dead are revived, though they are without speech. The dead may not speak of what they have seen in death's kingdom because they suffer only one death, while the initiate poet suffers "the second death" of initiation and so can speak the riddling tongue of initiates—a language incomprehensible to noninitiates (see chapter 7). Strabo, the Greek historian, writes of similar rites practiced by Germanic tribes: Prisoners of war are slain over a cauldron by prophetesses—such a scene is depicted on the Gundestrup cauldron.[38] In the Irish story "The Second Battle of Mag Tuired," the healer Diancecht and his children similarly revive the slain Tuatha de Danaan by throwing them into the well named Slane.[148]

(18) Efnissien's only redress is to break the cauldron's power by entering it as a living man; he is neither dead nor an initiate of the mysteries and so has no right to be "cauldron born." We guess at his likely motivation, however, and lament his actions. Efnissien's death is a noble one, though it brings hollow victory to Britain.

(19) Only seven men escape from Ireland: Pryderi, Manawyddan, Glifieu Eil Taran, Taliesin, Ynawg, Gruddyeu ap Muriel, and Heilyn ap Gwyn Hen. Likewise, only seven escape with Arthur after he has plundered Annwfn in the poem "Preiddeu Annwfn" (see chapter 6). Significantly, Taliesin is the survivor of both expeditions, to sing of these exploits to those who come after. The oracular head of Bran is discussed below.

(20) The parallels between Branwen and Kriemhild of the Germanic *Nibelungenlied* are pointed.[67, 79] Kriemhild marries the barbaric Etzel in the hope of avenging her husband Siegfried's death. Siegfried's murderer, Hagen, visits Kriemhild and slays her son, which is the signal for mass slaughter and the burning down of the hall. Although Branwen is rescued by Bran, her heart is broken. Triad 95 speaks of her as "one of the three who died of bewilderment."[5] Like the Irish Deirdrui of the Sorrows, who looks upon the two kings who are fated to share her body after her husband's death and who commits suicide, Branwen looks between the two countries laid waste for her and expires of grief. In Geoffrey of Monmouth we read that Lear's daughter Cordelia—whom Branwen much resembles—buries her father in an underground chamber dedicated to the god Janus (he of the head which looks both ways). Echoes of Branwen are very loud, since Branwen herself is buried in a "four-sided" grave on the banks of the Alaw. And although Branwen, unlike Shakespeare's Cordelia, does not commit suicide, the succession of sovereignty is likewise confused; it is virtually interred with the body of Branwen and the head of Bran.[37]

(21) In the absence of the host, Caswallawn has usurped the kingship by overcoming the seven guardians left in Bran's stead through means of his magic mantle of invisibility. (This mantle appears in the list of the Thirteen Treasures of Britain, page 56.) Like the invisible knight Garlon, who causes the Dolorous Blow in the Grail legends, so Caswallawn is responsible for causing disaster. Pendaran escapes to become Pryderi's foster father in a previous story, although Pryderi is himself one of the survivors, a disparity noted in the last chapter. Caradawg, Bran's son, is the second person whose heart, like Branwen's, is broken from bewilderment (Triad 95).

(22) The two feasts at Harlech and Gwales (identified as Grassholm, off Pembrokeshire) last eighty-seven years in total, though the Assembly of the Noble Head really takes place in the Otherworld, where time does

not run. The appearance of the birds of Rhiannon, the messengers of hope and otherworldly bliss, grant the gift of forgetfulness, the very same gift which Greek Lethe gives to the dead. These birds sing on the Tree of Knowledge and Memory in the Celtic paradise. The oracular and otherworldly gift of the Irish *filidh*, the vision-poets, was denoted by the silver branch hung with little bells, which was held over the heads of Celtic master-poets as part of their insignia—a branch from the paradisal tree. Otherworldly birds and cauldrons appear in "The Tragic Death of Cú Roi mac Daire" (see the section Guarding the Hallows, below).

(23) Britain is also called the Island of the Strong Door in the poem "Preiddeu Annwfn," indicating not only the strength of defense against oppression, but also the strong door standing between the worlds: Once that door is open, the spell of the Otherworld is lifted as time and remembrance return in a painful flood. The head of Bran remains uncorrupted as long as the door is closed.

(24) This passage refers to Triad 37, the three fortunate concealments, in which "the Head of Bran the Blessed . . . was concealed in the White Hill in London, with its face towards France. And as long as it was in the position in which it was put there, no Saxon oppression would ever come to this island."

Juxtaposed to these are the three unfortunate disclosures: "Arthur disclosed the Head of Bran the Blessed from the White Hill, because it did not seem right to him that this Island should be defended by the strength of anyone but by his own."[5]

The Tower of London, or the White Mount, is still the province of ravens; their disappearance is said to betoken invasion and the conquest of Britain, for which reason their wings are kept clipped, though recently they have been successfully bred in captivity. They are the totem bird of Bran, whose own name means quite simply "raven." The concealment and disinterment of Bran's head has a deeper significance in relation to the British mysteries. A literal reading of these triads shows Arthur possessed of hubris, yet in the succession of the Pendragons, Arthur's visit to Annwfn is a necessary one in which he must possess the hallows of Sovereignty, which are guided by the last great kingly sacrifice, Bran himself (see chapter 9). These British Isles have been known since classical times as the prison or sleeping place of Cronos, the great Titan of time and transmutation. We shall be discussing Bran as a type of Cronos in the commentary in the section Cronos and the Sleeping Lord, below.

(25) This story appears in the Irish *Book of Invasions* and neatly explains why Ireland was anciently split into five provinces.

(26) From this medley of titles and from the numerous cross-referenced triads, the story of Branwen clearly has primary place in the storyteller's repertoire.

## Guarding the Hallows

The richness of themes within "Branwen, Daughter of Llyr" makes it difficult for us to survey it fully. The reader will be struck perhaps by the universal elements common to many European folk stories and mythologies, especially in relation to the Greek legends about the family of Achilles and to both Norse and Germanic cycles.[79] Although Branwen is the eponymous heroine, the story really turns on the possession of the Cauldron of Rebirth—the Pair Dedani.

The cauldron is the prototype of the Grail itself, the otherworldly vessel whose gifts include healing, rebirth, knowledge, spiritual fulfillment, paradisal bliss, and magical power, as well as the provision of physical nourishment. The cauldron is the pagan resonance of the Grail, which has been identified with the redemptive symbol of Christ's new covenant. Both Grail and cauldron dispense the draught of salvation, the waters of everlastingness; both are vessels that have otherworldly provenance; both are attainable only by people of sovereign power or heroes of daring courage. Death—physical and spiritual—is written into the scenario of the quest for both Grail and cauldron: Those who fail are slain; those who win die to the world and are reborn or initiated into a different state of life.

The cauldron in "Branwen" comes from the Otherworld to Ireland and then Wales to become a vessel of contending kings. Matholwch despises its gifts, losing both the vessel and his life. Bran, on the other hand, accepts its gifts wholeheartedly to the extent that he lays down his life to become its guardian. The Irish employ the cauldron to revive their warriors, yet the seven British survivors of the slaughter are nourished by its bounty during the Assembly of the Noble Head, when, like the Grail elders, they sit with Bran's head for company, listening to the birds of Rhiannon and supping from the cauldron whose waters keep them alive yet free from aging.

The appearance of the cauldron and the paradisal birds is a theme of the Irish story "The Tragic Death of Cú Roi mac Daire," in which we observe resonances between the stories of both Branwen and Math. After the siege of Fir Falgae, there is contention over the spoils, including the woman Blathnat, the three cows of Tuchna, and the three birds which perch in the cows' ears, causing them to give into a cauldron the milk of thirty cows. Cú Roi is given nothing though he had helped the Ulstermen while disguised in a gray mantle. He therefore picks up the cows, thrusts the birds into his belt, puts Blathnat under one arm, and carries off the cauldron over his back. Cú Chulainn alone challenges him, and Cú Roi buries him up to the armpits in mud, shaves his head with a sword, and anoints him with cow dung for his trouble.

Cú Chulainn then seeks revenge on the disguised stranger. For shame of his appearance he does not appear at court but follows a flock of blackbirds, beheading one of them in every country he journeys through. Finally he reaches Srub Brain (raven's beak) in the West, near Cú Roi's fort, when he guesses the identity of his opponent. He manages to speak to Blathnat, with whom he is secretly in love, and together they plan Cú Roi's death. Diverting his men, Blathnat bathes

Cú Roi in the river into which she pours the milk from the cauldron as a signal for Cú Chulainn to attack, then she binds her abductor to the bedpost by his hair, where the Ulstermen behead him.

Cú Roi's poet, Fercetne, asks where Blathnat might be and is told, "She was only delivered because Cú Roi's head was struck off." Fercetne then seizes his master's betrayer and hurls both himself and her over a cliff to their deaths.[28]

In this story the cauldron is an otherworldly spoil over which rival kings contend. Cú Roi is identifiable with Bran, a titan of power and magical strength, though his role differs radically from Bran's. Cú Chulainn beheads blackbirds on his journey and realizes at Srub Brain who the stranger is. Blathnat is released only by Cú Roi's beheading. The meaning of her name and that of Blodeuwedd in "Math, Son of Mathonwy" are identical, as their Delilah-like betrayal suggests: They are both flower women of Otherworld provenance. Fercetne, the killer of Blathnat, is in Efnissien's place. Interestingly, the otherworldly spoils include a woman as well as a cauldron. In the Irish king cycles, otherworldly women frequently act as the Lady of Sovereignty and bestow kingship on heroes, just as we have suggested Branwen does to Matholwch.

In British legend the woman representing Sovereignty is rarely present in an obvious sense. More clearly present is the cauldron or other items forming the regalia of Sovereignty, the hallows themselves. The hallows, as the holy items of kingly regalia are termed, must be possessed by the rightful monarch, who is thus able to administer his lands with earthly discernment and otherworldly knowledge. This is the fundamental *raison d'etre* of "Branwen," a theme which is further underlined in "Culhwch and Olwen" and in the "Preiddeu Annwfn," in which Arthur and his companions journey ostensibly to Ireland to fetch certain objects, though it is clear that Ireland merely stands in the place of the Underworld, where these objects are secreted. This is part of the succession of the Pendragons—the kingly candidate must enter the Underworld and fetch the hallows from their guardian—and is a feature discernible from early British legend, later to be replaced by the quests of Arthur's knights for the hallows of the Grail: the spear, sword, cup, and dish.[72]

What were these hallows originally? Fortunately we possess a manuscript which lists the Thirteen Treasures of Britain. Like the triads, these items refer to stories we sometimes know little about, and they are often confused and repetitious. It is said that Myrddin (Merlin) obtained all thirteen of them and that he took them to his glass house on Bardsey Island, where they remain forever.[5] This fits well with Myrddin's role as guardian of Britain, the initiate who has withdrawn from this world into the Otherworld, where, like Bran, he keeps a careful eye upon the flow of energy between the two worlds.

## The Thirteen Treasures of Britain

1. Dyrnwyn (white hilt), the sword of Rhydderch the Generous. If a nobleman drew this, the blade burst into flames. It came into the hand of anyone who asked for it, but everyone rejected it because of this ability.

2. The hamper of Gwyddno Garanhir. If food enough for one was placed in this, food for a hundred could be taken from it.

3. The horn of Bran the Niggard from the North. This contained whatever drink anyone desired.

4. The chariot of Morgan the Wealthy. This carried a man quickly to the place of his desire.

5. The halter of Clydno Eiddyn, which was fastened by a staple to the foot of Clydno's bed. The horse of a man's desire could be found in the halter.

6. The knife of Llawfnodedd the Horseman. This served twenty-four men.

7. The cauldron of Dyrnwch the Giant. This boiled the meat of a hero, but not that of a coward.

8. The whetstone of Tudwal Tydglyd. If a hero sharpened his sword on this, his opponents bled to death; if a coward did so, his opponent was no worse.

9. The coat of Padaen Red Coat. This was the right size for any nobleman, but did not fit a peasant.

10.,11. The crock and dish of Rhygenydd the Cleric. These provided the food of anyone's desire.

12. The chessboard of Gwenddolau ap Ceidio. The men were of silver, the board of gold, and the pieces would play by themselves.

13. The mantle of Arthur in Cornwall. This made the wearer invisible, though he could see everyone.[5]

Clearly items 2, 3, 10, and 11 serve much the same purpose, one which is shared by the Grail. The sword of Rhydderch is the Glaive or sword of light, a weapon which is wielded with great effect in the quest for the Underworld cauldron (see chapter 6). The horn of Bran the Niggard is clearly a corrupted reference to the cauldron of Bran the Blessed. The mantle of Arthur is worn by Caswallawn in "Branwen" and is used in the killing of Bran's son and the seven guardians of Britain.

The chessboard of Gwenddolau appears in the *Mabinogion* in "Peredur," "The Dream of Rhonabwy," and "The Dream of Macsen Wledig." The magical chessboard is a paradigm of the land of Britain over which the contending sides battle. The Welsh and Irish gaming board differed from the modern game of chess: The board was sometimes seven squares by seven squares. In Irish the game was called *brandubh* and the pieces were made up of one king and eight opponents. *Brandubh* translates as "black Bran"; the game was also called *brannabh* which may be a corruption of Bran Naomh (blessed Bran). It is tempting to see the brandubh board as a paradigm of the hall at Harlech and Gwales, where the surviving seven feast with their king.

This list of hallows is medieval and does not represent the true treasures, some of which descend complete into the later Grail stories while others can be found in the early story of "Culhwch and Olwen" (see chapter 6). They remain echoes of the symbols of sovereignty, which must be won from their inner guardian by the rightful king. So why do we consider Bran to be such a guardian and on what evidence? To discover this we must look at the textured levels of an ancient tradition where a figure even older than Bran guards his golden horde in the timeless realms lying behind the Island of Britain.

## Cronos and the Sleeping Lord

The titanic stature of Bran the Blessed indicates that he is indeed one of the primordial and archetypal guardians of Britain. Arthur is clearly his successor on the list of mighty ancestors who have kept these shores free from oppression, and many such guardians follow him. But how did this tradition start—and by what authority? And why does Britain have such an important role in the world of the mysteries?

There is an authentic tradition stemming from classical sources which indicates Britain as a known otherworldly locus wherein is chained the last and greatest of the Titans: Cronos. Cronos's father, Uranus, begot many children with Gaia, but he never let them see the light of day, instead imprisoning them in the depths of the earth. Gaia helped her son Cronos castrate his father. But Cronos followed the same pattern when he came to maturity, swallowing up the children of his wife, Rhea, as they came from the womb. Rhea bore Zeus secretly and hid him, giving Cronos a stone in the child's place. When Zeus grew up he liberated his brothers and sisters and chained Cronos at the outermost edge of the world on the Isles of the Blest, identified as the British Isles.[40, 57] Thus far, the classical story.

In Plutarch's "The Silence of Oracles" there is a report from an official called Demetrius who visited Britain and learned many of the ancient religious traditions of these islands, including the following:

There is one island there where Cronos is a prisoner guarded by
Briareus in his sleep—sleep was the fetters designed for Cronos, and
many daimones lie around him as servants and followers.[60]

In another passage of Plutarch from "The Face of the Moon," a
Carthaginian antiquarian, Sextus Sylla, observes:

The natives have a story that in one of these [islands] Cronos has
been confined by Zeus, but that he, having a son for gaoler, is left sovereign lord of those islands . . . Cronos himself sleeps within a deep
cave resting on rock which looks like gold . . . birds fly in at the top-
most part of the rock, and bear him ambrosia, and the whole island
is pervaded by the fragrance shed from the rock.[11, 85]

Not only the scent pervades, but so does the evidence of tradition.
Cronos's myth is Greek, yet Bran's is British. We cannot say that one
preceded the other, but we may conclude that there were parallel or
shared traditions. Cronos rules the lost Golden Age—a timeless era corresponding to the otherworldly dimension. His very name means
"time." Zeus stops time by anchoring his father in the cave of sleep, but
father and son still interact, according to Plutarch. Cronos's companions are said to give forth utterances of prophetic power: "[B]ut the
greatest and those about the greatest issues, they announce when they
return as dreams of Cronos; for the things which Zeus premeditates,
Cronos dreams."[11]

This passage is central to the theme of Mabon and the succession
of the Pendragons, for it presupposes an interaction between the otherworldly kingdom of the Sleeping Lord and the realm of the worldly
king or ruler.

It is evident from "Branwen, Daughter of Llyr" that Bran's effect
does not end at death; rather it starts a new cycle of occurrence. Bran's
head, like that of the floating oracular head of Orpheus,[40] gives counsel after death; moreover, it is guardian of Britain against oppression
and guardian of the life-giving cauldron, which is itself a vessel of otherworldly, or, we might say, Golden Age power.

Bran entertains his seven companions on the island of Gwales in a place outside time, just as Arthur in legend sleeps with his companions under many hills, ready to rise at his country's need. Similarly, Cronos and his attendant "daimones" sleep in an otherworldly cave, awaiting their release. Bran guards the cauldron; Arthur guards a golden treasure, it is said; and Cronos guards the Golden Age itself and his very presence impregnates the land with the sweet odors of the Otherworld—a place of the ever-living, yet also of the mighty dead. These resonances reveal a strong tradition forming one of the central mysteries of Britain: that of the Sleeping Lord who is wounded, yet does not die; one who passes into the Avalonian realms to await the blowing of the mystic horn in a new time, when he will rise and come again, made young and strong, purged of age. Cronos is the lord of time and transmutation, the Titan who stands at the Strong Door, keeping at bay the destructive enchantments of an earlier time.

So, too, Bran guards Britain and its hallows. He is wounded, like the Grail guardian Brons, but he is enabled to pass on to his next phase by the coming of Arthur, who wins the hallows from Annwfn and promises to succeed to Bran's position as guardian when his time comes. After Camlann and the Last Battle, Arthur goes to Avalon, where his wounds will be healed and where he will hold the hallows in trust for the kingly candidate—the Pendragon—who comes after him. This is why Excalibur, one of many hallowed treasures of sovereignty, is cast back into the lake—only so may the kingly candidate win his regalia: by means of descent into Annwfn or by passing into Avalon.

If Arthur succeeds to Bran's position of Pen Annwfn, who succeeds to the post of Pendragon? The inner Pendragons are many and nameless, and like those knights who achieve the Grail, they are drawn from only the most worthy champions.

We must also ask: If Bran is no longer a Pen Annwfn, what does he pass on to become? What changes are wrought in the ancient titan during his golden sleep? We look to the land of Britain and wonder:

*Does the land wait the sleeping lord,*
*or is the wasted land*
*that very lord who sleeps?*'[118]

We must look to Mabon and his imprisonment if this mystery is to be revealed, else we will never know whether we are merely a dream of Bran/Cronos or a people unfettered by the subtle enchantments of stale tradition.

# 4
# Ⅲanawyddan, Son of Llyr

*Sospan fach yn berwi ar y tan,*
*Sospan fawr yn berwi ar a llawr.*
*A'r gath wedi crafu Joni bach.*
TRADITIONAL WELSH RUGBY SONG

*When Bron the Fisher King saw that Perceval*
*would ask nothing concerning the Grail he was*
*very sad. . . . When morning came Perceval*
*rose and went through the house and court but*
*found no one there, and he felt very sorrowful.*
DIDOT PERCEVAL

## The Story of the Hay Collars and the Doorknockers

This branch sees the continuing story of Bran's brother, Manawyddan, and his alliance with the family of Pryderi by marriage to Pwyll's widow, Rhiannon. Underlying the charmingly interwoven folk stories here are mighty mysteries which the reader might overlook. These include the imprisonment of Mabon; the Dolorous Blow, which causes the wasteland; and the quest for the Grail or the Cauldron of Rebirth. So although this story seems lightweight compared with the mighty matters of "Branwen" and "Pwyll," this effect is actually deceptive, brought about by a far more self-conscious storyteller than the one who transcribed the previous branches.

We shall be examining the nature of Pryderi's imprisonment and that of other famous prisoners who are pressed into servile duties, as well as pointing out the parallels between the raising of the enchantments of Dyfed and the quest for the Grail.

If the story has the shifting opacity of an object under water, we should not be too surprised, for its chief protagonist, Manawyddan, Son of the Sea, is a renowned shapeshifter in Celtic tradition. In Irish myth he is Manannán mac Lír, the King of the Otherworld, which appears as an island in the western seas, from whence he comes to gift mortals with the Cup of Truth.[28] His greatness is considerably muted in this branch in which he becomes an aging mortal, weary of earth's sorrows though still cunning and resourceful enough to defeat the enchantments besetting the land and his adoptive family.

The alternative title of this branch, "Mabinogi Mynnweir a Mynord" (The Story of the Hay Collars and the Doorknockers), reminds us that the underlying theme is the imprisonment of Mabon and the punishment of Modron, and is a restatement of the blows and wonders from the story of Pwyll.

## Synopsis of "Manawyddan, Son of Llyr"

(1) After the seven survivors have returned to Britain from Ireland and have buried Bran's head at the White Mount, Manawyddan exclaims that he alone has no place to lodge for the night. Pryderi comforts him with the thought that Bran's cousin Caswallawn is now king, but Manawyddan cannot share a house with the usurper of his brother. Pryderi proposes that Manawyddan return to Dyfed and marry his widowed mother, Rhiannon, whose dowry includes seven cantrefs of

land. (2) Rhiannon agrees to the marriage, and after feasting, Pryderi
goes to Oxford and pays homage to Caswallawn.

(3) One night, Pryderi and Cigfa, his wife, go with Manawyddan
and Rhiannon to sit on the Mound of Arberth. A mist descends,
thunder sounds, and when the mist rises they find the countryside
bare of people and dwellings. They are left to support themselves as
best they can. After two years they grow weary and (4) go into England
to live by a craft. Manawyddan makes saddles with Pryderi's help, but
the saddles are so well enameled and of such good quality that no
other saddler can sell his own products. The saddlers agree to kill
Manawyddan and Pryderi, but the two are warned and travel on. In
another town Manawyddan makes shields, and the resident shield-
makers are similarly done out of business. They again escape and
become shoemakers. The resident cobblers cannot compete against
their rivals' gold-buckled shoes and Manawyddan and Pryderi escape
once more. (5) On each occasion, Manawyddan restrains Pryderi from
taking revenge on their rivals, saying that freedom is better than
imprisonment, and that Caswallawn would hear of it.

They return to Dyfed and support themselves by hunting, as before.
(6) They encounter a pure white boar that lures men and dogs to follow
it. They chase it to a newly appeared castle; Pryderi enters it, despite
Manawyddan's warnings. (7) The castle is empty inside, but at its center, attached by chains reaching to the sky, there is a marble fountain
with a golden bowl on a marble slab. Entranced by the workmanship,
Pryderi lays hands on it and finds his hands are stuck to the bowl and
his feet to the marble slab. (8) Manawyddan waits for his return all day
and travels homeward, where Rhiannon berates him for leaving her son.
She goes to the castle and becomes similarly stuck to the bowl and slab.
Thunder and mist strike again and the castle vanishes.

(9) Cigfa and Manawyddan are now alone. Cigfa weeps for fear of
her chastity, but Manawyddan swears pure friendship to his stepson's
wife. They return to England, having lost their dogs and being unable
to hunt anymore, where Manawyddan (10) lives as a shoemaker once

more, much to Cigfa's disgust. The other cobblers threaten him and they return to Dyfed, settling at Arberth, where Manawyddan farms. (11) He sows three fields with wheat, inspecting each by turns every night only to find the stalks empty of grain. He then stands watch on the third field and sees a host of mice descend on the grain. He is unable to catch any of the creatures save one which is slower than the rest, and this one he confines in his glove. (12) He leaves the glove on a peg and informs Cigfa that he will hang the offender. She is horrified at his concern for such vermin.

(13) Manawyddan sets up a miniature gallows on the Mound of Arberth. (14) A poor scholar passes by, much to Manawyddan's surprise, for no living being has been seen in Dyfed for seven years, and offers to ransom the mouse with payment of a pound. Manawyddan refuses. A mounted priest passes by and offers three pounds for the release of the mouse. Last comes a bishop, with his entourage, who offers seven pounds for its release. At Manawyddan's refusal, he increases the offer to twenty-four pounds. He then asks Manawyddan's price, which is the release of Rhiannon and Pryderi, the removal of the enchantment on Dyfed, and the identity of the mouse.

(15) The bishop replies that he is Llwyd ap Cil Coed, cousin of Gwawl ap Clud, Rhiannon's former suitor, and that the enchantments are his in revenge for his cousin's insult. The three fields have been ravaged by his court, all of whom he turned into mice, but this mouse, his wife, was pregnant and slower than the rest. Manawyddan makes him further swear never to repeat the enchantments on Dyfed and promise that Rhiannon and Pryderi will be free of additional reprisals and that he himself will be so exempt. The mouse-wife is released at the same time as Rhiannon and her son. The land is restored to more than its former bounty. (16) It is revealed that the punishment of Rhiannon while imprisoned by Llwyd ap Cil had been to wear about her neck the hay collars of the asses after they had hauled hay and that Pryderi's was to carry about his neck the knockers of the court gates—which is why this branch is called "Mabinogi Mynnweir a Mynord."

## Commentary

(1) Manawyddan is named in Triad 8 as one of the three disinherited chieftains "because he would not seek an inheritance." In Irish legend, Manannán mac Lír, although later associated with the Tuatha de Danaan, is not mentioned as one of their number in earlier texts. He is a man apart in this story because he will not be part of Caswallawn's triumph over his brother, Bran.

(2) Caswallawn is a usurper by means of his cloak of enchantment. This garment ranks him with those other enemies of Britain who put the land under enchantment (see the section The Enchantments of Britain, below). In Geoffrey of Monmouth, Caswallawn, called Cassilivaunus, replaces his elder brother Lud, or Lludd, the founder of Lud's Town, or London, just as in "Branwen" Caswallawn replaces Bran, whose head is buried under the White Mount.[37] There are significant parallels between Manawyddan and Caswallawn suggesting a hidden or lost story, for both men are named in the triads as two of the three golden shoemakers. In this hidden story, which can be guessed at from the triads, Caswallawn disputes with Julius Caesar over a maiden, Fflur (flower), and pays homage to Caesar in order to secure Fflur's safety. Fflur appears to be another representative of Britain's sovereignty; she is championed by Caswallawn just as Cigfa is by Manawyddan or Branwen by Efnissien.[5] I have attempted to reconstruct this lost story in Celtic Love, under the title "The Golden Shoemaker."[135] There are strong correlatives between Caswallawn and Fflur and Cú Roi mac Daire (see chapter 3).

Rhiannon's marriage to Manawyddan makes her husband a landed man once more. The association of the Queen of the Underworld and the Lord of the Sea has already been noted, and Rhiannon has been shown to correspond to Demeter Erinys while Manawyddan corresponds closely to Poseidon. In Irish tradition, this partnership is paralleled by the marriage of Manannán mac Lír to Cliodna, who, like Rhiannon, has three otherworldly birds whose singing causes their hearers to weep, laugh, and sleep.

(3) The fateful Mound of Arberth becomes operative once more. When Manawyddan and his adopted family sit there, they contact the malevolent otherworldly power of their ancient enemy. This action corresponds closely to the Grail knight who sits upon the Perilous Seat and so causes the wounding of the Fisher King and the wasting of the land. This is discussed more fully in the section The Enchantments of Britain, below. Curiously, Pryderi gives over the actual administration of his lordship to Manawyddan. This substitution parallels that of Pwyll for Arawn in the First Branch.

(4) A Celtic nobleman did not work at servile tasks, yet Manawyddan works leather to make saddles, shields, and shoes. The tanner's trade was only slightly less smelly and ignoble than the fuller's, and dealing in hides was considered as shameful for a nobleman as swineherding, an occupation totally barred to those of gentle birth. Pigsties had to be out of smelling and even viewing range of a nobleman's house, according to Irish law. Yet, as we will see in chapters 5 and 6, the pig plays a central part in both "Math, Son of Mathonwy" and "Culhwch and Olwen."

Manawyddan is the master of any craft he picks up and Pryderi is his reluctant apprentice. As neither Rhiannon nor Cigfa is mentioned here (and as Cigfa would most certainly register the strongest objections to her husband performing menial labor, if her later remarks are anything to go by), we may assume that the women are either lodged separately from the men or do not travel with them.

(5) Pryderi bears his servitude with ill grace and is determined to seek a nobleman's revenge against the craftsmen. He suffers loss of face here—but later, despite Manawyddan's words of warning, he suffers imprisonment in yet more servile bondage.

(6) As Pryderi's father was lured into the otherworldly realms by means of a white stag, so Pryderi himself is lured by means of a white boar. Arawn's gift of pigs here seduces Pryderi back into the Otherworld.

(7) The theme of becoming stuck to an object is well known through-out folk tradition; however, in this instance, the cauldronlike golden bowl and its castle relate directly to the Grail story and the achieving of the Grail knight, as we will see.

(8) Rhiannon and Pryderi now undergo an almost exact rerun of the events in "Pwyll," in which they suffer abduction and imprisonment together. Like the British warriors cast into the Cauldron of Rebirth in "Branwen," they lose the power of speech.

(9) The storyteller has given Cigfa a very medieval modesty in the face of this situation. In Irish legend, Manannán has the reputation for being a night visitor of women who fathers many heroes, a fact which the storyteller might well have had at the back of his mind.[87]
This incident parallels the chaste friendship of Pwyll and Arawn's wife in the First Branch. Here Manawyddan substitutes for Pryderi, as Pwyll did for Arawn.

(10) Here is the reason that Manawyddan is called one of the three golden shoemakers (Triad 67): He ornaments his shoes with golden buckles. Similarly, he ennobles an ignoble profession for one of his rank by employing precious dyes and enamel, or Calch Llassar, a craft learned from Llassar Laes Gwfnewid, the same Underworld being who brought the Cauldron of Rebirth from the Irish lake.

(11) Just as Teyrnon in "Pwyll" lost one foal every May Eve, so does Manawyddan lose each of his three fields of wheat. Both men keep watch on the final occasion of loss.

(12) As Gwawl was tied up in a bag and belabored in "Pwyll," so here is the mouse imprisoned in Manawyddan's glove. The Irish Manannán is famed for his possession of a crane bag—a marvelous receptacle hold-ing treasures visible at high tide but which appeared empty at ebb tide.

These treasures correspond to the hallows of sovereignty or of the Grail, and to the Thirteen Treasures of Britain.[91]

(13) The fateful Mound of Arberth reverts to its original role as a place of assembly and judgment: All the ills, enchantments, and blows emanate from this Otherworld gateway and here, at last, they are resolved by the arbitrator. We have already mentioned the connections between Bran and Cronos, yet Cronos rules the Otherworld, according to classical tradition, with his brother Rhadamanthys, lord of the dead and judgment. Manawyddan rightfully stands in the place of Rhadamanthys because he is now married to the queen of the dead, Rhiannon, the mistress of the Underworld.

(14) Manawyddan provokes one of the Mound of Arberth's strange properties of either giving blows or showing a great wonder. He witnesses the miraculous reappearance of people after the countryside has been deserted for seven years. It is possible that in earlier oral versions the disguise of Llwyd might have been that of a wandering bard, a druid, or a judge. Manawyddan bargains ruthlessly for the release of his wife and stepson, for their release means the lifting of the enchantment.

(15) The true connections between the First and Third Branches are now clearly apparent. Gwawl, Rhiannon's former suitor who promised not to avenge himself on Pwyll, has been vindicated by his cousin Llwyd. Just as Gwawl was struck in "Pwyll" (though by whom, he knew not), so Pryderi and Rhiannon are stricken with a Dolorous Blow by being imprisoned in the Otherworld while their land suffers enchantment.

(16) The land is restored from wasteland to its accustomed fertility at the moment of Rhiannon and Pryderi's release. Their notable and shadowy imprisonment is deeply connected with the Mabinogi of Mabon and Modron (see chapter 9). There are parallels between the Third Branch and the motif of the mule without a bridle, which

became widespread in later French romances: While the bridle is missing, the enchanted person cannot resume his or her former shape.[58, 63] There are also innumerable British and Irish folk stories concerning the enchantment of a woman into a mare.

## The Enchantments of Britain

Part of this story's mysterious action takes place in the Otherworld, in the Hollow Hills, which is where the unwary find themselves if they travel unprepared. Just as we know little about the possessor of the great claw which attacks Teyrnon's foal in "Pwyll, Prince of Dyfed," so also are we ignorant of the place of Rhiannon and Pryderi's imprisonment. Throughout the first three branches, magic mists and mysterious disappearances abound. Yet the influence of the Otherworld is not evil in itself: Pwyll gains the friendship of Arawn and himself succeeds to Arawn's title, and he marries the Underworld woman Rhiannon, whose magic singing birds bring refreshment and forgetfulness to Bran's surviving companions. But beneath this friendship is set the constant enmity of Gwawl, Rhiannon's intended suitor. The Otherworld threshold of the Mound of Arberth bestows wonders and blows impartially.

The arch enchanter of the land of Dyfed is Llwyd ap Cil Coed, cousin of Gwawl, who causes mist to appear and engulf the land, people to disappear, and the mysterious castle with the marble fountain to appear. He, like his cousin, is an otherworldly lord of great power. We have already noted that Caswallawn is called an enchanter because his mantle of invisibility helped him slay Bran's son. He likewise causes devastation of the land in "Branwen, Daughter of Llyr." The appearance of both men in the Third Branch doubly reinforces the enchantment upon the land. The mist and the mantle of invisibility seem to be of the same provenance, and both render the countryside a wasteland empty of people. Yet the enchantment of Dyfed is brought about by Pryderi and his family sitting upon the Mound of Arberth.

There are two stories which help point to the parallels between this branch and the motifs of the quest for the Grail, the making of the land into a wasteland, and the descent into Hades for an Otherworld bride (as in Pwyll's quest for Rhiannon, by which the tangled web of enchantments is set upon the loom). These stories are the classical tale "Theseus and Peirithous" and the Grail texts of *Perlesvaus,* or the *Didot Perceval.*

Peirithous the Lapith was said to be a son of Zeus, the god who mated with Dia while disguised as a stallion. Peirithous made a pact of friendship with Theseus and invited him to his wedding to Hippodameia (horse tamer). But the centaurs who also attended the feast were unused to wine and one raped the bride. Peirithous and his friend Theseus leapt to her rescue, cutting off the ears and nose of the offending centaur. After Hippodameia's subsequent death, Peirithous and Theseus sought daughters of Zeus as brides. Theseus sought Helen of Sparta, and then helped Peirithous to obtain Persephone, accompanying him to Tartarus, where Hades received them and bade them sit on the chair before them. They sat, unsuspecting, on the Chair of Lethe, "forgetfulness," which welded itself to their flesh so that they could not rise from it. They remained in torment until Hercules came to complete his last Labor and was permitted to release Theseus but not Peirithous, who had blasphemously attempted to seize the queen of the Underworld.[40, 57]

It would be impossible to superimpose this Greek legend over the Third Branch and bring forth direct parallels, yet it is possible to see a tangled relationship between Pwyll or Pryderi and Peirithous, whose family retains an interest in ladies of an equine nature or underworldly disposition. The disastrous marriage feast with the drunken centaurs resembles more the feast of Gwern's succession in "Branwen, Daughter of Llyr," when so many men are killed—there is even an echo of Efnissien's mutilation of Matholwch's horses in the mutilation of the centaur. The trip to Tartarus in order to obtain Persephone ends in the two friends stuck firmly by their backsides to Lethe's chair, from which only Theseus is finally released while Peirithous remains a prisoner. This echoes the fixing of Rhiannon and Pryderi to the golden bowl in the otherworldly castle. Pwyll's attempt to marry Rhiannon brings him to the Underworld, where he must defeat by guile a rival suitor from whom he extracts humiliating terms. Yet Gwawl is aptly avenged on Pwyll's son and widow.

To pinpoint the moment at which the enchantments of Dyfed begin, we must return to the First Branch in which Pwyll sits for the first time on the Mound of Arberth. Two events recur when anyone sits there: Thunder sounds and a mist descends—the Otherworld reaches out and impinges upon the world of every day. Such events also occur in the story *Didot Perceval* in which, on arriving at Arthur's court, Perceval takes for himself the forbidden Perilous Seat:

> As soon as he was seated, the stone split beneath him and broke with such an agonising sound that it seemed to all that the world might sink into the abyss. And . . . there issued such a great shadowy cloud that for more than a league they could not see each other.[95]

The voice from the cloud exclaims that in sitting in the Perilous Seat, Perceval has performed the rashest act ever known and has barely escaped destruction. The story also reveals that Bron, the Fisher King, cannot be healed of his wound until the best knight seeks the Fisher King's court and answers the Grail question. Only then will he be cured, will the stone be reunited with its place at the Round Table, and will the enchantments fall from the land of Britain.[95]

Perceval, after many adventures, does find the court but fails to answer the question, and when he awakes he finds the countryside empty of people, just as Pryderi and his family do on the Mound of Arberth. He does, however, eventually achieve his quest. Bron (a later resonance of Bran, who likewise guards a cauldron and who awaits a successor) gives the Grail into Perceval's keeping and all hear the melody which issues from the vessel. Bron then dies, leaving Perceval to guard the Grail. The two halves of the stone seat are reunited, and the enchantments of Britain are relieved. Perceval is given the title of the Fisher King.

By sitting on the Perilous Mound of Arberth, Pryderi ruptures the stasis between the worlds, and the true cause of the enchantments is known. Pryderi likewise succeeds to his father's role of Pen Annwfn, but only after he has been proved worthy through humiliation and imprisonment. Bron, like Bran, is a willing prisoner chained to mortality by his unhealing wound—itself a paradigm of the land's condition, barren, Grailless, and laid waste by enchantment. But only in the castle of the Grail can the truth be made known. The chained cauldronlike bowl of the mysterious castle where Rhiannon and Pryderi are imprisoned is not of this dimension. One of the best-crafted Grail stories will help us see its function more clearly.

In *Perlesvaus,* Perceval, nearing the end of his quest, is taken to an otherworldly island, to a hall hung with depictions of Christ and his disciples. Thirty-three men enter, each dressed in white with a red cross on his chest. As they sit down to eat, Perceval sees:

[a] golden chain descending and from the middle hung a golden crown . . . it was attached to nothing save the will of Our Lord. As soon as the masters saw it descend they opened a great wide pit in the middle of the hall . . . the greatest and most lamentable cries ever heard rose up from below; and when the worthy men heard them they raised their hands to Our Lord and all began to weep.[20]

The chain is withdrawn after the meal and the pit is covered up. The crown is intended for Perceval, who is told that he will be made king of the Isle of Plenty, the former king having succeeded to a greater kingdom. The conditions of his service state that he must see "that the isle is well provided for; if you do not, the crown will be taken from you and you will be placed on the Isle of Need, whose people you heard crying in this hall."[20] At length, Perceval becomes the guardian of the Grail and departs on a ship for his destined kingship.

Striking here are the resonances between this otherworldly company of Grail initiates and the Assembly of the Noble Head. Although there is no cauldronlike bowl of gold, the masters wash in a great golden basin before the chain descends, attached, as in "Manawyddan," to thin air. The vision Perceval sees is directly related to the succession of the Pendragons, those worthy guardians of sovereignty whose part is to ensure the bounty of the land. Those who serve faithfully will be allowed to succeed to another kingdom, while those who fail will be as those lamentable souls in the pit who, like Mabon, the immemorial prisoner, grieve unceasingly. In *Perlesvaus,* rather than hypocritical rejoicing at the fate of these prisoners, there is compassion and a willingness to end their torment. Such is the fate of the Titans like Cronos, who exceed their role and become the scourge of their land. Yet there is hope even for him in succession of the ages. As the poet Taliesin says,

> *Perfect is my seat in Caer Sidi,*
> *Nor plague nor age harms him who dwells therein.*
> *Manawyd and Pryderi know it.*[101]

Are they both masters at this feast, who contemplate unendingly the mysteries of the Grail and the Noble Head?

The parallels between Perceval and Pryderi show that both men are rash in their actions, inconsiderate of important tasks, and correspondingly humiliated in their failure. Yet while Perceval is a prisoner of his own ignorance, he is not physically imprisoned as Pryderi is. Unlike Perceval, Pryderi is himself a ruler of a country at the beginning of the story, although he has passed the kingship into the hands of Manawyddan. He has sat with the other six survivors around the head of Bendigeid Bran (blessed Bran), and has known the sorrow of mortality and the remembrance of when the otherworldly door has been opened. If Pryderi has ever been connected with the quest for the Grail or cauldron, then that episode appears only in relation to "Branwen, Daughter of Llyr," although, according to the Irish translation of the ninth-century chronicler Nennius, Manaal is the keeper of a perpetual cauldron.[63] In "Manawyddan," Pryderi is an immature ruler who needs the cautious support of his stepfather. Surely few characters can have had more fathers than Pryderi, who is born of Pwyll, brought up by Teyrnon, fostered by Pendaran, and, last, gains Manawyddan for a stepfather! It is only within "Math, Son of Mathonwy" that he appears as a mature ruler, and even there he is easily duped by Gwydion, yet another enchanter.

Gruffydd has suggested that Manawyddan and Teyrnon Twrf Liant (lord of the raging sea) are doublets of each other and that Teyrnon, not Pwyll, is really the father of Pryderi. His theory centers on the derivation of Rhiannon's and Teyrnon's names from the Celtic Rigantona (great queen) and Tigernonos (great lord)—which are titles, as are Mabon's and Modron's names. Certainly Manawyddan is a substitute father, for Pwyll has succeeded to his destined role as Pen Annwfn, Lord of the Underworld. We have also the evidence of Pausanius to cement the union of the sea god with the Queen of the Underworld (see pages 36–37).

After Poseidon raped Demeter while they were both in the shape of horses, she gave birth to twins. The wooden statue of Demeter Melaina at Phygalia showed her having a mare's head from which issued serpents and other animals. In one hand she held a dolphin, the symbol of Poseidon, and in the other a dove, a symbol of Persephone. Try as we might, we cannot escape the mare and her foal.

One further story will show how Pryderi's servile punishment accords with both that of Mabon and of another god: Apollo.

## The Powerful Herdsman

We are not told precisely what Pryderi's punishment is while he is enchanted by Llwyd; we only know that the doorknockers or hammers of the gate are about his neck, but this seems to be a symbol of the punishment, not the punishment itself. So what can this punishment be? There may be a hint in Triad 26, where we are told of:

Pryderi, son of Pwyll, Lord of Annwfn, tending the swine of Pendaran Dyfed, his foster father. These swine were the seven animals which Pwyll Lord of Annwfn brought, and gave them to Pendaran Dyfed, his foster father. And the place where he used to keep them was in Glyn Cuch in Emlyn. And this is why he was called a powerful swineherd; because no one was able either to deceive or to force him.[5]

This descriptive yet elliptical triad both reveals and obscures something of our story. Let us leave it to one side for a while and consider clues from the classical tradition—Apollo's servitude to King Admetus.

In this story, Apollo must do penance for an act variously described as: (a) the slaying of the oracular serpent, Delphyne; (b) the slaying of Zeus's smiths and herdsmen, the Cyclopes; and (c) the tricking of Thanatos (death) out of a destined victim.[5, 57]

For each of these outrages, Apollo's penance is identical:

> Zeus would have hurled him to Tartarus; however, at the intercession
> of Latona (Leto) he ordered him to serve as thrall to a man for a year.
> So he went to Admetus, son of Pheres . . . and served him as a herds-
> man, and caused all the cows to drop twins.[8]

The name Admetus means "invincible," and is one of the titles of Hades—the Greek Pen Annwfn. This period of servile bondage seems to have been part of Apollo's cult when, according to the Delphic religious calendar, Apollo is said to be absent in the land of the Hyperboreans—the place beyond the north wind, associated with the Celtic paradise or Elysium where Cronos is similarly put out to grass. Plutarch interpreted this yearly absence as Apollo's annual descent to the realm of the dead, a necessary event in his cult's calendar. We notice that it is only at the advice of Latona (or Leto), the mother of Apollo, that he is spared the torments of Tartarus. Instead he is punished by servile bondage to a lord of the Underworld.

Is it possible that the punishment of Pryderi was of a similar kind? He is the son of Pwyll, Pen Annwfn, and a lady of the Underworld who was abducted from the land of the dead through trickery—a transgression committed by Pwyll, but avenged upon his son. But in what manner can Apollo and Pryderi have any possible connection?

To anticipate the argument in chapter 9, we can note that Pryderi stands in the place of Mabon as an embodiment of Mabon's power and further, that Mabon/Maponos was closely identified with Hyperborean

Apollo. The connection between Pryderi and the immemorial prisoner Mabon is deftly given in the poem "Preiddeu Annwfn," by Taliesin, which states:

> *Complete was the prison of Gwair in Caer Sidi,*
> *According to the story of Pwyll and Pryderi.*

Gwair is one of the names of Mabon, the mysterious prisoner who must be released. So famous was this theme that the comparison between Gwair and the stories of Pwyll and his son could be drawn upon by poets to indicate the nature of Mabon's imprisonment in the Underworld castle of enchantment.

If we look again at the alternative title of this branch, "Mabinogi Mynnweir a Mynord," and contemplate the nature of Rhiannon and Pryderi's imprisonment, we will note a few interesting facts:

> Pryderi has had the knockers of the gate of my court about his neck,
> and Rhiannon has had the collars of the asses, after they have been
> carrying hay, about her neck. And such have been their fetters.[4]

There is a mystery hidden within this part of the story which only the initiate poet could penetrate: The asses have been carrying *gweir,* or hay, in a literal sense, but Rhiannon's dual penance is to become the pack mare and portress at the gate in both the First Branch and the Third Branch, and really the bearer of Gweir/Gwair, or Pryderi, who is a type of Mabon.

The collars which fetter them to the Underworld are the chains by which the golden cauldron, or bowl, is attached to its lord, the chains of enchantment making them both prisoners and porters at Llwyd's gate. As the "Preiddeu Annwfn" goes on to relate of Gweir:

> *None before him was sent into it,*
> *Into the heavy blue chain which bound the youth.*

This indicates that Gweir's imprisonment is the first, but by no means the last, of its kind. Present also within this poem is a mysterious reference to a guarded beast whose destiny is closely woven with that of the prisoner.

Pryderi's totem beast is the foal bound up with his birth and conception, but on his father's side he inherits the swine of Annwfn, which are the gifts of Arawn to Pwyll in token of their everlasting friendship. As we have been told by the triad, it is Pryderi, not Pwyll, who is one of three powerful swineherds. Further we note that the swine are given to Pendaran Dyfed in trust for Pryderi, and that these swine are the magical seven in number—which is the number of men who are redeemed from the visit to Ireland with Bran as well as from the harrowing of Annwfn with Arthur (see chapter 6).

We can only speculate, given these facts, that Pryderi is indeed like Apollo: He undergoes a necessary sojourn in the Underworld as a prisoner, tied to a task which is normally demeaning to one of his nobility, but which establishes his willingness to stand at the gate between the worlds of the living and the dead. Destined to be a sorrow to his mother, Gwri Golden Hair leaves behind his childhood to become Pryderi, "anxiety," a name arrived at by his mother's first utterance upon being reunited with him and confirmed by Pendaran Dyfed, whose herds he guards. Last, he becomes one of three powerful swineherds whom no one can deceive because he has already suffered his term in the realms of the Underworld. The scene is set for Pryderi's last appearance, and for a new Mabon to appear.

# **5**

# ⁵
# Ⓜath, Son of Mathonwy

*Few there are who know where the magic wand*
*of Mathonwy grows in the woods.*

ANONYMOUS WELSH POEM, *DARONWY*

*Did he and his back-room team*
*contrive this gleaming spoil from fungus by*
*Virgil's arts in Merlin's Maridunum?*

DAVID JONES, *THE ANATHEMATA*

## **The Enchanter's Nephew**

In the Fourth and final Branch of the *Mabinogion*, we take leave of
Pryderi and witness the birth of another hero: Llew. The First and
Fourth Branches are not only the longest stories, but also the most
complex, interwoven, and forgotten tales, full of unexplained themes
to tantalize the reader. These branches are connected by a circuitous
chain of cause and effect: Pwyll befriends Arawn and receives the
Underworld swine as a gift; Gwydion steals them through trickery in

order to cause war and to satisfy his brother's lust. Thus one hero perishes and another is conceived.

In the other branches the conflict has been between this world and the Otherworld or between Britain and Ireland, but here Gwynedd and Dyfed, North and South Wales, are opposed. The events of the *Mabinogion* seem to leap from otherworldly time into real time where the tawdry enchantments of Gwydion are motivated by lust, greed, pride, and jealousy, and where the ancient values of kingship and sacrifice, as typified by Math, are in decline.

Gwydion and his brothers and sister are children of Don (see figure 3, below) about whom we have no information. Scholars have pointed out the parallels between this family and that of the Irish Tuatha de Danaan, or the family of Danu, a similar shadowy ancestress whose descendants' names match those of Don's almost exactly. In each case, both sets of descendants are known as children of their mother, not their father—except for Arianrhod, who, according to Triad 35, is the daughter of Don by Beli. This same triad makes Arianrhod at least a half sister of Caswallawn and perhaps hints at other familial connections not necessarily made plain in the family tree derived from this branch.

## Synopsis of "Math, Son of Mathonwy"

(1) Math ap Mathonwy is Lord of Gwynedd and Pryderi is Lord of Dyfed. When he is not at war, Math has his feet held by the Goewin, the footholder, which is an appointment only a virgin can maintain.

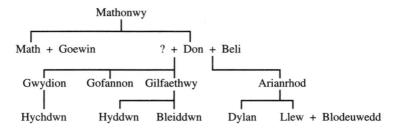

Figure 3. The family tree of Math

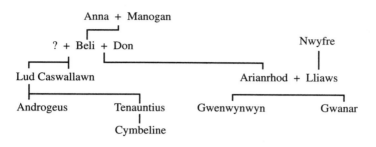

Figure 4. The family tree of Don

(2) Only Gwydion and Gilfaethwy, Math's nephews, are able to go on circuit in place of their uncle. (3) Gilfaethwy lusts after Goewin, yet she is never out of Math's sight. Accordingly, Gwydion plans to help his brother by making war. (4) He petitions Math to let him go and ask for the pigs which Pryderi has and which came originally from Annwfn.

(5) Disguising themselves as poets, Gwydion and Gilfaethwy sing for Pryderi and ask for the pigs as their fee. Pryderi is bound not to give any away until they have bred and have increased their number twice. Gwydion, using his magic, then creates thirteen steeds and twelve hounds and offers to exchange these and their accoutrements for the pigs. Taking the swine, Gwydion and his retinue head for home. But his enchanted gifts, now in Pryderi's possession, resume their former shape, that of mushrooms. Gwydion and Gilfaethwy are then pursued by Pryderi's host and arrive in Gwynedd to find their kinsmen mar-shaling for war.

(6) In the uproar, Gilfaethwy rapes Goewin. War commences between Gwynedd and Dyfed. (7) Pryderi suffers a defeat and gives hostages to Gwynedd. Then, to prevent needless slaughter, he offers to fight Gwydion in single combat to decide the outcome of the war. Gwydion wins by using magic. (8) Returning to the court, Math finds that Goewin is no longer a virgin and immediately offers her marriage in reparation. He then forbids his people to give shelter to or feed his nephews, who are forced to submit to his judgment. He strikes them with his wand, turning them into deer—Gilfaethwy into a hind,

Gwydion into a stag—and bids them live in the wilderness, mate and produce young, and return to court in a year's time. At the end of the year, they return together with a fawn whom Math changes into a human child before further enchanting his nephew Gwydion into a sow and Gilfaethwy into a boar. A piglet is born of this union and is similarly made human. The last enchantment sees Gilfaethwy as a bitch wolf and Gwydion as a wolf who return with a cub. All three children are raised by Math.

(9) The nephews are forgiven. Math asks their advice about who should succeed the footholder. (10) Gwydion suggests Arianrhod, his sister. As a test of her virginity, she steps over Math's wand and immediately gives birth to a yellow-haired boy. On leaving the court, she drops something which Gwydion picks up and hides. (11) The boy, baptized Dylan, makes for the sea and swims away. (12) Meanwhile, Gwydion finds that what he has hidden in the chest at the foot of his bed has become a boy, whom he puts out to fosterage until the child is four years old.

(13) He takes the boy to Caer Arianrhod, where his mother refuses to name him and lays on him a *geis* that none shall name him but herself. Gwydion and the boy later return to Caer Arianhod in a boat, both disguised as shoemakers. No shoe will fit Arianrhod until she presents herself in person. She sees the boy cast a stone at a wren and exclaims: "The fair-haired one has hit it with a skillful hand." After this Gwydion names him Llew Llaw Gyffes and both discard their disguises. Arianrhod then swears that none but she shall arm him as a man. Disguised this time as poets, Gwydion and Llew travel to Arianrhod's castle again, where Gwydion summons the illusion of an enemy host. Arianrhod then arms Llew, but Gwydion lifts the enchantment and she swears that Llew shall never have a wife of humankind.

(14) Together Math and Gwydion fashion out of flowers a woman called Blodeuwedd. Math gives Llew estates in Ardudwy. One day, while Llew is absent at court, Blodeuwedd sees a hunter, and offering him hospitality, she falls in love with him. Together they plan Llew's death.

(15) She feigns anxiety as Llew tells her the conditions under which he can be slain: He can be killed only with a spear that has been fashioned on Sunday while Mass is said, but the murder must be accomplished neither inside nor outside, neither on horseback nor on foot. It can occur only if a bath with a roof frame over it is made on the riverbank and he himself stands with one foot on the edge of the bath and the other on the back of a goat.

Blodeuwedd informs Gronw, her lover, of these conditions, and then, a year later, begs Llew to calm her anxiety by showing her how difficult such a death would be. (16) He complies and Gronw casts the spear, killing Llew and taking both Blodeuwedd and Llew's estates. Llew disappears in the shape of an eagle. (17) Gwydion scours the land to find him, and eventually comes to a cottage where a swineherd is having difficulty penning or guarding his sow. Gwydion follows the sow to a tree in Nantilew beneath which she feeds on rotten flesh falling from an eagle in the treetop. (18) Gwydion sings three *englyns* to entice it down, and then strikes the bird with his wand. It is the wasted body of Llew, whom he takes back to the court to be cured.

(19) In revenge, Gwydion pursues Blodeuwedd. Her maidens all drown in a lake, while she is transformed into an owl, doomed ever to hunt by night. Gronw asks if he can pay compensation to Llew, but is refused. (20) Llew demands that Gronw suffer the same stroke under the same conditions as the one he had received from Gronw. He allows Gronw to place a stone between his body and the blow, but Llew pierces both the stone and Gronw. (21) Llew eventually succeeds to Math's kingdom.

## Commentary

(1) The post of *troedawc,* or footholder, was named in the Welsh laws: The troedawc was entitled to rent-free lands and perquisites. "His duty is to hold the king's feet in his lap from the time he begins to sit at the carousal until he goes to sleep, and it is his duty to scratch the king."[45] It was clearly a position of honor, roughly equivalent to the present lady

and gentleman of the royal chamber. Goewin also seems to represent the Goddess of Sovereignty in that while Math's feet are in her lap, the land is not at war. There is a venerable tradition of young women who, like Goewin, serve aged kings: King David had Abishag to give him heat in his old age (I Kings 1:1–4) while, in the East, young women are taken into the beds of sages as a test of the males' continence and as a means of absorbing the life-giving Shakti, or female power, a custom practiced by Gandhi. In medieval poetic tradition there was clearly a variant story in which Arianrhod was Math's footholder; in a fifteenth-century poem by Lewis Mon, she is described as sharing Math's bed.[45]

(2) In the succession of Celtic kingship, it is the king's nephew, not the king's son, who has precedence. The blood of the mother, not the father, confers royal status, hence the king's sister produces the heir. Matrilinear succession is clearly an ancient practice which is still observable within Arthurian tradition and within the *Mabinogion* long after the introduction of primogeniture among the Norman kings governing England and Wales. As we will see, it is Arthur's nephews who figure largely in the heroic stories of his court, while his son, Medraut or Mordred, is his opponent.

The custom of going on circuit was followed by all professional classes. Druids, judges, poets, and kings went on circuit to inspect the good government of the land, administer justice, settle disputes, tell stories, and so forth. This custom helped spread responsibility for feeding the court, whose provisioning must have been gargantuan. Although Math is the maintainer of the realm, the active role of administrator of justice has fallen to his nephews.

(3) Math is able, like the Coraniad in the story "Lludd and Llefelys," to hear news on the wind. While he is attended by his footholder, he is omniscient, rooted in the very heart of his land. Yet Gwydion is also able to divine Gilfaethwy's complaint very easily. Gwydion is virtually Math's successor, in both magic and cunning, yet he lacks Math's sta-

bility. He exemplifies the sterile black magician within this story, one who destroys because he cannot create anything out of love.

(4) The pig was a beast of great importance to the Celts, both as a staple food and as an emblematic beast of the Underworld. Choice cuts from the pig were served to selected heroes at feasts to honor their exploits, yet at the same time there existed the curious ban on nobles having anything to do with their herding. We have seen that Pryderi is named as one of the three powerful swineherds and one who is in contact with Annwfn and the sometimes overwhelming Underworld powers. The older gods and heroes frequently have this underworldly connection, acting as doorkeepers for those who travel to these realms (see chapter 8). The hunting of the boar by the boy born in a pig run is the theme of "Culhwch and Olwen," which features the earliest correlative of the Grail quest: the harrowing of Annwfn to gain its treasures. Gwydion wishes to have the Underworld's treasures for his own people, and like Arthur and others who travel to Annwfn, he is willing to steal them at the cost of many lives.

(5) Here is yet another of the many substitutions which afflict Pwyll's family. Pwyll changes places with Arawn in the First Branch. Manawyddan refuses to exchange the mouse-wife of Llwyd for a retinue of horses and greyhounds in the Third Branch. Unfortunately, Pryderi is not so cautious; he accepts Gwydion's enchanted offer and so breaks his promise to Arawn. The pigs, however, are a dangerous commodity, bringing into the lives of the men of Gwynedd the terrors of war and otherworldly disruption.

(6) The rape of Goewin is the rape of Sovereignty, for war is declared and the land is set in uproar. Although Goewin is the one raped, it is Arianrhod who bears the children (see note 10, below).

(7) Pryderi gives Gwrgi Gwastad to the north as a hostage to peace.

Gwrgi's name is suspiciously like that of Gwri, Pryderi's childhood alias. The text also tells us that Gwrgi is a youth. After Pryderi's death, he and his companions are freed from their imprisonment at Gwydion's suggestion. With Pryderi's ignoble death, his story, which has bound the Four Branches together, transfers to another level of consciousness: He becomes an inner guardian, which we will address further. The combat between Pryderi and Gwydion echoes the earlier combat between Pwyll and Hafgan.

(8) Math's redress and punishment are both radical. Goewin is restored to her former honor, becoming queen, in fact. Gwydion and Gilfaethwy both suffer punishments for greed and lust by becoming animals themselves and bearing children to each other. In addition, they are both seen by the court while in this condition, just as Arianrhod is later shamed.

(9) Presumably Math has spent some three years without his footholder, a discrepancy which the storyteller conveniently glosses over.

(10) Arianrhod's name means "silver wheel," which may make reference to her citadel. Taliesin speaks of serving three periods of imprisonment within Arianrhod's prison. Caer Arianrhod is the name for the Corona Borealis, and is sometimes conflated with the revolving or spiral tower of Caer Sidi.[147] W. J. Gruffydd further suggests that because her name is often spelled Arianrad, it may also mean "silver fortress."[45] She is an otherworldly queen and has strong connections with Ceridwen as the mistress of initiation (see chapter 7). She seems to have undergone a curious rationalization into an enchantress of malign intention in this story. The tangled sources for this transformation from possible footholder of Math into a wicked mother are dealt with in more detail in the section One-Eye and the Skillful Hand, below.

Tests of chastity were much beloved of the medieval *conteurs*, but here Math's wand, in a rather Freudian way, becomes the instrument of Arianrhod's undoing. She is, of course, one of the royal women from whom the rightful heir can descend because she is Math's niece. The wand of Math has the ability to reveal the truth, as we have seen from his transformation of Gwydion and Gilfaethwy. With Arianrhod his wand effects a twin birth, suggesting that her qualification to be a virgin footholder is somewhat dubious. The mystery of the children's father is never solved in the story, though many commentators have discerned a subtextual incestuous union between Gwydion and his sister. One child is nearer term than the other, if we are not to consider the second "small something" as the placenta, which Gwydion magically incubates and turns into Llew.

Triad 78 names Arianrhod as one of three fair maidens of Britain. One of the others is Creirwy, the daughter of Ceridwen, further strengthening the link between Arianrhod and Ceridwen as initiatory women.

(11) Dylan's lost story is known only from a similarly lost triad here referred to as the three unfortunate blows. His death at the hands of his uncle Gofannon is partially reconstructed here (see the section One-Eye and the Skillful Hand, below).

(12) Gruffydd cites many instances in folklore where the placenta is considered to be the double of the child.[45] Gwydion shows himself incapable of creating anything himself; he must always use some kind of raw material to effect his enchantment, as when he creates horses and hounds from mushrooms and leaves. The story of Fionn Mac Cumhail's secret upbringing is particularly relevant to Llew's and is given in the section One-Eye and the Skillful Hand, below. The rapid development of Llew is parallel to that of Pryderi and indicates that we are witnessing a new hero in the mold of Mabon.

(13) A *geis* (plural *geasa*) in Irish tradition is a binding injunction or prohibition placed upon one person by another. Generally, geasa protect the life, gifts, or honor of the person who bears them. The geasa upon

Llew strongly prevent his acknowledgment by society, for without a name, arms, or a wife, he would be a nonentity.[138] Because Gwydion has taken away her own reputation, or name, Arianrhod refuses to name Llew. Her reluctance to name him is perhaps also due to the fact that he is the child of her brother. The incestuous parentage of the hero is well attested in Celtic folklore.[87] Such a union produces a special child with superhuman abilities, yet he is generally outcast by being thrown into the sea, as in the case of Mordred or Taliesin. Here, of course, it is Llew's brother, Dylan, who takes to the sea.

Both Llew and Manawyddan are named as two of three golden shoemakers in Triad 67 (although it is Gwydion who makes the shoes here). The third, Caswallawn, is somewhat of a mystery, for his story has been lost. Like Llew, Caswallawn marries a Flower Bride in Fflur. There is probably an ancient tradition of Llew and shoemaking because the Gaulish god Lugus was the patron of shoemaking.[45]

Llew's name, like Pryderi's, is taken from his mother's first expostulation. Both Llew and his Irish counterpart, Lugh, are renowned for their skillful aim—Balor names Lugh in exactly the same way as Arianrhod names Pryderi. In Llew's killing of a wren, traditionally an oracular bird, we see another reference to the succession of the Pendragons: In folklore, the wren, symbolizing the old king, is killed at midwinter in much the same way that the Irish god Lugh slays his grandfather, Balor, who is Math's Irish counterpart. The implication of Llew's killing of the wren is that he shows himself worthy to replace the wise old king, Math. It was an Irish folk custom corresponding to the winter death of the old year, or king. The Wren Boys would then go about singing a carol, showing the dead wren hung from a pole, and demanding payment in the immemorial way of itinerant players.[135]

Because Llew and Lugh both have associations with the spear or sword, it is likely that an original version of the story would have mentioned this weapon in the arming of Llew. As it is, Llew's skill is transposed to the first geis and his spear to the third part of the story where he is killed by it. This weapon seems also to have been the cause of

Dylan's unfortunate death (see the section One-Eye and the Skillful Hand, below). The arming of the son by the mother was an important part of Celtic society when young men "took valor" or were recognized as marriageable men of adult status. By denying him this right, Arianrhod dooms Llew to perpetual youth.

(14) This last geis is the most difficult to accomplish and is beyond even Gwydion's skill. It is Math who is skilled in creation. The creation of Blodeuwedd from the flowers of oak, broom, and meadowsweet is well annotated and appears as a first-person interpolation with the "Cad Goddeu" attributed to Taliesin.

> *Not of mother, nor of father was my creation.*
> *I was made from the ninefold elements:*
> *From fruit-trees, from paradisal fruit;*
> *From primroses and hillflowers,*
> *From blossom of the trees and bushes;*
> *From the roots of the earth I was made;*
> *From the bloom of the nettle;*
> *From water of the ninth wave.*
> *Math enchanted me before I was made immortal;*
> *Gwydion created me by his magic wand;*
> *From Eurwys and Euron, from Euron and*
>     *Modron,*
> *From five fifties of magicians and masters like*
>     *Math was I made.*
> *I was made by the master in his highest ecstasy;*
> *By the wisest of druids I was made before the*
>     *world began.*[147]

We do not know who Eurwys and Euron are in this poem, but the juxtaposition of Euron and Modron makes us wonder whether Euron is a scribal error for Mabon. The "Cad Goddeu" credits Blodeuwedd's existence before her conjuration. While Math's great enchantment can create a physical body of living molecules, it cannot ensoul his nephew's intended wife. She is totally otherworldly, incapable of human morality, and hence, unworthy of Gwydion's harsh punishment.

(15) The old Delilah ruse of feigning anxiety over the possible cause of a husband's death is here employed by Blodeuwedd. Her betrayal of Llew is like that of Blathnait (see chapter 3). No one inquires whether she loves Llew; she is merely given to him. A late Welsh story relates how the wife of Huan plotted to kill her husband. Huan's father, Gwydion, eventually found him in Caer Gwydion (i.e., in the stars), to which his son's soul had flown. Gwydion turned the daughter into a bird. The story is called "Huan's Deceiving" ("Twyll Huan"). Tylluan is also Welsh for "owl." This story gives corroborative evidence that Gwydion is Llew's father, not only his uncle.[45]

(16) Llew very stupidly breaks his own life-protecting geis by accomplishing two of the three conditions for his death. It is interesting that, although he is given the geasa of namelessness, the state of being unarmed, and wifelessness, he should be aware of the conditions by which his life may be ended. Because Gwydion incubated him and partly created him, this information was also vouchsafed to him. Such impossible conditions are common in folklore where the protagonist must appear neither sitting nor standing, neither clothed nor naked, neither inside nor outside, neither running nor walking. In this instance the conditions are clearly as follows: neither inside nor outside, neither riding nor on foot, with the additional condition of being neither clothed nor naked, for a bathtub is mentioned. Llew straddles the tub half-clothed—we may wonder whether an original detail had him clothed in a fishing net, but such watery details have all been transposed to Dylan, his brother.

(17) As once Teyrnon watched anxiously for his foal's safety in "Pwyll, Prince of Dyfed" as once Manawyddan watched the burgeoning of his

crops, so Gwydion follows the progress of the sow in order to find Llew, who does not die from Gronw's blow, but is instead transformed into his totem bird, the eagle. In times of stress and when under the influence of the Otherworld, the characters within the *Mabinogion* revert to their totemic shapes. Here the appearance of the sow is significant; Gwydion, in his earlier transformation under Math's wand, appears as a sow and so knows all the ways of this creature. The sow, a most ferocious and dangerous beast, is one of the fearsome forms of the goddess Ceridwen. Sows, like many other mammals, are quite capable of eating their offspring if they are disturbed or endangered. Here the sow may be seen as an extension or representative of Arianrhod, who wishes her son's destruction in this story.

(18) The three englyns are worth examination and meditation. Gwydion here employs the authentic magic of the poet, rather than the tawdry enchantment of his magic. He uses music to once more attract the soul of his protégé from the edge of death to the threshold of life. Gwydion stresses the real-world location to him and identifies the eagle as Llew, thus helping Llew to bring his soul from the state of limbo between the worlds, where it is trapped.

(19) The revenge of Gwydion upon the body of the woman he helped to create is without mercy or compassion. Blodeuwedd is transformed into an owl, a night-hunting bird which other birds shun. Alan Garner's great reworking of this romance, "The Owl Service," revolves around this very point of revenge or mercy: "She wants to be flowers, but you make her owls," cries the crushed and penitent descendant of Gwydion, Hugh Half-Bacon, who has lived through the triple destruction of Llew, Gronw, and Blodeuwedd times without number and witnessed his own loveless defeat.[110]

(20) Llew's revenge has the tempered quality of his great-uncle, Math. He allows Gronw the shelter of a stone when he casts the spear for the

reciprocal blow, though this in no way alters the inevitable outcome of Gronw's death at Llew's hands.

(21) Because Arianrhod denies him a bride, Llew cannot become a true king, wedded to his sovereignty. Blodeuwedd is an otherworldly woman, and in this human world of the Fourth Branch, she can confer nothing on her husband. Llew's own birth was caused by the loss of Goewin's sovereignty and by his mother's loss of reputation. His subsequent sufferings are the working out of a hard destiny in which he will eventually succeed to his great-uncle's throne and his uncle/father's magic.

## One-Eye and the Skillful Hand

All the signs indicate that the Fourth Branch is of later composition than the other three. The world of Gwynedd, though still replete with enchantment, has less direct contact with the Otherworld, and though there are still many ancient themes buried within it, this story has the greatest number of rationalizations of character. Because of this aspect, it is the one which most readers find easiest to identify with. The terrible rejections and revenges exacted here are wholly human and, as such, they are the most tragic and unendurable. The only people for whom Gwydion shows any love—Gilfaethwy and Llew—suffer from his jealous affections; and those who oppose the objects of his affection—Pryderi, Blodeuwedd, and Gronw—are subjected to terrible revenge and merciless death.

This branch is composed of three connected narratives: the theft of Pryderi's pigs and the rape of Goewin; Llew's childhood and the lifting of his geasa; and the betrayal of Blodeuwedd. Beneath these tales are even more ancient ones which we are able to uncover with the help of many Irish folk stories and so solve the mysteries of Dylan's death, Arianrhod's lover, and the nature of Gwydion and Llew's relationship. We are indeed fortunate that so many variant stories directly relating to the birth and destiny of Llew's Irish counterpart, Lugh, have survived within the oral tradition. A common tradition underlies the families of Don and Danu, the Irish evidence of which was recorded at a much earlier date than the transcription of the *Mabinogion,* but this does not necessarily make it older in essence.

The surviving folk stories relating to Balor and his grandson, Lugh, are correspondingly very late from the point of transcription, for J. F. Campbell and Jeremiah Curtin recorded the oral tales of Ireland and Scotland in the nineteenth century.[24, 30] These stories are also relevant to our study of "Culhwch and Olwen" because it draws on the same oral tradition. Gruffydd, in his monumental study of Math, has fully demonstrated the stages by which common Welsh and Irish themes were synthesized, so we will content ourselves with a brief retelling of the relevant Irish stories. The main source is "Balor on Tory Island."[30]

King Balor lives on Tory Island because it is prophesied that he will be killed by the son of his only daughter. This prompts him to imprison her in a tower on Tory with twelve women to guard her. Opposite on the mainland lives a smith, Gavidim, who owns a magical cow, the only such beast in all Ireland which can fill any vessel with milk. Balor wants the cow and sends his agents to fetch it, but they are refused. The three sons of Ceanfaeligh come to Gavidim to have swords made for themselves, and each promises to take turns in guarding the cow. Fin, the youngest brother, is responsible for losing the cow, which is captured by Balor's agents. Gavidim demands that Fin return it, then threatens to behead him. Fin asks the help of an otherworldly man called Gial Dubh (or Mathgen, in another variant). Together they go to Balor's castle, where Fin submits to impossible tasks which Gial Dubh achieves magically. He helps Fin sleep with Balor's daughter, counseling him to lie with the twelve guardian women as well so that they might not warn Balor out of jealousy of each other. Fin obtains the cow and returns it to Gavidim.

Before the end of the year, Fin returns to Tory and rescues the thirteen children which the women had borne. Twelve fall overboard and become seals and the thirteenth is Balor's grandson, who does not thrive until taken back to his mother's breast. Gial Dubh creates a magical forest around the island to hide the child from Balor, but a wind blows it down and Balor kills Fin. Not knowing himself to be Balor's grandson, the boy determines to kill his father's murderer. In another variant, the boy becomes the gardener's assistant and because he is able to pick up many apples, Balor cries out "Tog leat Lui Lamfada" or "Take them away, Little Long Hand." And so he receives his name.

Lui kills Balor's agents and escapes from the island. Balor pursues him to Gavidim's forge, where Lui waits with a red-hot spear. Balor has an eye in the middle of his head which he covers with nine shields that the world might not be blasted by his baleful glare. As he raises the last shield, Lui strikes him in the eye, and Balor then knows the identity of his opponent as his own grandson. He requests that Lui behead him and place the head over his own so that he will know everything and become invincible. Lui instead casts down the head, where it makes a hole in the earth deeper than the deepest lake.

Many similar aspects between this tale and the Fourth Branch are apparent, but the characters and their motivations are completely dissimilar. Gavidim the smith is Gofannon. Gial Dubh is Gwydion, who helps Fin with his magic—the variant name of Mathgen for Gial Dubh equates the magical roles of both Math and Gwydion in one character. Balor and Math are not at all alike. Balor appears again in the *Mabinogion* as the Cyclopean giant Yspaddaden in "Culhwch and Olwen," where again his death is dependent upon his daughter remaining unmarried. Balor's daughter is analogous to Arianrhod: Both women are associated with dwelling in a tower. Math's testing of Arianrhod's virginity would make more sense if, in an original source, Math were in the position of Balor. In "Balor on Tory Island," the daughter is impregnated through magical means. She bears a son by Fin, and her women each bear a child who swims off into the sea, just as Dylan does. In another variant, the smith Gavidim fosters Lui and it is he who forges the famous spear of the hero, which in Math becomes the weapon of both Llew's downfall and Gronw's death. In both instances, it is Gial Dubh or Fin who is the enabling magician who obtains the magical cow (pigs) and helps impregnate the imprisoned daughter.

Gruffydd has shown that Goewin is a late interpolation into the Fourth Branch and that Arianrhod originally fulfilled the role of footholder to Math. Tudor Aled, a fifteenth-century poet, spoke of Arianrhod thus: "Woe to him who looks upon her. . . . Over her . . . is a keeper as strong as the wall . . . there is her father with his eyes upon her . . . the lissom lady dare not jump on to the cliff."[45]

The fifteenth-century Welsh poet Lewis Mon wrote comparing his love with that of Arianrhod, clearly demonstrating that knowledge of other variant stories was still circulating long after the first transcription of the *Mabinogion*: "My plaint concerning a maid is greater than that of Math Hen, son of Mathonwy. The arm of a chaste white-armed maiden was every night his pillow, Arianrhod white as snow; that man might not live without her."[45]

Arianrhod's tower, Caer Sidi, has passed into the mysteries of Britain as the magical tower of poetic initiation and also the otherworldly caer of death and transformation. Folk tradition speaks of the inundation of the tower by the waters of Caernarvon Bay, where a reef of stones can be seen at low tide.[13] This legend is very like that of Ker Ys in Brittany; the pride of Ahes, a woman not unlike Arianrhod, caused its inundation.

Arianrhod is described in the triads as Beli's daughter. Beli and Balor may have a common derivation. In Irish legend Balor becomes the restrictive grandfather giant whose Cyclopean eye blasts all he looks upon, while in Welsh legend, Beli becomes a renowned ancestor whose name heads many genealogies. If we refer to the family trees of Math and Don (figures 3 and 4, pages 80 and 81), we will see that Beli's wife or mother is named as Don or Anna. Both names derive from a common Celtic source, and while later medieval commentators have tried to pass off Anna as identical with St. Anne, mother of the Blessed Virgin, it is evident that the lady in question is really Danu—Don or Anu, the ancestral goddess of both Irish and Welsh peoples.[5, 91]

Arianrhod has clearly inherited all of Balor/Math's characteristics from a lost original: She restricts her own son in an inexplicable manner, transferring to him the geasa which were likely once issued by Balor/Math. On her imprisonment and secret wooing, Math is silent. What remains is an unattractive enchantress whose malignancy is total.

The conception, birth, and upbringing of Dylan and Llew are strongly related to that of Fionn Mac Cumhail, whose own upbringing is kept necessarily secret. Fionn's mother bears two children, the second of whom is hidden by her brother, Gobhan Saor, in a tree trunk or among a magical enclosure of trees. *Gobha* is Irish for "smith," and clearly relates to Gofannon's role as foster father of Dylan, while the hiding of the child in a tree equates to Gwydion's hiding of Llew, or the hiding of Lui in the magical forest by Gial Dubh. In a folk story relating to Fionn, it is told how Fionn's father has to temper the sword he is making on the first thing to come through the smithy door, such is his skill at making deadly weapons. At these times, Fionn's mother hides away her son and sends a dog to the forge that the sword's venom might be spent on the beast and not the boy.[45] This perhaps gives us the necessary clues to Dylan's own untimely end. In the lost original, Gofannon, the master smith, is doubtless the forger of Llew's famous sword or spear. The following tentative reconstruction of this original should not be considered as definitive, but as one possible means of understanding the complex mysteries hidden within this story.

Math's rule is destined to end when his daughter marries. She is therefore imprisoned in a tower on an island. Math desires the magical pigs of Pryderi and sends his agents to fetch them. The youngest of these, Gilfaethwy, aided by the magic of Gwydion and the smithcraft of Gofannon, determines to supplant Math by sleeping with his daughter, Arianrhod. Gilfaethwy sleeps with her, while Gwydion sleeps with her women. When it is time to rescue the children, Dylan slips into the sea, whereupon Gwydion gifts him with the ability to turn into a seal so that the boy has two natures. The other boy, Llew, is weak, requiring his mother's milk. Gwydion disguises himself and Llew as gardeners and gains employment on the island of Math, where the boy is hidden among the trees.

Math suspects that his daughter has borne a child and submits her to a test of virginity. On finding she is no longer a virgin, he swears on her son the destiny that he should have no name and that he should bear no arms. Then he transforms the boy's father into a beast. Yet Math himself names the boy by remarking on his great dexterity and good aim, so that the boy is called Llew of the Long or Skillful Arm.

Math desires that a spear be made for him which should have great venom and kill the first thing entering the smithy door while it is cooling. Gofannon sets up the forge for such a weapon, but after it comes from the anvil, Dylan returns to his foster father's forge and is accidentally slain in place of Llew, for whom Math intended the spear.

Llew then seizes the spear and kills his grandfather, who swears a final destiny that Llew should have no woman of mortal stock for his wife. Gwydion is able to make a woman from flowers, but she is inhuman and betrays Llew with another man. Gwydion searches the stars for his foster son until he finds his soul. Llew is avenged upon his wife and her lover but, having no offspring, he dies and Gwydion sets him in the stars as the hero with the spear or sword of light who fights for those imprisoned beyond hope of release.

Lui, Lugh, and Llew are strongly related to the hero Llwch Lleminawc, whose brilliant sword of light wins the treasures in the poem "Preiddeu Annfwn" (see chapter 6). His name has been associated with the Celtic deity Lugus, who is remembered in many place-names such as Lugudunum (Lyon) and Luguvalium (Carlisle). Throughout Celtic legend, Lugh/Llew/Lugus is a sun god whose skills rank him supreme among the gods. His name is now lost to modern pantheons, but not his power, to which St. Michael now succeeds. In fact, T. C. Lethbridge's study has shown that many places once associated with Lugh were rededicated to St. Michael during the Christian era.[59] The bearer of the flaming spear still thrusts down into darkness those things of ancient evil and releases prisoners with his sword of light.

It is not only as a Christian saint that Llew has survived, but also as Lancelot, the queen's champion who is raised by the Lady of the Lake. In almost all versions of the Arthurian legend, the Lady is unnamed, yet in Layamon's *Brut*, she is called Argante, in which name we hear an echo of Arianrhod, who also inhabits a sea-girt island. Arianrhod and Llew, like Rhiannon and Pryderi, stand forth as the latest contenders for the titles of Modron and Mabon. Both women are shamed by their child's birth; both children are lost, are raised in secret, and return to perform great deeds.[143]

If the Arthurian overtones seem a little strained, we have only to consider that in *Lanzelet*, a twelfth-century German poem, Lancelot's foster mother, the Lady of the Lake, is named Modron whose son, Mabuz, becomes an evil magician in this version of the story.[105] Further, we can play a permutation game in which Arianrhod, Gwydion, and Llew become Igrayne, Merlin, and Arthur, but once one enters the vast field of Arthurian sources, it is easy to find correspondences—it is a virtual treasury where gold is so common one can stuff one's pockets full and still come back for more.

The Fourth Branch of the *Mabinogion* is as rich a field as we could wish for, in which the young sun god suffers a small eclipse only to rise brighter on the morrow and perform more splendid deeds of valor.

# 6
# Culhwch and Olwen

*My lords, a proven sooth it is that seven times
was the Court found in the seven Cloaks of the
story. But as yet ye know not what this may
signify . . . the seven Cloaks are in truth the
seven Wardens. Each of these Wardens in his
turn will tell you how he found the Court, and
before hand ought it not to be told.*

ELUCIDATION DE L'HYSTOIRE DU GRAAL

*Bring the sword of light that can never fail to
cut or give light, the bread that can never be
eaten and bottle of water that can never be
drained.*

COLDFEET AND THE QUEEN OF THE LONESOME ISLE,
A TRADITIONAL IRISH STORY

## Tasks and Heroes

With "Culhwch and Olwen" we leave the medieval retelling of the Four Branches of the *Mabinogion* and enter a deeper, more ancient world where the sources underpinning and complementing the Four Branches can be discerned. "Culhwch and Olwen" is virtually a compendium of stories dovetailed together to read as one sequence. Embedded within it are genuinely traditional portions of original storytellers' presentations. These are found in the riddling dialogues of Culhwch and the porter and in the repetitive utterances and sequences, as well as in the great artistic wordplay which describes Culhwch and Olwen themselves. Repetition of phrase and descriptions are a feature of orally transmitted stories, landmarks to guide the teller from one passage to another. We find them in the *Iliad* and the *Odyssey,* in which Homer draws on oral tradition, right down to the tales of the present *seanchaithe* and cyfarwyddiadd, who are the last guardians of the Irish and Welsh storytelling tradition. This story falls into the category of Six Who Go Through the World, a world folk device wherein a young hero gains the help of experts or specialists in their field, such as men who can breathe underwater or hear ants in another land or see great distances.

Compared with the medieval constraints which have fallen upon the retold Four Branches, "Culhwch and Olwen" has all the humor and immediacy of a folk story. It ranges from high tragedy to burlesque. We meet Arthur's court, which is made up of heroes from so many levels of tradition that we are surely halfway within the regions of the Otherworld itself. Beasts, birds, men and gods, witches, maidens, queens, and enchantments mingle in this most complex of tales which gives us virtually a roll call of the gods of Britain. The list of those in Arthur's court, including no fewer than 250 individuals, may disconcert non-Welsh speakers—which is a shame because, while some of these characters' names are merely nonsense or riddling epithets, others are very revealing.

Although this seems the most Welsh of stories, we should not be surprised to encounter distinct Cornish and Irish elements. The hero,

Culhwch, bears a strong relationship to both Tristan and Lugh, as we will see. But the major themes are those central to the British mysteries: the harrowing of Annwfn by Arthur to fetch the hallows; the finding of Mabon with the help of the oldest animals, a theme to be discussed more fully in chapters 8 and 9; and the defeating of the restrictive giant, which highlights Arthur's place in the succession of the Pendragons.

## Synopsis of "Culhwch and Olwen"

(1) Cilydd ap Celyddon Wledig married Goleuddydd ferch Anlawdd Wledig. While she was pregnant she ran mad. Near her time she returned from the wilderness and gave birth to her son in a pig run. He was subsequently known as Culhwch (pigsty). Goleuddydd fell ill and before her death forbade her husband to marry again until a two-headed brier grew on her grave. For seven years her tutor trimmed the grave, but at length he forgot and Cilydd finds such a brier growing upon it. (2) He then fights the neighboring King Doged, marries his widow, and takes his lands and his daughter. The new queen demands an old hag to tell her if her abductor has any children. On learning about his son, she bids Cilydd recall Culhwch from his place of fosterage. She then suggests to Culhwch that he wed her daughter, but he refuses. She lays a destiny on him that he might marry none save Yspaddaden Pencawr's daughter, Olwen. (3) Immediately, Culhwch conceives a love of Olwen, upon which his father sends him to Arthur to ask Arthur's help in obtaining her.

(4) Culhwch is prevented from entering the hall by Glewlwyd, Arthur's porter, (5) which leads Culhwch to threaten to satirize Arthur and lay waste the country with his complaint unless he gains entry. He is allowed in and demands of Arthur the rights of a king's heir (6) and that Arthur trim his hair for him. Arthur realizes their kinship instinctively and promises (7) to grant whatever Culhwch asks, save his personal gear and his wife. (8) Culhwch then, in the names of all at Arthur's court, demands Olwen.

After a year's search, she is not found. Cai, Bedwyr, and others with Culhwch go to a far land and meet (9) a giant herdsman called Custennin sitting on a mound; he has been dispossessed by Yspaddaden. (10) Culhwch gives him a ring which Custennin takes home to his wife. She realizes instinctively that Culhwch is her sister's son. The company comes to Custennin's house where Cai is nearly killed by the wife's joyful greeting. (11) The woman reveals her (unnamed) son hidden in a cupboard for fear of Yspaddaden, who has killed twenty-three of her sons. The boy becomes Cai's charge. The woman then arranges for Culhwch to see (12) Olwen, who comes to wash her hair every Saturday night at their place.

(13) Olwen tells Culhwch that she cannot marry him, having given her promise not to disobey her father, who would die if she married. She bids Culhwch accept any task or promise which her father might exact. (14) The company comes to Yspaddaden's hall and asks for Olwen's hand. (15) Yspaddaden must raise his eyelids with forks in order to see his guests, and he casts a poisoned stone spear at them; Bedwyr flings it back and pierces the giant in the knee. Culhwch's company returns to the hall a second time and is delayed by the answer that Olwen's great-grandparents must be consulted first. Yspaddaden casts a second spear and this time Menw casts it back, catching the giant in the chest. On the third visit to the hall, Culhwch himself casts back the spear and catches the giant in the eye.

(16) At last Yspaddaden heeds their request and sets Culhwch thirty-nine *anoethu,* or impossible tasks:

1. To clear a wood, plow the land, and sow it in a single day to provide the wedding feast.

2. To see that the field is plowed by Amathaon, son of Don.

3. To see that the irons for the plow are delivered personally by Gofannon, son of Don.

4. To see that the two oxen of Gwlwlwyd plow the field.

5. And that the yellow, pale white, and brindled oxen are yoked together.

6. To acquire the oxen who were once men, Nynnyaw and Peibyaw.

7. To sow a field with linseed, that a veil might be spun from it for Olwen's wedding.

8. To get the sweetest honey from a hive without drones or bees to make braggat mead.

9. To obtain the only cup capable of holding such strong drink: that of Llwyr, son of Llwyron.

10. To get the inexhaustible hamper of Gwyddno Long Shanks, which produces the food each man desires.

11. To get the horn of Gwlgawd of Gododdin.

12. To obtain the harp of Teirtu, which plays by itself.

13. To get the Birds of Rhiannon, who wake the dead and soothe the living.

14. To obtain the cauldron of Diwrnach the Irishman, steward to King Aedd, in which to boil the meat.

15. To obtain the tusk of Ysgithrwyn, chief boar, to shave the giant.

16. To summon Odgar, son of King Aedd, the only one capable of drawing the tusk.

17. To see that Caw of Scotland acts as the messenger for this task.

18. To obtain the blood of the pitch-black witch, daughter of the bright-white witch, to straighten the tangles in Yspaddaden's beard.

19. To acquire the thermos of Gwydolwyn the Dwarf to keep the blood warm.

20. To obtain the milk bottles of Rhynnon Stiff Beard to keep the milk for the feast from souring.

21. To get the comb and shears from between the ears of the boar Twrch Trwyth, in order to straighten the giant's hair.

22. To get Drudwyn, the whelp of Greid ap Eri, without whom the boar cannot be hunted.

23. To get the leash of Cors Hundred Claws to restrain Drudwyn.

24. To get the collar of Canhastyr Hundred Hands to collar Drudwyn.

25. To get the chain of Kilydd Hundred Holds to attach to the collar.

26. To release Mabon ap Modron, who was taken from his mother when he was three nights old and whose whereabouts no one knows, for only he can manage Drudwyn.

27. To get Gwynn Dun Mane, the horse of Gweddw, for Mabon to ride.

28. To release Eiddoel ap Ner, Mabon's cousin, without whom Mabon will not be found.

29. To get Garselid the Irishman, Master of Hounds, without whom Twrch Trwyth cannot be hunted.

30. To get the leash made of Dillus Farfawg's beard to hold the hounds—but the hair must be plucked out while Dillus is alive.

31. To get the wild man, Cynedyr, son of Hetwn the Leper.

32. To summon Gwynn ap Nudd, whose task is to prevent the destruction of the world but who has the untamable energy of spirits from Annwfn.

33. To get Du, horse of Moro Battle Leader, for Gwynn to ride.

34. To get Gwilenhin, King of France, to hunt Twrch Trwyth.

35. To get Alun of Dyfed to unleash the hounds.

36. To get the hounds of Rhymhi, Aned, and Aethlem, who, once loosed, always kill.

37. To persuade Arthur and his companions to help hunt Twrch Trwyth.

38. To get Bwlch, Cyfwlch, and Syfwlch, sons of Cilydd Cynfwlch, with their equipment and entourage, for when their three horns are blown, everyone will come.

39. To get the sword of Wrnach the Giant, who cannot be killed except by his own sword.

(17) Only fourteen tasks are achieved within the ensuing story. In order, the sword of Wrnach the Giant is acquired. (18) Eiddoel, Mabon's cousin, is released, as is Mabon ap Modron. The hounds of Rhymhi are obtained. (19) The field of linseed is sown for Olwen's veil and the leash is made of Dillus Farfawg's beard. (20) The whelp Drudwyn is found, Gwynn ap Nudd is summoned. The leash of Cors is obtained and Gwrgi Seferi and Odgar ap Aedh are summoned, and the tusk of Ysgithrwyn is obtained. (21) The cauldron of Diwrnach is obtained. (22) Twrch Trwyth is hunted with the help of those assembled, and the blood of the pitch-black witch is acquired.

(23) Then Yspaddaden is shaved, according to his request, with the comb and scissors from between the ears of the Twrch Trwyth. He then gives his daughter to Culhwch who, with the help of Arthur and his men, has fulfilled all conditions. Goreu, son of Custennin, then beheads the giant, and Culhwch is possessed of Olwen and her father's castle.

## Commentary

(1) This preliminary story of Culhwch's birth establishes his totemic name: "pig run" or "pigsty," which, at first glance, appears outrageous or merely comic. Because it is Culhwch's destiny, however, to defeat the two great boars, Ysgithrwyn and Twrch Trwyth, we may acknowledge his name's natural advantage. As we have already stated, the pig played

a great part in Celtic life both as a staple food and as a totemic creature of the Underworld. Additionally, the combination of pigs and madness is a repeating motif within Celtic literature. Merlin, in his madness, addresses his lamenting prophecies to a pig in "Coed Celyddon," thus showing himself to be one of the great swineherds or guardians of the totem beasts (see chapter 8). Here, Goleuddydd gives birth "for fear of the swine"; it is the chthonic pig that causes Culhwch to be born.

If pigs come from the Underworld, then their guardians, swineherds, often have an initiatory significance as Underworld guides. They show the way to health and prosperity, as instanced by King Bladdud's discovery of the hot springs over which the city of Bath was founded,[99] or by the swineherd who discovers the mysterious location of Cashel for the Eoghanacht kings of Munster in Ireland.[21]

Culhwch is found in a pigsty just as Pryderi is found in a stable; each hero's destiny is bound by this totemic association, as is that of the the Irish hero Diarmuid, whose destiny is woven with that of a white boar.[87] Culhwch acquires no other name, although he does gain a helper, Goreu, whose role is tied equally to Culhwch winning Olwen and the destiny of Mabon, as we shall see in chapter 9. There is a secret and undisclosed association between Culhwch and the mighty Twrch Trwyth perhaps hinted at in *Cormac's Glossary*, a tenth-century Irish etymology which tells us that in Irish, *torc* or *orc* and *triath* mean "boar" and "chieftain," respectively. *Triath* is the name of a king, while *orc triath* is the name for a king's son.[21] In Celtic times the pig was valued, yet the trade of pig-tending was disgraceful for noblemen. The role of swineherd was connected to both madness and exile, and as a result of its associations, it was often the trade taken up by banished or temporarily deranged heroes. Yet, as we have seen, it is a role which bestows hidden insights and often riches in folk stories. Part of the kingly candidate's training in many myths from that of Apollo to Pryderi consists of servile labors. Culhwch is no exception to this rule: He has to perform strange and impossible labors to placate the giant; he must kill Twrch Trwyth, which, according to the Irish gloss, means "king's son." In Culhwch, Arthur states that the giant boar was once a king, "but because of his sins, God turned him into a pig." The connections among our hero, the boar, and the giant will be further traced in note 23, below.

(2) In this story, Doged's widow enacts the role of the jealous step-mother determined to further the rights of her own child. Like Arianrhod, she lays a marriage geis upon Culhwch. Her dialogue with the old hag survives as late as the nineteenth century in the Irish folk-tale "Black Thief and King Conal's Three Horses," which parallels Culhwch almost exactly up to this point.[30]

(3) Culhwch is, according to the story, only seven years old at this time. His newfound adulthood is accelerated by two actions: the realization of Olwen and his love for her, and his shaving at the hands of Arthur. He loves Olwen the moment she is named, and as in "The Dream of Macsen Wledig," where Macsen cannot rest until he finds Elen, so Culhwch sets off on his quest. The description of his ride to the court, like the later description of Olwen, is one of the masterpieces of Celtic storytelling embellishment.

(4) The pattern of question and answer between Culhwch and Glewlwyd is very ancient indeed. It parallels almost exactly the exchange between Irish Lugh and the porter in the court of Nuadu of the Tuatha de Danaan, as told in "The Second Battle of Mag Tuired."[148] It is midwinter when Culhwch arrives at Arthur's court in need of help, but he is shut out. Glewlwyd, extolling the great deeds of Arthur, states that throughout two thirds of his life he has never met a more worthy man than Culhwch.

(5) Culhwch threatens to raise three shrieks which will blast the land's fertility, a very serious challenge to the rightful upholder of sover-eignty, King Arthur. In "Lludd and Llefelys," a dragon cries every May

Eve and similarly blights both land and animals. The theme of the land becoming a wasteland is slight within "Culhwch and Olwen," yet the unrestricted underworldly powers of Twrch Trwyth threaten to blight the Island of the Mighty. When Arthur aids Culhwch, he is strengthening and defending his own realm, for Yspaddaden, though acknowledging Arthur's might, tells Culhwch that the king is secretly under the giant's power.

(6) Culhwch is one of Arthur's many cousins. The cousins and nephews of a king were of greater importance in family precedence and succession than the king's sons. The family tree of Culhwch (figure 5, page 109) shows some important and revealing links.

It will be seen that Arthur's mother, Eigr, as the triads call Igerna, is the sister not only of Goleuddydd, Culhwch's mother, but also of Custennin's unnamed wife. These three sisters are none other than the famous Cornwall sisters of later Arthurian romance who, like the Parcae or Fates, use their magical arts to weave the fate of Arthur.

Culhwch's shaving is a rite of passage into manhood, administered by the most senior and most noble of his kin—Arthur himself. Hair and shaving are motifs throughout this story: Culhwch is shaved by Arthur, Olwen washes her hair in the house of her foster mother, a leash is made of Dillus's beard, and Yspaddaden demands extensive barbering with a variety of implements.

(7) Triad 93 describes Culhwch as one of three "who specified their dependency from Arthur as their gift." Arthur promises unreserved help, exempting only his ship, mantle, sword, spear, knife, and wife. An almost exact catalog of these items is given by Geoffrey of Monmouth: Arthur has a golden helmet whose crest is a dragon, and across his back is a shield called Pridwen on which is painted a likeness of the Blessed Virgin. His sword, Caliburn, is forged on the Island of Avalon, and his spear is called Ron.[37] Clearly, "Culhwch and Olwen" and Geoffrey's *Historia* have definite links.

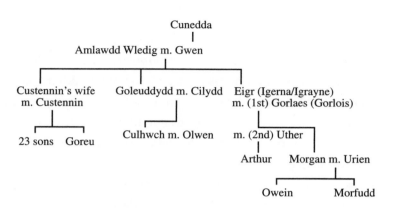

Figure 5. The family tree of Culhwch

(8) Culhwch's request leaves out nobody in Arthur's retinue. From the list which follows, it is clear that Arthur's court comprises famous Arthurian heroes as well as immortals, kings of adjoining lands, poets, and survivors of Camlann (from which Arthur himself was borne away to Avalon). Monsters and nonsense people abound, such as the daughters of Bwlch, Gyfwlch, and Sefwlch who are called Plague, Want, and Penury. The storyteller and his successors have included many characters from the entire Arthurian court, as well as favorites from other traditional stories current at the time. It is exceedingly valuable to study the names listed, in order to establish a fuller picture of the Dark Age Arthur.[73] Several names are mentioned more than once, noticeably that of Llwch Llenllawg, of whom we will speak later.

Nearly every branch of the *Mabinogion* is represented by one character, but most important are those men of special skills who are the enablers of Culhwch's quest. Each of these possesses a unique and otherworldly ability and these men form Culhwch's inner band of human helpers.

(9) Custennin is Yspaddaden's herdsman and porter. The text implies that these lands and the fortress once belonged to Custennin, who

says, "Because of my wife, Chief Giant Yspaddaden has ruined me."[3] We are not told what manner of claim the giant has on Custennin's wife nor why she has caused Custennin to lose his lands. We know that Yspaddaden has been assiduous in destroying any children she has so that he may not be overcome or replaced by them, which presupposes that she and her heirs are of royal or powerful descent. If we look to the family tree of Culhwch (figure 5, page 109), we immediately see grounds for suspecting the truth. Custennin's wife is Arthur's aunt, the senior of three royal sisters of the line of Cunedda, whose eight sons are each said to have established his dynasty in Wales. Cunedda is thought to have left the Old North, whence the Welsh originate, in the fifth century.[149] Do we have an ancient memory of the displacement of the aboriginal peoples of Wales who are depicted here as a titanic race?

But both Custennin and his wife themselves are described in titanic terms, as if they are related more to Yspaddaden's family than to Arthur's. The roles of herdsman and foster mother, which they jointly fulfill, are deeply involved in the initiation of the hero and heroine (see chapter 8). A similarly awesome herdsman figure appears in "The Lady of the Fountain," in which his role as guardian of the way between the worlds is clearly shown. Custennin's fortunes are in decline and can only be rescued by his remaining son, Goreu.

(10) The mysterious riddling dialogue between Custennin and his wife is quite baffling until we look at other parallel stories. Custennin pretends he acquired the ring from a washed-up corpse, but his wife immediately knows this is not so; like Arthur, she immediately realizes a deeper sense of kinship between herself and Culhwch. In "The Second Battle of Mag Tuired," Eri, a woman of the Tuatha de Danaan, conceives her son Bres after lying with a man who came out of the West in a magical boat. He leaves her a ring and bids her give it to none other than the one it should fit. When Bres grows up and becomes king of the Fomorians, he demands to know of his parentage: Eri gives him the ring, which fits perfectly, and sends him to his father.[148] Further to this,

we have the testimony of the Tristan legend, so close to the account of Culhwch's own upbringing. In it Tristan's mother gives a ring to her husband when she is near death after giving birth to Tristan. She bids him show the ring to King Mark so that he will know that the child is his sister's. It would seem, then, that Culhwch gives his mother's ring as a token and Custennin's wife, being sister to Goleuddydd, immediately recognizes it.

(11) In this episode in which Cai is nearly strangled by the woman's greeting, we see Cai in his accustomed role as buffoon, deflecting the danger of the otherworldly powers. However, he accepts Custennin's son in the spirit of true fosterage. The boy in the cupboard is called Goreu, whose name means "the best." This singular incident in the middle of the text, also giving us the finding of Mabon, is not insignificant. Goreu is hidden right under the giant's nose, within his own household, and is released into the custody of Cai, with whom he performs great deeds. The terms of Cai's care imply that the boy's life will be as long as his own. This is important if we consider Cai's later action of freeing Mabon and carrying him away on his back. Goreu and Mabon have very close relationships and may be seen as aspects of each other. Both are hidden or imprisoned and both do deeds of great glory. Cai is the enabler of each and so has an important role in turning the wheel of the succession of the Pendragons. Heroes do not become kings without the help of such willing enablers.

(12) Olwen and Culhwch are never described in mundane terms; they are the peerless protagonists of this story. Olwen's name means "white track," after the white clover which springs up behind her as she walks. It is clear that she is a Flower Bride, like Blodeuwedd or Blathnat (see chapter 3). Her relationship with Custennin's wife is very close, though whether it is as aunt and niece or nurse and foster daughter is not entirely clear.

(13) Although she is the giant's daughter, Olwen is not a giant herself. Like Bran and Branwen, who have similarly disparate sizes, Olwen and her father come from very different levels of proto-Celtic story. Whenever flowers or flower names are associated with female protagonists, we become aware that we are in the presence of a sovereignty-bearing woman. Olwen is one such, with the very earth responding to her every step, while, obversely, Yspaddaden is a titan whose negative underworldly restriction keeps everything locked up. Although Olwen does not follow the pattern of other giants' daughters by actively helping her suitor, it is possible that she does give magical assistance to Culhwch and his helpers. Sworn never to disobey her father's orders, Olwen knows that her marriage will mean his death.

The motif of the giant's daughter is discussed further in the section Freeing the Giant's Daughter, below.

(14) The fort is ringed by nine gates and guarded by nine porters, and nine mastiffs wait, all of whom are killed by Culhwch and his men. Like many other features of this compendious story, which restate certain themes in ways resembling musical motifs, Yspaddaden's court seems analogous to Annwfn itself and to the complex descent which Arthur's men and Culhwch are making (see figure 6, page 131).

(15) Yspaddaden is clearly a Balor figure, even down to the baleful single eye. From the Cyclops of the *Odyssey* onwards, this motif recurs in the stories of many cultures. The giant has a stone spear, the barbarous weapon of a native pre-metal-age titan. Yet the poisoned spears which are deadly to mortals are as mere barbs to giants; like a cartoon baddie, Yspaddaden complains with exaggerated peevishness at the inconvenience caused by having spears in his knee, chest, and eye.

(16) Yspaddaden sets Culhwch thirty-nine impossible tasks *(anoethu)*, which are clearly stories in themselves. The full oral telling of this tale must originally have filled many nights. Only fourteen tasks are actu-

ally achieved in this telling. The first tasks (numbers 1–14) involve the provision of food, drink, music, and clothing for the wedding. Of these, only tasks 7 and 14 are achieved: Obtained are the veil for Olwen, which is made with the help of an ant colony that Gwythyr ap Greidawl saves from a fire, and the cauldron of Diwrnach, which is none other than the cauldron of Annwfn. Tasks 15–39 concern the assembling of men, horses, and hounds in order to obtain the tusk of Ysgithrwyn and the comb and scissors from between the ears of Twrch Trwyth. With these last items Yspaddaden will be shaved and his hair will be cut, signaling his imminent death. The obtaining of these items is totally dependent upon Culhwch's ability to assemble men of appropriate gifts, abilities, and aptitudes to accomplish the anoethu.

(17) In task 39, which is performed first, the sword of light is won from Wrnach, a fellow giant of Yspaddaden's ilk. The dialogue between the porter and Cai is exactly the same as between Glewlwyd and Culhwch. Custennin's son, hitherto unnamed, wins his name, Goreu the Best, by his exploit of crossing three courtyards and defeating their guardians. Just as Culhwch becomes an adult at Arthur's court, so Goreu becomes a man in the court of Wrnach.

(18) Task 28 consists of freeing Eiddoel ap Ner, Mabon's cousin, without whom Mabon cannot be found. Interestingly, Eiddoel is himself imprisoned in the fortress of Glini. We have information about neither character from any other source. Glini says of his castle to Arthur, "I have neither good nor pleasure here, no wheat or oats," so that Arthur should not turn envious eyes upon his abode. This may be significant, for the root of Eiddoel's name gives us words meaning "desire," "vigor," and "jealousy."

Because the memory of men is deficient, the freeing of Mabon is accomplished with the help of the totem beasts who lead Culhwch and his helpers through a succession of animals to the source of their quest. The particular reason that Culhwch is seeking him is because

Mabon is the only man capable of handing Drudwen (the brave white one), the hound of Greid ap Eri. Mabon's rescue is told in chapter 8, where its full implications are considered.

(19) The preparation of the field that must be cleared and sown to provide Olwen's wedding veil requires the help of two sons of Don, Amathaon and Gofannon who, respectively, govern cultivation and smithcraft. Amathaon, according to Triad 84, stole a white roebuck and greyhound pup from Annwfn, an act which provoked the Cad Goddeu or Battle of the Trees between the children of Don and Arawn, King of Annwfn.[5, 2] While Amathaon is seen as the original plowman, his brother Gofannon is known as the original smith.

(20) Task 32 involves obtaining the services of Gwynn ap Nudd, but this is delayed because of the dispute between Gwynn and Gwythyr ap Greidawl over the possession of Creiddylad. This ancient theme of the fight of the Summer King and the Winter King over the hand of the Spring Maiden is deeply rooted in the British mysteries. To some extent, Rhiannon is fought over by Gwawl and Pwyll according to this pattern. The combat between Tristan and the Morholt over the hand of Iseult merely reinforces the links between this story and "Culhwch and Olwen." This combat is also a feature of later Arthurian romance in which Guinevere is abducted by Melwas of the Summer Country from Arthur, who plays the part of the Winter King.[49]

Gwynn ap Nudd is King of the Underworld, and plays the Winter King here, and while Gwythyr's antecedents are unknown, his epithet, Greidawl, derives from "scorch" and so he is likely to be the Summer King of this fray. Creiddylad is none other than Cordelia in disguise. Her father is Llydd Llaw Ereint (King Lear); he is a doublet of Nuadu of the Silver Hand, who loses sovereignty because of his disability.

In order to judge between the Gwynn and Gwythyr, Arthur rules that every May Day they shall contend for Creiddylad, but none shall win until Judgment Day, until which time she remains with her father.

But as we said earlier, this is unlikely to be, since Gwynn ap Nudd's task is to prevent the destruction of the world. It is Gwynn ap Nudd who is responsible for the imprisonment of Greid ap Eri (the finding of whose hound, Drudwen, is task 22). Gwynn also causes Cynedyr (who is sought in task 31) to become a wild man by making him eat his father's heart. Gwynn is traditionally one of the many leaders of the Wild Hunt, which, led by its fierce, unyielding chief, is an otherworldly retributive troop that rides down those who have done deeds against humanity.

(21) Task 14 concerns the harrowing of Annwfn by Arthur. Although the cauldron of Diwrnach is in Ireland, we may see it as a resonance for the Underworld. In Celtic legend, neighboring islands are often recognized as the abode of the dead; thus they are ferried by a gray-clad, hooded boatman. The ship of the dead sails still in Celtic imagination in both Brittany and Cornwall, as well as in many other places. A fuller discussion of this task follows in the section The Spoils of Annwfn, below.

(22) Task 21 sees the pursuit of Twrch Trwyth and his seven piglets. Arthur sends Gwrhyr, who knows the speech of beasts, to parley with the swine, and learns that the boar was once a king, the son of Prince Taredd, condemned to boar shape for his sins. This legend has a direct parallel in Irish tradition where a druid, Cian Mac Cainte, the father of Lugh, bewitches his pupils into beasts of the chase and hunts them himself, in the form of a hound. The children of Turenn strike him with his own magic wand and turn him into a black pig. Cian the druid then begins a rampage of fury across Ireland until he plunges into the sea off Donegal—whence the Clad na Muice or "Black Pig's Dike" in Northern Ireland, the great defensive earthwork which can be seen today and which ends in Donegal.[148]

Just as the dangerous power of Matholwch's cauldron from Ireland in "Branwen, Daughter of Llyr" the boar Twrch Trwyth represents the potentially destructive power of the Underworld when it is let loose in Britain. Because it is an unbalanced force, only the most ancient archetypal characters of Arthur's court can catch and subdue it. It is chased from Ireland, to Wales, down the Severn, and into Cornwall, where it vanishes into the sea.

(23) The shaving of Yspaddaden is done by Caw of Scotland, another giant of British mythology. Yspaddaden is killed not by Culhwch or Arthur, but by Goreu, Custennin's son, who avenges his father's disgrace and his brothers' deaths. The retributive and satisfactory conclusion of the story hides one of the major patterns in the succession of the Pendragons: that of the substitution of one character for another's role (see chapter 9). In many folk stories, giants can be overcome only if their exterior soul is found and destroyed. In Yspaddaden's case, his power lies in his hair. Here we see that the instruments to curb Yspaddaden's titanic powers are the shears and comb, which are found between the ears of the ravening boar, Twrch Trwyth.

## Freeing the Giant's Daughter

The sources for "Culhwch and Olwen" are so numerous they would fill a book, never mind a chapter. The three main sources or parallel texts derive from folk story as partially integrated tradition, from the legend of Tristan, and from the myths of Lugh.

Central to the story is the motif of the giant's daughter, which may be summarized as follows. The hero's father makes a bargain with an otherworldly being before his son's birth so that the boy is destined for difficulties and possible imprisonment. The hero is driven into the service of the giant because his father has remarried and his stepmother wishes to dispossess him in favor of her own children. During this employment the hero falls in love with the giant's daughter. He may win her only by performing impossible tasks, such as mucking out a byre left dirty for seven years and thatching a roof with birds' feathers. He is aided by the giant's daughter, who has her father's magical powers, or by companions whose abilities are unusual—for instance, the ability to drink all the water in a lake or eat all the food filling a barn (the device known as Six Go through the World). Alternatively, the hero is aided by animals whom he has rescued. Having achieved the tasks, he must identify the daughter from a roomful of identical women. She is identified by some disfigurement caused in the completion of the tasks; a portion of a finger, for example, is missing. They are married and are then pursued by the giant, who is overthrown by his own enchantments. Often it is necessary to find the hiding place of his heart or soul, which is then broken along with his power.[30, 53]

The anoethu which Culhwch performs to win Olwen are clearly akin to the Labors of Hercules; the power of Yspaddaden resides in his hair and so he must be shaved, like Samson, before his destined death. The giant's daughter motif occurs in many example of world folk story; but it is in two particularly Celtic sources that we find the closest parallels to "Culhwch and Olwen."

We have already mentioned the Cornish connections of "Culhwch and Olwen." Not only is the hunt of Twrch Trwyth completed in Cornwall, but traces of that most Cornish hero, Tristan, are readily apparent. The Tristan legend has its parallels in the Irish Diarmuid and Grainne story and must have one of the widest distributions of any Celtic tale, appearing in Welsh, Icelandic, Danish, German, and even Serbo-Russian texts. Only fragments of the Welsh texts remain, but these are very revealing.[49]

In them Tristan is called Drystan and his father is Tallwch or Talorc. We will remember the Irish gloss which tells us that *orc triath* is the name for a king's son; accordingly, that makes Tallwch "first boar" or "chief boar." We should not be surprised that, apart from his father's name, Drystan has closer connections with pigs. He is named with Pryderi in Triad 26 as one of the three powerful swineherds, one who tended the swine of March ap Meirchyawn (King Mark) while the official swineherd went with a message to Essylt (Iseult). The triad alludes to an unsuccessful expedition on the part of Arthur to steal these pigs, but the story is now lost.[5] What is interesting is that Drystan becomes a substitute swineherd, and that he elopes with Essylt to Coed Celyddon—the very place where Merlin addresses pigs in his madness.[96] This story also corresponds to the details of the Summer King's and Winter King's combat for the hand of the Spring Queen. Arthur hears both sides of the argument from Drystan and King Mark, each of whom wants Essylt, ruling that she should go to Drystan when leaves are on the trees, but to Mark when the trees are bare. Essylt's reply may well indeed be that of Creiddylad's in the most ancient version of Gwynn ap Nudd's and Gwythyr's combat for her:

> Blessed be the judgment and he who gave it! There are three trees that are good of their kind, holly and ivy and yew, which keep their leaves as long as they live. I am Trystan's as long as he lives.[49, 135]

The circumstances of Tristan's birth are similar to those of Culhwch in nearly every respect, for Tristan's mother also runs mad and delivers her son in a pigsty. But while she is called Blanchfleur in most medieval versions, Culhwch's mother's name is derived from Essylt's companion in the Welsh Tristan story. Goleuddydd means "bright day"; in the Tristan story, Essylt's companion is called Golwg Hafddydd (shining summer's day). The coincidences are too consistent for mere accidental transmission of one story to another.

It is even possible to see connections between Custennin's wife and the roles played by both Iseult's mother and Brangwain in the later Tristan stories: All three are wise women, foster mothers to the young Flower Bride who is wed to a man whose attributes make him every bit as restrictive as Yspaddaden to his daughter. All three older women are willing to smooth the bride's way with magic or with a potent cup of desire to extinguish the differences of age.

But while these charming medieval excursions are of interest, we must look for another more obvious parallel with Culhwch: the god Lugh of the Shining Spear. Between these two, the correspondences are manifestly apparent. Both Culhwch and Lugh/Llew share an uncertain birth; both go to a great king's court and become empowered by his authority; both overcome a one-eyed giant; and both win a Flower Bride. It is almost possible to see the invisible join between the stories of Culhwch and Math when we look at the Irish text of "The Second Battle of Mag Tuired," in which Lugh is the champion of the Tuatha de Danaan and defeats his enemy and grandfather, Balor of the Fomorians. As we have stated, the Tuatha de Danaan and the children of Don are of the same lineage; although Irish and Welsh traditions name family members differently, a number are recognizably the same person—for example, Lugh and Llew and Goibniu and Gofannon.

At the beginning of the story, the king of the Tuatha de Danann, Nuadu, loses his hand in battle and so his kingship is forfeit under the rules of Celtic kingship, which state that no blemished man should reign. The kingship is passed to Bres, the son of a Tuatha woman and a Fomorian man. The Fomorians gain ascendancy and put the Tuatha to servile tasks. The great god, the Dagda, has to build the Fomorians' fort and suffers many iniquities.

When the oppression is at its height, a stranger comes to the hall of Nuadu. He seeks entrance in a way that parallels almost exactly the exchange at the gate between Culhwch and Glewlwyd. The stranger is Lugh, the son of Ethniu. (Ethniu is the daughter of Balor the Fomorian and of Cian, son of Diancecht of the Tuatha.) The porter will allow no man to enter unless he is a man of skill. Lugh vouchsafes himself to be not only a wright, but also a smith, a champion, a harper, a hero, a poet, a historian, a sorcerer, a healer, a cupbearer, and a fire-maker. Although Nuadu has men possessed of these abilities, Lugh is admitted because he combines them all, for he is *samildanach*, "many-gifted." After a test of his various skills, Nuadu cedes place to him and goes to consult with his council for a year.

The result of this council is an assembly of men each of whom will perform some particularly wonderful deed by which the Fomorians can be defeated: The druid Mathgen says he will cast the twelve principal mountains of Ireland on their enemies' heads; and the cupbearer will withhold water from the Fomor men. A great battle is prepared, but Lugh is restrained from entering it by the Tuatha, who fear his early death, for he is clearly gifted by the gods. However, he escapes his guardians and encounters his grandfather Balor, whose evil eye he pierces with a stone thrown from a sling. The battle is won, but Nuadu is slain. Lugh then takes up his place.[148]

While Lugh is here possessed of many special skills, he nevertheless draws on a great host of other specially equipped men, just as Culhwch does. The Dagda is like Custennin in description, and is put in so similarly a servile position as guardian and builder of what was once his own property that it is not hard to make the connection. Although Culhwch seems to have acquired a more subsidiary role, the qualities of Lugh are still visible in his makeup: He is a satirist, a hero, nephew to a great king, and he is the one who wounds Yspaddaden in the eye with a spear. Others of Lugh's qualities are discernible in different characters within "Culhwch and Olwen": Goreu and Mabon share the role of Wondrous Youth, while Taliesin is the harper and poet. The Irish myth gives us Lugh the samildanach or many-gifted one; the Welsh story gives us Culhwch who is helped by men of many skills.

To discover the mysteries of "Culhwch and Olwen," the treasures that we seek, we must plunge ever deeper into the confines of Annwfn.

## The Spoils of Annwfn

The hunting of Twrch Trwyth, the shaving and death of Yspaddaden, and the harrowing of Annwfn are three closely related themes central to the mysteries of Britain. The first two themes are clearly stated in the text of "Culhwch and Olwen," yet the implications of the last are not fully developed within the story. We read that Arthur sends Menw into Ireland "to see if the treasures were between the ears of Twrch Trwyth" and that he then sails to Ireland in his ship *Prydwen* in order to fetch the cauldron of Diwrnach. From the list of Thirteen Treasures of Britain, we know that this cauldron would not boil the meat of a coward, but only that of a hero (see chapter 3, page 56). The finding of the cauldron occupies three paragraphs of the text, where it is listed as only one of many anoethu, yet it is crucial to our understanding of "Culhwch and Olwen."

The importance of this episode would remain unclear if we did not have the evidence of a ninth-century Welsh poem, the "Preiddeu Annwfn" or "The Spoils of Annwfn," in which Arthur goes to Annwfn to rescue a prisoner and to gain certain of the hallows, notably the cauldron of Annwfn. Welsh scholars universally attest to this poem's obscurity and have been more interested in its philology than in its mythic implications. Interested readers are directed to consult both the Welsh original and the English translation in R. S. Loomis's *Wales and the Arthurian Legend,*[64] and Marged Haycock's "Preiddeu Annwfn and the Figure of Taliesin."[130] Taliesin is our narrator of the story of this perilous voyage, a firsthand account of the mighty deeds of Arthur in the Underworld. The following version of the "Preiddeu Annwfn" is my own new translation of the original Welsh text.

> *I praise the Mighty One, Pendragon of the kingly*
>    *land,*
> *Who encompasses the margins of the world!*
>
> *Predestined was Gweir's captivity in Caer Sidi,*
> *According to the tale of Pwyll and Pryderi.*
> 5 *None before him was sent into it,*
> *Into the heavy blue chain which bound the*
>    *youth.*
> *From before the reeving of Annwfn he has*
>    *groaned,*
> *Until the ending of the world this prayer of poets:*
> *Three shipburdens of* Prydwen *entered the*
>    *Spiral City*
> 10 *Except seven, none returned from Caer Sidi.*

*Is not my song worthily to be heard*
*In the four-square Caer, four times revolving?*
*I draw my knowledge from the famous cauldron,*
*The breath of nine maidens keeps it boiling.*

15    *Is not the Head of Annwfn's cauldron so shaped:*
*Ridged with enamel, rimmed with pearl?*
*It will not boil the cowardly traitor's portion.*
*The sword of Lleawc flashed before it*
*And in the hand of Lleminawc was it wielded.*

20    *Before hell's gate the lights were lifted*
*When with Arthur we went to the harrowing.*
*Except seven, none returned from Caer Feddwit.*

*Is not my song fit recital for kings*
*In the four-square Caer, in the Island of the*
      *Strong Door,*

25    *Where noon and night make half-light,*
*Where bright wine is brought before the host?*
*Three shipburdens of* Prydwen *took to sea:*
*Except seven, none returned from Caer Rigor.*

*I sing not for those exiled of tradition*

30    *Who beyond Caer Wydyr saw not Arthur's valor.*
*Six thousand men there stood upon the wall,*
*Hard it was to parley with their sentinel.*
*Three shipburdens of* Prydwen *we went with*
      *Arthur:*
*Except seven, none returned from Caer Goludd.*

35    *I sing not for those whose shield arms droop,*
*Who know not day nor hour nor causation*
*Nor when the glorious Son of Light is born,*
*Nor who prevents his journey to Dol Defwy.*
*They know not whose the brindled, harnessed ox*

40    *With seven score links upon his collar.*
*When we went with Arthur on difficult errand;*
*Except seven, none returned from Caer Fandwy.*

*I sing not for those not of our companions,*
*Who know not on what day the chief was born,*
45    *Who do not know the hour of his kingship,*
*Nor of the silver-headed beast they guard for him.*
*When we went with Arthur of mournful mien:*
*Except seven,, none returned from Caer Ochren.*

*Monks howl like a pack of wolves*
50    *At the meeting of magicians;*
*Unknowing of the wind's course, or of the sea's*
     *depths,*
*Unknowing of the fire's sparking, or its unyield-*
     *ing tumult.*

*Monks howl like a pack of wolves*
*At the meeting of magicians;*
55    *Unknowing of the track of midnight or of dawn,*
*Unknowing of the course or whence the attack*
*Of the wind's career or what land it strikes,*
*How many saints are in suffering, how many*
     *are on earth.*

*I praise the Mighty One, the great Pendragon.*
60    *May sadness leave me: Christ is my guerdon.*

On this epic voyage, Arthur and his many men steal the cauldron belonging to the Lord of Annwfn and pass through seven *caers*, or castles, on their ship, *Prydwen*. But only seven return, as in "Branwen," in which only seven men return from Ireland. In both these stories, Taliesin is one of the survivors.

Underlying and echoing the epic theme of this poem is Taliesin's own agenda: revealing his poetic conflict with clerical orthodoxy, where metaphorical and monastic understanding clash, where druidic and clerical knowledge radically diverge from each other. (See lines 35–40 and 49–58 in the "Preiddeu Annwfn.") Let us examine the themes, stories, and locations of this voyage in more detail.

Seven or possibly eight caers (castles) are named, depending on whether or not Caer Pedryfan is considered part of the sequence. The meanings of their titles are obscure even to scholars, especially caers 3, 6, and 7 (Caer Rigor, Caer Fandwy, and Caer Ochren). When other-worldly locations appear in sequence, as in the Irish text *Immram Maelduin (The Voyage of Maelduin)* in which the blessed islands of the western Atlantic each represent a station of the otherworldly voyage, there are distinct states, moods, or conditions attached to each location.[134] Such a pattern is discernible among the caers of Annwfn:

1. **Caer Sidi, the Revolving Castle.** Cahirconree, in Kerry, is said to be the location of Cú Rói mac Daire's fort, which revolves every night after dark so that none can find the gateway the next day. In "Hanes Taliesin," Taliesin speaks of three periods of time spent in the prison of Caer Arianrhod, an otherworldly locus that is the place of incubatory assimilation of poetic wisdom. Caer Arianrhod is associated with the Corona Borealis, or Crown of the North in Welsh star lore, whereas Caer Sidi is located in the Underworld. In *Immram Maelduin,* there is an island upon which a mill grinds into fine flour everything that has been grudgingly given.[134] Mills and turning towers fulfill the purpose of grinding things down and often appear in Celtic myth as places of assimilation or of after-death purgatorial refinement. Gweir, the prisoner, is detained in Caer Sidi, though it is worth noting that his chains may not be literal ones, but rather the "chain" of the sea that encircles this castle. The mood of Caer Sidi is one of perpetual or repetitive patterns of suffering.

2. **Caer Feddwit, Castle of Mead.** As we might expect from a place that houses the cauldron of Pen Annwfn, Caer Feddwit is a castle

of carousal, where intoxicating mead is served—the place where Pen Annwfn's company of heroes may be nourished. It is a place of light and fire, the mood heavy with enchanting knowledge until Lleminawc draws Arthur's sword to steal the cauldron.

**3., 4. Caer Pedryfan, Four Square Castle,** and **Caer Rigor, Castle of Indominability.** The word *rigor* denotes "hardness," "inflexibility," "firm determination," or "indomitability." Taliesin tells us that the song of his voyage to Annwfn is fit material to be sung in Caer Pedryfan, the Four Square Castle within the Island of the Strong Door. This is an epithet for the island of Britain, which is depicted on early maps by classical cartographers as a four-sided, trapezoidal shape. The island fortress of Britain, surrounded on each of its coastlines by the barrier of the sea, is indeed a four-square citadel wherein an otherworldly hero or guardian maintains its defense. This role is now popularly assigned to King Arthur, but ancient tradition recognized other heroes who predate him.

We have already discussed the notion of Bran as a type of Cronos or guardian sleeper, one whose head is a palladium against the invasion of Britain, but here we experience the formidable nature of this part of Annwfn, which, like many otherworldly regions, blends night and day into a kind of twilight. With Bran to guard it, the land and all that lies under it is firmly and indomitably guarded. Line 25 may be translated two ways: *Echwyd a muchyd* means "flowing water" and "jet," and also "noon" and "darkness," with the interesting note that *echwydd* is a resting place for oxen, which is significant if considered in the light of lines 39–46. There are many allusive mentions of an ox or other horned beast which is the destined possession of a special otherworldly hero.

The abiding and unchanging quality of these two caers echo the static and unyielding nature of Pen Annwfn. If Caer Pedryfan is an epithet for Britain, to be considered separately from the caers of Annwfn, then the unchanging and eternally guarded realm of Caer Rigor may be its underworldly complement.

5., 6. **Caer Wydyr, Glass Castle,** and **Caer Goludd, Castle of Riches.** Caer Wydyr may be made of glass or may be as transparent as glass, as in *Immram Maelduin*, in which the Irish heroes, to their great terror, pass over a sea as clear as glass.[134] The clarity of Caer Wydyr enables the Arthurian heroes to see the great host arrayed against them, but because these foes are of otherworldly kind, or maybe because they are reborn from the cauldron and have no speech, Arthur's host cannot parley with them.

Glass was not in common usage in Britain, but rather a fabulously costly luxury. It is therefore associated with otherworldly states of almost hallucinogenic clarity. In medieval Welsh romance, Ynys Gutrin, the Island of Glass, is where the ninefold sisters live, a realm analogous to Geoffrey of Monmouth's Inis Avallonis. By the twelfth century, Ynys Gutrin had been identified with Glastonbury. In the Celtic languages, *glas* is not "glass" but rather "sea color," described variously as gray, green, or blue depending upon the speaker's intention. Again, we find echoes of the "heavy blue chain" from line 6. The riches of Caer Goludd are frustratingly well guarded in this part of Annwfn, where the verse seems to convey a mood of exaltation mixed with terror.

7. **Caer Fandwy, Castle of the High God.** Many scholars have tried to stretch the likeness between the name Fandwy and that of Manawyddan, but Fandwy may actually derive from Ban-dwy or "high god," where the Welsh initial consonant has mutated from *B* to *F*. Such a translation can be supported by the context of this caer, which discusses the epiphany of the Son of Light, the title for the hero who will come to actively defend the land. We can associate this mythic personage with Mabon. The verse hints at the mysteries of his appearance and his arrested manifestation in

Dol Defwy, or the Valley of Awakening. The brindled ox of this caer is the same one that is the object of Culhwch's fourth and fifth tasks. With the yellow and pale white, the brindled Ox must be yoked and set to plowing by Amathaon, son of Don. These beasts are also mentioned in Triad 45.[5] The mood here is one of high mystery, stressing the importance of knowing the coordinates of Mabon's epiphany and revelation.

8. **Caer Ochren, Enclosed Castle,** or **Castle of Keys.** *Ochren* may derive from *ochr* or "key," or from *awch*, "edge." If Ochren is a scribal error for Achren, this would give us Castle of Trees, but perhaps Enclosed Castle is the most likely translation, for this caer seems so edged about with mystery. We may compare it to the Island of the Four Fences in *Immram Maelduin*, which is internally divided into compartments.[134] The beast that is guarded for the Son of Light is said to be an ox, but it is unclear whether this is the same as the "silver-headed beast" that is guarded for the Son of Light.

In many of the Irish cattle-raid stories—notably "Táin Bó Flidais" and "Táin Bó Froech"—cattle, a woman, and a cauldron are stolen.[148] These spoils are sought by the Son of Light and their possession validates and confirms his reign, as here, where Arthur himself is engaged in a quest on behalf of Culhwch. An ancient pre-Christian Irish prayer for long life invokes "the Silver Champion" who can sustain life, a compelling characteristic of the Son of Light. This invocation highlights once more the matter of Mabon's birth and his assumption of power. The mood is again secretive, exclusive to those with the understanding of these mysteries.

The poem begins and ends with an invocation to God, who is described as a great king. Druidic philosophy influenced Celtic Christian thought, which conceived of Christ as king of the elements, a theme that this poem echoes. In pre-medieval Christian lore, knowledge of the elements and movements of the universe was obligatory for all learned people, as the Irish text *Saltair na Rann* tells us: "Five things a wise person should know: the day of the solar month, the age of the moon, the tides of the sea, the day of the week, the calendar of holy days."[136] From line 49 on, Taliesin is scathing to monks who are ignorant of the mysteries of their own tradition and land and who make distinction between one tradition and another, thus separating rather than reuniting their wisdom. The clerical inability to comprehend the mythic resonances between the deepest wisdom of both traditions grates upon him. The coming of the Son of Light is a matter for the initiates and people of all traditions, though the saving story of that coming is couched in the native myths and stories of every land.

Lines 3–9 refer specifically to the prisoner of Annwfn, here named Gweir, which is one of Mabon's aliases. The fate of this prisoner will be discussed in chapter 9, but we note that in the poem, Taliesin refers to the redemptive appearance of the Son of Light in line 37, and concludes the poem with a prayer for his own inclusion within that redemption. In this he reveals not an orthodox acceptance of the Christian message so much as a druidic comprehension of the role of Mabon. Somehow, Arthur's action of entering Annwfn touches upon the motif of the eternal prisoner, Gweir or Mabon, the one who awaits liberation. The groaning of Gweir, like the moaning of Mabon, echoes hugely throughout this poem; the affliction that he suffers is experienced by Arthur himself, and is poetically underscored by the repetitive last line of the main stanzas, "except seven, none returned."

Line 58 is highly significant, implying that clerics are ignorant of the saints who are suffering, literally, "in perdition" *(yn difant)*. This reminds us of the harrowing of hell, the redemptive descent of Christ into purgatory to release the souls of the just who died before his incarnation, which is instanced in the portion of the Creed stating, "he descended into the hell." This concept is also present in the British theme of the Sleepers in the Land or guardian spirits who protect the land for every era and who are accompanied by a number of warriors standing ready to defend the land. Each succeeding generation has had such palladium spirits whose sole duty is to maintain the Island of the Strong Door, as Britain is called in this poem. This role has been ascribed to historical figures such as Arthur himself, Sir Frances Drake, Lord Kitchener, and Winston Churchill, and they are each accompanied by a body of warriors who fight with them. In druidic terms they are the Sleepers in the Land; in mystery terms they are "the greater dead." In this poem, Arthur leaves many of his own men within Annwfn. It is only in later legend that he joins them as their leader, the once and future king who will rise to defend his land.

The Pen Annwfn, or Sleeper in the Land—himself a withdrawn Pendragon—must maintain a company of warriors within the Underworld that is capable of defense. Only the greatest, bravest heroes can accompany Arthur, only the greater dead may imbibe the nurture of the stolen cauldron. It is not kept boiling by a mere fire, but by the breath of nine maidens, the ninefold sisters whom we shall meet again in *King Arthur and the Goddess of the Land*. They are the native British muses, guardians, and sibyls of the land's creative life.

Lines 11–17 refer to the object of Arthur's quest, the cauldron of Pen Annwfn, which is described as the cauldron of Diwrnach in "Culhwch and Olwen." In the "Preiddeu Annwfn," Taliesin alludes also to the cauldron of Ceridwen, which inspired him, but rather than identifying it as the same cauldron, he is merely reminded of it. Let us differentiate the cauldrons of the *Mabinogion* to be entirely clear: The brew of Ceridwen's cauldron exists solely to distill the three drops of *awen*, or "inspiration"; the rest of the broth is poisonous. This long-brewed elixir is responsible for Gwion's rebirth as Taliesin. Bran's cauldron, which derives from Ireland, gives rebirth to the dead. The cauldron of Diwrnach is also Irish, and as we are told in the list of the Thirteen Treasures of Britain (chapter 3, page 56), it will not boil the meat of a coward, a property which also belongs to the cauldron of Pen Annwfn, which is guarded by nine maidens whose breath maintains its heat. These cauldrons therefore enable knowledge, rebirth, or the nourishment of heroes.

Lines 16–17 refer to the hero whose sword of light enables Arthur's men to snatch up the cauldron. In "Culhwch and Olwen," the sword is called Caledfwlch, Arthur's Excalibur, which is wielded by Llenlleawg, or Lleminawc, the Irishman, as Arthur's champion. Who is this hero? We are told in "Culhwch and Olwen" that Llenlleawg swings Arthur's sword in a circle and so kills Diwrnach and his entire retinue, enabling Arthur's company to depart with the cauldron. The name Lleminawc means "leaping one" but also means "the foretelling one" or "the pre-destined one." In medieval Welsh prophetic verse, the name Lleminawg is often used as an epithet for Mab Darogan or the Son of Destiny, the hero who will vindicate the British people over the English, the one who leaps out of the ground from the ancestral land to liberate his people. This is crucial in our understanding of Mabon's role.

The sword of light is one of the hallows of the land still enshrined within British and Irish folk story as the instrument by which the hero is identified. We may recall that the true candidate for Irish kingship is recognized by the roar of acclamation that issues from the Lia Fail or Stone of Destiny when sat upon by the rightful hero. Arthur's own kingship, in medieval legend, is established by his feat of pulling forth the sword sheathed in the stone. Is the one who leaps out to acclaim the theft of the cauldron the youth who is held in Annfwn's captivity? The wielder of the sword of light in "Culhwch and Olwen" is not Culhwch himself but Goreu, Custennin's son; it is he who leaps across three courtyards and who beheads Yspaddaden. It would seem that Goreu performs the function of king's champion, which, in "The Second Battle of Mag Tuired," Lugh performs for Nuadu. Goreu, who has been hidden away, unnamed and forgotten, acts as a type of Mabon in this greatest of stories.[148] The release of the prisoner from Annwfn is therefore of the greatest importance.

We may now see the accomplishment of Culhwch's anoethu as the means of release for the Son of Light, as a mythic epiphany of great complexity and heroic endeavor requiring the entire complement of mortals and immortals and the assembly of the hallows of Britain and

| Caer | "Preiddeu Annwfn" | | Culhwch's Progress |
|------|-------------------|---|--------------------|
| Caer Sidi | imprisonment of Gweir | | Culhwch is fated to seek Olwen |
| Caer Pedryfan | cauldron of Pen Annwfn | | He seeks protection of the Pendragon |
| Caer Feddwit | sword of light | | He is acknowledged as adult by Arthur |
| Caer Rigor | the court of Pen Annwfn | The Path of Goreu | Yspaddaden sets the thirty-nine anoethu |
| Caer Wydyr | the innumerable host of Pen Annwfn | | Culhwch is aided by Arthur's host |
| Caer Goludd | the brindled ox | | Twrch Trwyth |
| Caer Fandwy | high god's refuge | | Mabon is found and released |
| Caer Ochren | the prophesied hero | | Yspaddaden is overcome |

Figure 6. The caers of Annwfn and Culhwch's progress

their guardians and animals. The intricate weaving of the shared themes of "Preiddeu Annwfn" and "Culhwch and Olwen" can best be appreciated if we see Culhwch's progress in the story as a series of levels with certain protagonists standing as porters at the gates of each level, as shown in figure 6, above. Just as Arthur cannot gain the cauldron of Diwrnach without passing through the seven caers or fortresses of Annwfn, Culhwch cannot gain Olwen unless he descends through the levels of Annwfn. This descent is marked by encounters which give Culhwch the necessary maturity and experience, and incidentally help both Arthur and Mabon take their rightful place in the succession of the Pendragons.

In the context of "Culhwch and Olwen," Culhwch is the loyal youth, the prisoner who is bound by a cruel fate. He is catapulted from boyhood into adulthood by the awakening of his passion for Olwen. To win her he must achieve manly status at the hands of Arthur and over-come the thirty-nine anoethu which Yspadadden lays upon him. The straight path to the depths of Annwfn is taken by Goreu, who wields the sword of light as Arthur's champion. It is he who acts as a rescuer to Arthur himself, as we will see in chapter 9. Readers may wish to compare the path of Goreu with R. J. Stewart's "Path of the Thief" in his *Underworld Initiation*.[98] A hint of this path is given in the episode of "Culhwch and Olwen" where Goreu crosses three courtyards. In the course of this quest, Arthur makes the perilous descent to Annwfn, setting in motion the turning of the succession of the Pendragons.

Three roles emerge: Mabon, the heir apparent of the Pendragons; the Pendragon, who is the ruler of the land of Britain; and the Pen Annwfn or Lord of the Underworld, who rules in the Otherworld. At the beginning of "Culhwch and Olwen" the pattern is as follows:

| Position/Role | Role Player |
| --- | --- |
| Mabon | Culhwch |
| Pendragon | Arthur |
| Pen Annwfn | Yspaddaden |

But this pattern soon changes radically and we begin to see the succession in action. Culhwch passes from being a child and becomes Arthur's champion; his destiny is bound up with that of Twrch Trwyth, which makes a wasteland of the land of Britain in its rampage through the country. Arthur is Pendragon, the ruler of his land, but the unbalanced forces of the Underworld are abroad and threaten his reign. We can see a similar theme in "The Second Battle of Mag Tuired," in which Nuadu is the Wounded King who receives Lugh at his court.[148] Lugh takes Nuadu's place on the throne and in battle, eventually succeeding to his place permanently. In "Culhwch and Olwen," we see an Arthur who is past his prime; his men frequently strive to prevent him from exposing himself to combat. Traditionally, he passes to the other-worldly realm of Avalon, where his wounds are healed and he becomes

an Otherworld guardian. Arthur's Avalon has been frequently fused
with the Underworld; both are accessible by water.

Last, we may see Yspaddaden himself as a restrictive Underworld
king in the mold of Cronos, the Pen Annwfn of the piece. In fact, if we
superimpose the myth of Cronos and Rhea upon him and Custennin's
wife, much of the story becomes clear. Custennin's wife bears twenty-
four sons, twenty-three of whom are slain by Yspaddaden. She hides
the last, Goreu, whose Zeus-like task is to kill his oppressor, which he
indeed fulfills as well as helps the prisoners of Annwfn escape.

Yspaddaden is called Pencawr, or "chief giant." Twrch Trwyth and
Ysgithrwyn, or "chief boar," seem to be the totemic doubles of the
giant. It is the treasures possessed by these boars which bring about
Yspaddaden's death. From the evidence of folk story, the giant cannot
be killed until his daughter marries or until his heart or soul is discovered. The hiding place of the heart or soul is often guarded by fierce
animals and impossible tasks which the suitor-champion must master.

We have already noted the similarities and resonances between
Lugh and Culhwch. With regard to Yspaddaden, we see that he is analogous to Balor, whom Lugh slays. Culhwch, although he is not the
giant's grandson, but only his son-in-law, nevertheless casts a spear
through the giant's eye, just as Lugh does.

The new pattern in the succession of the Pendragons at the conclusion of Culhwch is subtly altered:

| Position/Role | Role Player |
| --- | --- |
| Mabon | Mabon, who is released from the toils of Annwfn |
| Pendragon | Culhwch, who frees the land and gains the sovereignty of Olwen |
| Pen Annwfn | Arthur, who harrows Annwfn and gains its treasures |

Each character becomes the guardian of the state he has mastered.
Mabon passes from baby to kingly champion; Culhwch passes from

child to champion to Pendragon, if we follow the parallel story of Lugh; Arthur passes from being king of Britain to being king of the Underworld, the inner guardian of the hallows, which he watches over until the coming of the next Pendragon. Yspaddaden, at the end of his term of office, is disestablished. Although it is not stated in the story, the giant is responsible for the imprisonment of Mabon and prolongs the duration of the cycle beyond its limits. He therefore loses his place in the succession, and gives way to Mabon (see chapters 9 and 10).

In "Culhwch and Olwen," Mabon earns the name Goreu, although he has other names in other stories. If we need further evidence of this succession, we may recall that one of Arthur's ancient titles is the Boar of Cornwall—a name which confers its own honor:

> because this was the Day
> of the Passion of the Men of Britain
> when they hunted the Hog
> life for life.[118]

# 7
# Taliesin

Who was Taliesin? I did not ask, but Pryderi
  breathed the answer:
"Mabon." I should have known. This was indeed
  the Glorious Youth.
JOHN JAMES, NOT FOR ALL THE GOLD IN IRELAND

Gwion: He who would seek the Muse, he who
  would seek
To marry himself to any kind of sovereignty,
Must make the descent down to the earth's centre,
To face his utmost fears, and his most secret anxieties.
JOHN HEATH-STUBBS, ARTORIUS

## The Luck of the Weir

In this story, we encounter the Wondrous Youth Taliesin, the poet-seer and rescuer of his patron, Elphin. As his story is not found in either *The Red Book of Hergest* nor *The White Book of Rhydderch* (the manuscripts from which the rest of the *Mabinogion* was derived), many translations of the *Mabinogion* omit "Hanes Taliesin," which is a great shame because few readers have the opportunity of studying it for themselves unless they possess the Lady Charlotte Guest edition,[4] or the more recent translation by Patrick K. Ford.[2] The manuscripts which contain versions of "Taliesin" are generally late copies and there is much dispute about authenticity and order of presentation. I have drawn upon both editions mentioned above. Readers can also consult John Matthews's *Taliesin* for in-depth commentary and translations of poetry attributed to Taliesin.[147]

Taliesin Ben Beirdd, chief poet and one of the *cynfeirdd,* or first poets of Wales, was a historical character who was poet to Urien Rheged in the sixth century. Fragments of his poetry turn up at all levels of Welsh literature, but his main work is found in the thirteenth-century manuscript *The Book of Taliesin.* The poetry shows strongly the nature of ancient poetic discipline and inner knowledge of the mysteries, although these are hidden under the hand of clerical transcribers. There is also the problem of false ascription; the work of many lesser poets has been ascribed to Taliesin. These problems aside, in the story of Taliesin we are at the root of the poet's initiatory quest. His escape from Ceridwen reveals to us the mystery of the turning of the totems (see chapter 8); his concern with Elphin's freedom is a resonance of Mabon's release; and his utterances about the elemental changes of the initiate put us in touch with the primal mysteries of creation of which Ceridwen is the mistress and chief alchemist.

### Synopsis of "Taliesin"

(1) In the days of Arthur there lived a man called Tegid Foel and his wife, Ceridwen. (2) Their daughter, Creirwy, was the most beautiful

maiden, but their son, Morfran (great crow), was so ugly that he was nicknamed Afagddu (utter darkness). In order to compensate for his appearance, Ceridwen prepared a (3) cauldron of inspiration so that he might be possessed of prophetic insight and secret knowledge. Its contents were distilled from numerous herbs and plants, and the cauldron was to be kept boiling for a year and a day. (4) She set Gwion Bach, son of Gwreang of Llanfair in Powys, to stir it and an old man, Morda, to tend the fire under it. (5) Near the end of the year, three drops flew out of the boiling cauldron and fell on Gwion's finger. To cool the scald, he put his fingers in his mouth and so received the inspiration intended for Morfran. (6) The cauldron burst in two, for the remainder of its contents was poisonous. The liquor flowed into a stream, and so the horses of Gwyddno Garanhir were poisoned.

(7) Perceiving Ceridwen's wrath, Gwion fled in the shape of a hare, but Ceridwen followed as a greyhound. He became a fish, she an otter. He turned into a bird, she changed into a hawk. Finally he fell from the sky into a pile of wheat, becoming a grain himself, but Ceridwen became a hen and swallowed him. (8) He was born of her womb nine months later, and so great was his beauty that she did not kill him, but instead set him adrift in a coracle on April 29.

(9) Gwyddno's son, Elphin, was a spendthrift courtier in the service of King Maelgwn. His luck and fortunes were so bad that his father allowed him to go and catch the salmon which were annually caught in the weir on May Eve, for their value was one hundred pounds. Elphin saw nothing but a coracle in the weir. Opening its leather wrappings, he exclaimed, "Behold the radiant brow!" *(tal iesin)*, and so the child was named. The child sang to Elphin, consoling him for the loss of the salmon and prophesying that what he had found would be worth far more. (10) When asked who he was, Taliesin sang of his transformations. Elphin's fortunes improved, and the child was given to his wife to nurse.

(11) Thirteen years passed. Elphin went to his uncle Maelgwn's Christmas court. Maelgwn's twenty-four poets praised above all others

the king and his possessions, but Elphin was moved to boast that his wife was as chaste as the queen and his poet better than the king's. He was instantly imprisoned until a test could be made of this. (12) Rhun, a notorious lecher, was dispatched to debauch Elphin's wife, but Taliesin, who knew everything, had her exchange shape with a kitchen maid. Rhun made the maid drunk and cut off her finger on which she wore Elphin's ring. This was later produced as proof positive of his wife's disgrace. Elphin refuted it on three points, however: The finger was too large to be his wife's; its nail had not been cut for a month, which was uncustomary for his wife; and it had been kneading dough, something his wife had never done. Elphin was imprisoned again until his second boast could be proved.

(13) With a satire on his tongue dispraising Rhun and Maelgwn, Taliesin set out for the court to refute the poets. He sat in a corner playing *blerwm, blerwm* on his lips with a finger. When the poets came to sing before Maelgwn, they did likewise, to their own confusion. Maelgwn had the chief poet struck for impudence, but he blamed the poet's behavior on Taliesin. (14) Maelgwn inquired who Taliesin was and where he came from. In a lengthy poem, Taliesin explained in prophetic and analeptic verse his true nature: He had been existent since the creation of the world, present at all its works; he knew all knowledge; he should be until the end of the world. (*Analepsis* is the art of revealing unknown matters from the past, from a time before the revealer's birth.) The poets could make no reply. (15) Taliesin then asked for the release of Elphin from his chains. He challenged the poets to answer riddles that seemed impossible to them. He then sang the wind and other elements so that Maelgwn speedily called for Elphin's release. Because the poets could not answer him, Taliesin satirized them while upholding the princeliness of true poetry.

(16) He then bade Elphin wager Maelgwn that his horse was the better. A race was arranged at Morfa Rhiannedd, the king having twenty-four horses in the race. Taliesin gave Elphin's jockey twenty-four holly sticks with their ends blackened, and told him to strike each of

Maelgwn's mounts as he overtook them and throw down his cap at the point where his horse finished. At this place, men were set to dig and in time they discovered a cauldron full of gold, which Taliesin gave to Elphin in recompense for his barren night at the weir.

(17) Taliesin was then brought before Maelgwn to sing of the Creation. He sang of Adam and Eve, of the Fall, and of the mystery of Christ's sacrifice. He sang of the fate of Troy's descendants, the invasion of the Saxons, the servitude of the Britons, and of their final liberation.

## Commentary

(1) Tegid the Bald makes no further appearance in this story. His name survives in the Welsh lake Llyn Tegid, a typical cauldron lake such as Llassar Llaesgyfnewid and his wife emerge from in "Branwen." In this instance the cauldron belongs to Ceridwen, one of the titanic aspects of the Goddess. The mythology of Ceridwen is scant, but it can be related directly to that of the mountain mothers of Scottish and Irish tradition,[71] the *cailleachs*, who drop stones from their aprons to form mountain ranges and who play an important role in the annual chase of the god of youth by the old hag.

(2) Creirwy is named in Triad 78 as one of the fairest maidens of Britain. She stands in the place of Kore to Ceridwen's Demeter. Morfran, the ugly son, we have already encountered in "Culhwch and Olwen," where he appears as one who was not slain at Camlann because all who saw him believed him to be a devil, not a man. But though the cauldron is prepared for his benefit, it is Gwion who becomes a seer-poet and, incidentally, Ceridwen's child.

(3) The text invests Ceridwen with the mantle of a medieval alchemist consulting her planetary hours and culling herbs under the phases of the moon. She is said to prepare the brew according to the books of the Fferyllt, which has often been translated as the "faeries," but in Welsh it has the connotation of "chemist," "alchemist," or "magician,"

especially referring to Virgil who, in medieval mythology, became associated less with his poetic achievements and more with the magical arts. It is interesting to compare this cauldron with the one which nine muses cool with their breath in the "Preiddeu Annwfn" (see chapter 6). Both are cauldrons of Underworld deities, both are vessels of poetic or prophetic inspiration. The vessel is kept boiling for a year and a day—the same duration in which the spear that slays Llew is forged. There is a reference to a similarly prepared cauldron in "The Second Battle of Mag Tuired,"[148] but more generally in Celtic myth, the food which bestows knowledge is the salmon. As we will see, this motif is not absent from "Taliesin."

(4) Gwion the Small and Blind Morda tend the cauldron: extreme youth and extreme age. Ceridwen beats Morda so hard when the cauldron's contents are lost that he loses an eye—a feature of Balor's story as well: He loses the sight of one eye in spying on a similar cauldron. Instead of receiving wisdom, however, Balor is poisoned by the steam from the vessel.[28]

Gwion is fated to become Taliesin, the seer-poet. Throughout this story it is necessary to look below the levels of the text because more than the surface meaning is present. As with many another Wondrous Youth, Taliesin has his childhood name. The sense of creative continuity motivating his verse makes it impossible to see the poet and Gwion as two different people; they share the same identity.

(5) The cooling of the burned finger is a universal folk motif, but one central to all Celtic traditions. In the next section we will discuss the thumb of knowledge in relation to other texts.

(6) Gwyddno Garanhir, Elphin's father, appears in many Welsh texts and is often associated with the kingdom of Rheged—the court of which gave the historical Taliesin his patronage. Gwyddno is also associated with the inundation of land in Cardigan Bay; folk tradition

speaks of a lost cantref, or region, and makes him the ruler over it. He also seems to have had trouble with Gwynn ap Nudd, according to an early dialogue poem.[5] Both of these events may be hinted at in the episode in which his horses are poisoned and his lands are lost or made barren by an Underworld deity. Most important, we must note that Gwyddno appears in the list of the Thirteen Treasures of Britain (see chapter 3, page 56) as the possessor of a miraculous hamper into which food for one could be placed, and from which food for a hundred could be taken.[5]

(7) The transformations which Gwion and Ceridwen undergo are part of an initiatory sequence. Other shape-changes are hinted at in the songs Taliesin sings at Maelgwn's court. These changes correspond to certain levels of poetic training during which the initiate is given deeper and deeper insights into the nature of creation. And although on one level Ceridwen appears as his aggressor, she is in fact his initiator, forcing him to deeper levels of understanding until he reaches the primal essence of life itself, here symbolized by a grain of wheat (see the section The Hag and the Poet, below, and chapter 8).

(8) This mysterious rebirth of the initiate as a weak and helpless baby is connected to the incubation period during which the mysteries are learned. There must always be a period of withdrawal and assimilation after the receipt of a mystery, which, like a seed, burrows into the depths and must be allowed to germinate undisturbed. Ceridwen does not name her child but puts him into a womb-shaped coracle and leaves him to the mercy of the waves. He is on his own. The Ford text says, "He had been floating in the pouch from the beginning of Arthur's time until about the beginning of Maelgwn's time."[2] This is reckoned at forty years. In many mythologies, children who have a hard destiny are often cast adrift on the sea in a form of boat or basket, like Moses, to find their own luck.

(9) Elphin is known as the unfortunate youth in all stories which include him. His luck seems to be at an even lower ebb when, instead of a run of salmon, he finds a baby poet floating in the weir. But he is destined to better fortune yet. The Ford text says that this annual run of salmon is caught on All Hallows Eve, or Samhain, whereas in Guest's text Elphin comes to the weir on May Eve, or Beltane. But whether the salmon are on their upstream mating run or their downstream return to the Gulf Stream does not matter. Elphin goes expecting salmon and catches the Salmon of Wisdom himself. This is Taliesin's own totem and it is one of the essential identities of all seer-poets. He gains his name in much the same way as Pryderi, Llew, or Goreu: from the first utterance of the person who has responsibility for fostering him.

(10) The many poems occurring in the text of the story appear in different manuscripts. The Guest translation has often interspersed these poems in a random way. In any case, like the obscure "Preiddeu Annwfn," Taliesin's verse is translatable only by analeptic means and by one whose knowledge of early Welsh surpasses any scholar now alive. So much of its inner meaning is lost in translation that it is doubtful whether we will ever fully comprehend the esoteric references and internal puns.[147]

Taliesin's inspired utterances are as far beyond poetry as ordinary poetry is beyond prose. Because he shares the nature of the Blessed Ones, he is able, while still a baby, to reveal his transformations:

> *In the court of Ceridwen I have done penance . . .*
> *I have fled as a chain,*
> *I have fled as a roe into an entangled thicket;*
> *I have fled as a fierce bull, bitterly fighting,*
> *I have fled as a bristling boar seen in a ravine,*
> *I have fled as a white grain of pure wheat,*
> *On the skirt of a hempen sheet entangled,*
> *That seemed of the size of a mare's foal,*
> *That is filling like a ship on the waters. . . .*[4]

These references are clearly not to be understood as rational state-
ments; indeed, in the last three lines, we may discern a faint reference
to the Mabon-like theft of Pryderi from his mother.

(11) King Maelgwn was a historical figure; according to the *Annales
Cambriae*, he died of the yellow plague in 547 C.E.[94] In one of his satires,
Taliesin proclaims:

> *And I will tell your king what will befall him,*
> *A most strange creature will come from the sea-*
> *marsh of Rhianedd*
> *As a punishment of iniquity on Maelgwn*
> *Gwynedd;*
> *His hair, his teeth, and his eyes being as gold. . . .*[4]

Elphin's boast is curiously like that of Crunnchu mac Agnoman in
"The Debility of the Ulstermen" (see chapter 2). It certainly draws
down disaster on his head, for Elphin is imprisoned and chained (with
silver chains because of his nobility) by Maelgwn, who has a kingly reputation to uphold.

(12) The chastity test is exactly that which Shakespeare uses in his
strangely haunting retelling of one of our national stories, *Cymbeline*.
In this play, Iachimo secretes himself in Imogen's chamber and steals a
bracelet. The Elphin of this story is Posthumus; only here Imogen, his
wife, is his liberator, taking the name Fidele and, dressed as a boy, res-
cuing her husband and brothers from imprisonment and death. This
theme is followed closely in Beethoven's working of the female liberator, Fidelio, who releases all the captives imprisoned with her husband.
This is a very potent motif when compared with the release of Mabon.
In *Cymbeline*, the eponymous king is in the place of Tegid, while his
queen stands in for Ceridwen. Her loathsome son, Cloten, is analogous
to Afagddu. In "Taliesin," Elphin vindicates his wife by a piece of neat

detective work. But as Elphin once freed Taliesin from the leather bag, now it is up to Taliesin to release him.

(13) The thirteen-year-old seer-poet now pits his considerable wits against Maelgwn's twenty-four poets, starting with the use of some sympathetic magic. Idiot-like, he plays on his lips with his finger and Maelgwn's poets make the same unpoetic utterances before their kingly patron! This passage is part of the manifestation of Mabon (see chapter 9), where the Wondrous Youth confronts his elders and betters and confounds their combined wits. This pattern is observable in the lives of Christ and of Merlin who, while still youths, confound the elders in the Temple and the magicians of Vortigern, respectively.

(14) The parallels with Merlin are extremely close, as Taliesin himself attests in his reply to Maelgwn's ill-placed inquiry about his antecedents:

> *Primary chief bard am I to Elphin,*
> *And my original country in the region of the*
>   *summer stars;*
> *Idno and Heinin called me Merlin,*
> *At length every king will call me Taliesin.*[4]

This statement is curiously like that of Christ to his disciples: "Who do people say is the Son of Man?" The disciples respond, "Some say he is John the Baptist, some Elijah, and others Jeremiah or one of the prophets." (Matt. 16:14). It is also suspiciously similar to the words uttered by Wisdom in Proverbs and the other wisdom texts of the Bible and Apocrypha. We need not suspect, however, the hand of a zealous clerical copyist, necessarily. Taliesin's boasts ("I have been . . . ") are a prophetic sequence relating to his initiation and participation in the whole of creation. He has been to no less than the highest heavens as well as through the gates of Annwfn. He has companioned Christ, the prophets, and Mary Magdalene, and has been in the court of Don, the prison of Arianrhod, and on the White Hill with the head of Bran. Maelgwn should have known better than to ask!

(15) The freeing of Elphin is accomplished. This episode bears comparison again with the freeing of Gweir from Annwfn in the "Preiddeu Annwfn" (see chapter 6), for there, "a heavy blue chain bound the youth," whereas Elphin is "released from the golden fetter." The magical nature of Celtic poetry lives uniquely in "Taliesin," where the poet is shaman, one whose words become powerfully manifest. The puny bards of Maelgwn's court can offer only barren words which have no effect, whereas Taliesin is able to raise even the elements to do his bidding.

(16) In the succeeding race this prophetic insight is upheld. Taliesin instructs Elphin's jockey to overtake the other horses by striking them with twenty-four blackened holly staves. Without resorting to the semantic word games of Robert Graves's *White Goddess*, might these staves be engraved *oghams*—wooden billets inscribed with the alphabet?[41] Taliesin wins by the power of speech. He overcomes twenty-four poets with his eloquence. He then overcomes twenty-four horses.

Holly is the wood sacred to the Green Man of Knowledge, a character appearing in Celtic folk story who is analogous both to the Green Knight of the Gawain cycle and to the seer-poet of earlier Celtic story. The cauldron of gold is the guerdon of poets, the poet's fee, but instead of Elphin giving it to Taliesin, Taliesin gives it to his master. Elphin's reward comes belatedly at the hands of his fosterling.

(17) Taliesin's last poem bears comparison with the prophecies of Merlin, which it much resembles.[96, 97] It starts with the creation of humanity: Adam and Eve are outcast and made to break the earth for bread. The lines following relate the mystical levels on which the grain of wheat can be understood, from the stark bread of toil and disobedience to the mysterious transubstantiation of the host on the altar of

the Cross. The poem then relates the descent of esoteric knowledge through to the race of Troy, of which remnant Taliesin sees himself as prophet. The final victory of the Britons over their invaders is hinted at, and the restored sovereignty is implied.

This poem and Merlin's prophecies are apocalyptic and full of mystery, telling of a world before this and of a time which comes after our own.

## The Thumb of Knowledge

In Taliesin we see one of the last great seer-poets, the remnant of a mighty professional class whose utterances were of magical origin, not merely a product of the intellectual faculty. The roots of seer-poet and shaman are very close. Throughout the twilight of the classical period of Irish history (c. 450–900 C.E.) it is possible to see the progressive demise of the seer-poet. Evidences of the Irish texts—Ireland maintained the seer-poet longer than Britain—give us the laws and customs of poets in great detail. The evidences of Welsh manuscript sources are far more slender. The once-great class of poets who were able to diagnose and divine, foretell destiny and shapeshift, were gradually stripped of their powers until the greatest thing they could accomplish was the blighting of a reluctant patron with a satire. Fear of the satire, which could raise blotches on the victim's face or drive him insane, was the cause of the famous assembly at Drumkett in Ireland in 574 C.E., at which kings and nobles determined to have the whole order of poets suppressed. St. Columba represented the poets and saved the day, but their power was considerably lessened.

Taliesin seems to leap from the depths of the ancestral past, for not only can he satirize his opponents, but he also has "birds' knowledge"— the allusive and often instinctual understanding that is common to seers. He shows such complete accord with the whole of creation that he can identify with it with poetic omniscience. The three drops which fall upon his finger are echoed in a parallel Irish tradition recounted in "The Boyhood Deeds of Fionn."[142] Fionn Mac Cumhail lives in Irish tradition—much as Arthur does in British tradition—as a mighty war leader with his band of champions, who is troubled with an unfaithful wife. However, the boyhood of Fionn is particularly relevant to the story of Taliesin.

Fionn is secretly raised by two women warriors and a druidess. His boyhood name is Demne. He has to be hidden because the sons of Morna, his hereditary enemies and the slayers of his father, will kill him; thus he is kept ignorant of his ancestors. During a hurling match he overcomes many noble youths, and the chief of that place calls him a shapely, fair youth, whence his name Fionn (meaning "fair"). His identity is revealed and Fionn catches up with the enemy who has killed his father and taken his treasure bag. He then goes to the sage Finneces to be taught poetry. The poet watches the salmon of Fec's Pool on the Boyne for seven years because it has been prophesied that Finneces would eat of it and know everything. The salmon is found and Fionn is set to cook it, but he burns his thumb and, warned to eat none of the fish, he puts the thumb under his tongue to cool it. Finneces then willingly gives Fionn the whole salmon to eat because he realizes with druidic insight that the young man is indeed the one destined to its knowledge. Fionn thereby learns the three things which make a poet: the techniques of *teinm laegda, imbas forosna,* and *dichetul dichennaib.*[142] The story further tells how Fionn captures a faery woman *(bean sidi)* who gives him "a vessel full of gold, of glorious silver," which he distributes among his *fian* (war band).[93]

The Salmon of Wisdom which swims in the Fountain of Nine Hazels is, of course, the source of all wisdom in Irish tradition. It is one of the oldest beasts, having the richest store of wisdom, and is often the prime totem of the seer-poet who seeks its wisdom. The person who watches for it and who often catches it is rarely the one who acquires its knowledge. Just as Ceridwen and Finneces—both seers of considerable power—prepare the brew or salmon only to have it tasted by an apprentice, so too Elphin loses his valuable run of salmon. The cauldron of Ceridwen is analogous to the Fountain of Nine Hazels, a drink of which gives memory of the past and knowledge of the future. It is also clear from the subtext of our story that Taliesin is the Salmon of Wisdom. He says of himself, "It is not known whether my body is flesh or fish."

We have little direct knowledge of the poet's training, but this is hinted at in Fionn's story. Much ink has been spilled over the true meanings of the three techniques he acquires.[80, 93] The ancient laws of Ireland state that all three are necessary for an *ollamh* poet (a doctor of poetry); until the fourteenth century they remained the criteria by which a true *filidh*, or seer-poet, could be discerned. They may be summarized as follows:

1. *Teinm laegda.* Literally, "the heating up of the poem." Fionn, in order to have access to his gift, has to chew upon his thumb, but the method actually involved a series of trancelike incantations by which uncertain matters were orally brought to light, thereby allowing access to levels of intuitive or inherent wisdom.

2. *Imbas forosna.* Literally, "the inspiration of the great tradition." *Cormac's Glossary* tells us that this was achieved by chewing on the flesh of an animal and by certain ritual invocations, after which the poet would send himself into an incubation of meditative sleep or on a shamanic spirit journey. This method gave access to the wisdom of ancestors and totems.

3. *Dichetul dichennaib.* Literally, "the augury from the ends of one's fingers." The poet could spontaneously compose a poem upon meeting an unknown person, upon touching a person with his staff, or after picking up an object of unknown provenance and telling its history through a process akin to psychometry. This method gave access to analeptic wisdom—that which cannot be known by rational means.

All these techniques, except the last, were outlawed in Ireland after the time of St. Patrick because they could not be performed without offerings to spirits.

I have detailed these techniques in order to show the parallels to them within Taliesin's own poetic methods. It is known that throughout the Gaelic countries until the eighteenth and nineteenth centuries, poets still followed a curious incubation method akin to imbas forosna. In order to compose a poem, a poet would lie in a darkened room with a mantle over his head. The act of composing outdoors was frequently satirized as a newfangled art by eighteenth-century Irish poets.[142] This gives us, perhaps, some clues as to Taliesin's period of incubation, for "three periods in the prison of Arianrhod" are on one level the three-times-three months spent in the womb of Ceridwen. Arianrhod and Ceridwen are both referenced by Taliesin as muselike inspiratices. The variant texts say also that his coracle floated for forty years—long enough, perhaps, to learn the wisdom of the totems and that of the masters of wisdom? Prior to his great "I have been" boast, he plays *blerwm, blerwm* on his lips with the ends of his fingers, as in teinm laegda; here he reveals his true inherent identity. And by means of dichetul dichennaib, analeptic wisdom, he tells of future events as well as relating the nature of creation.

By such techniques the seer-poet can answer impossible questions and see into the heart of things relating their history and destiny. He is enabled to change shape and to travel between the worlds, for their thresholds are open to him. This door-opening ability is demonstrated in a variant to the Salmon of Wisdom story: We are told how Fionn Mac Cumail traps his finger in a faery mound, which becomes his source of wisdom. Forever afterwards he chews upon this finger to stimulate knowledge and learn the necessary resonances between this world and that. The connection between the sense of taste and the gaining of primordial wisdom can be traced from the Garden of Eden onwards: A forbidden knowledge is accessed through innocence, resulting in a theft of knowledge that can be shared with the world, which is then changed or transformed. The finger upon the lip is the universal emblem of the initiate who has gained wisdom that cannot yet be shared with others because it is not accessible to normal reason. We see such a figure in the Egyptian deity Harpocrates, the child with his finger upon his mouth, enjoining silence.

Fionn is closely associated with ogham—the inscribed alphabet of Irish poets. Tree ogham, as popularized in Graves's *The White Goddess*, is only one form of many.[41, 137] *The Scholar's Primer* gives many alternative ogham alphabets, such as bird ogham, king ogham, and sow ogham. Among the many methods of inscribing these are: Fionn's window—a circular ogham formation, Fionn's ladder, and the tooth ogham of Fionn, in which each character is shaped like a tooth.[22] Yet while these word games are interesting, they are merely the tools of the poet. It is poetic omniscience which alone discerns the truth, and this cannot be learned by intellectual means. It is received by those who have been through the mill of the Goddess and who have drunk the few precious drops from her wisdom-giving cauldron.

## The Hag and the Poet

The pursuit of the youthful god by the hag is a perennial theme in Celtic tradition. The initiate recognizes the hag or *cailleach*, typified by Ceridwen, as the mother of creation whose role is that of an initiator of the candidate, the Son of Wisdom, here typified by Gwion. He is pursued throughout all his transformations just as a tutor pushes a student through harder and more varied forms of learning until a synthesis of knowledge is acquired. Only then does the hag rest and send the newborn seer-poet into the world.

Ceridwen's cauldron is both the fountain of wisdom and the womb of life. It also has its place in the native scheme of alchemy as a vessel of transformation where the catabolic or deconstructive action of the Goddess breaks down all that she encounters into its essential constituents. The pursuit of Gwion through many shapes is not a retributive action but an initiatory sequence, which we can call the turning of the totems. Each one of the beasts which Gwion becomes represents a deeper level of experience, as we shall see in the next chapter. Many further shape-changings and related experiences are detailed in Taliesin's own poetry.

The Gospel of John tells us that "unless a grain of wheat falls on the ground and dies, it remains only a single grain; but if it dies, it yields a rich harvest (John 12:24). This mystery saying is common to many cultures. In his final transformation, Gwion becomes such a grain of wheat and is fermented with many other elements to become the drink of initiates. In his last poem, Taliesin speaks lyrically of Christ's formation from such a brew:

> *From wheat of true privilege,*
> *From red wine generous and privileged*
> *Is made the finely molded body*
> *Of Christ son of Alpha.*
>
> *From the wafer is the flesh,*
> *From the wine is the flow of blood*
> *And the words of the Trinity*
> *Consecrated him.*[2]

These verses are not a later Christian interpolation, but true understandings of the initiatory state of the seer-poet. Noninitiates die only once at their physical death. Initiates die twice: once to the flesh and once to the world, being reborn as the Blessed Ones. Taliesin is such a being and subtly refers to his own state within this poem. As Christ is the living bread who must be consumed for initiates of his cult to be reborn to the heavenly state, so, for the British tradition, Taliesin is the living fish, an exemplar of the Salmon of Wisdom, who must also be consumed by the next seer-poet at his initiation. Always one wisdom-bearer must give way to the next.

We have seen how the succession of the Pendragons can be applied to the kingship. A similar pattern is also discernible among the poet-kind. This is the Poet's Wheel which the candidate seer-poet undergoes. There are such close resonances between the two cycles that it is perhaps unnecessary to distinguish but roughly between them. The kingly cycle

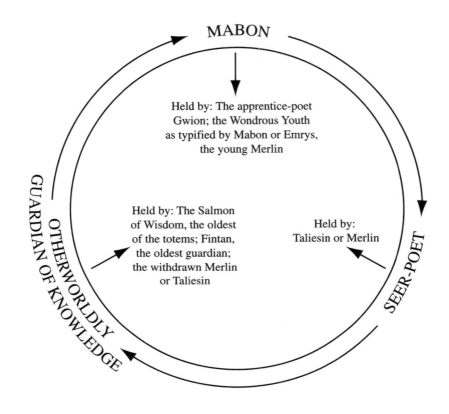

Figure 7. The Poet's Wheel

affects the king's champion, the king, and the inner guardian of the hallows. Figure 7, above, depicts the pattern of poets, or Poet's Wheel.

Corresponding with the Poet's Wheel is a set of roles which are filled by the representatives of the initiatory Goddess. Figure 8 (page 153) depicts these as they appear in "Taliesin."

Both the succession of the Pendragons and the Poet's Wheel start with a Mabon position because Mabon holds the dual roles of hunter and harper. The female pattern works in a similar way within the succession of the Pendragons, as we will explore further in chapter 9. Ceridwen is the transforming hag, changing to her maiden aspect in the shape of her daughter, Creirwy, the most beautiful maiden.

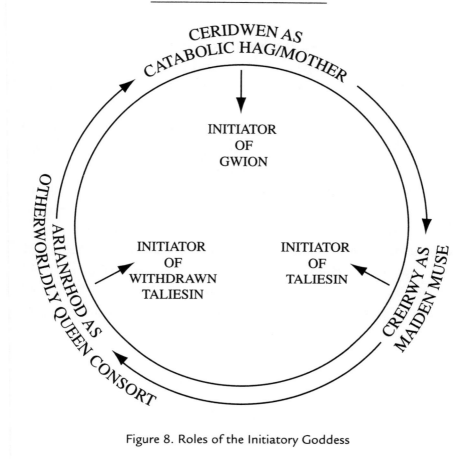

Figure 8. Roles of the Initiatory Goddess

Finally she manifests as Arianrhod, the queen of the otherworldly Caer Sidi, itself a faery kingdom where the riches of knowledge are guarded by her wisdom-bearer and consort, Taliesin, the Salmon of Wisdom who swims among the summer stars. In all traditions there is a withdrawn guardian who holds the wisdom until another comes to take his place.

It will be seen from the mythic subtext of this story that Ceridwen is not a cruel mother; she merely sends her son "to learn his gramarie" in another world, giving him the opportunity of initiation and receiving him as her consort when he at last dies to the world and is born once again in the Otherworld.

The final mystery story of Gwion Bach may be reconstituted and summarized as follows: Set to stir the cauldron of inspiration, Gwion licks the three drops from his oracular finger. He undergoes the initiation of the turning of the totems until he finally becomes the Salmon of Wisdom, the totem of all knowledge. He swims into the Cauldron of Rebirth, into the fountain of knowledge, which is the womb of Ceridwen, the creator and re-creator of worlds. He flows forth on the birth waters into the sea, still in his caul of incubation, and so into the realms of manifestation, whence he is taken by Elphin, his patron. He comes to set free prisoners from ignorance, pride, and despair. He comes to succor the unfortunate and to chastise the unworthy. He knows all wisdom. He was, from the beginning of the world, the child of Modron the Goddess. He will be until the end of time the liberator of the lost. No more a Wondrous Youth or a seer-poet, he swims in the fountain of knowledge, waiting for a worthy successor to attain his store of knowledge.

# 8
# The Totem Beasts of Britain

*Through my voice the Son of the Morning
speaks. Cronos is his name . . . and my
animals and my birds and my fishes hear
his voice and rejoice.*

J. C. POWYS, *PORIUS*

*He became a silvan man just as though
devoted to the woods. For a whole summer
after this, hidden like a wild animal, he
remained buried in the woods, found by
no one and forgetful of himself and of
his kindred.*

GEOFFREY OF MONMOUTH, *VITA MERLINI*

## Mabon and the Oldest Animals

Armed with the evidence of Taliesin's transformations, we can begin to view Mabon's story in some detail, particularly in relation to the totems. What is a totem beast? It is an animal emblematic of a tribe or person which has its reality in and draws its being and power from the Otherworld. A tribe might acquire a totem by virtue of a famous ancestor's exploits or through some inherent affinity with a beast. Such a totem would appear as a standard in battle and play an important role in the tribal mysteries. In later ages, when heraldry took over the old formulas of the tribal genealogist, the animal found its way on to the arms and livery of a family; different families were therefore distinguishable in battle and assembly by their totemic sign. Heraldic armorials portray mythical and realistic beasts along with a motto or device embodying the virtue of that animal, such as "touch not the cat but a glaive," of the Scottish Clan Chattan, whose emblem is a wild cat.

Within the *Mabinogion,* totems have a deeper mystery significance. The totem beast is an otherworldly helper whose power resonates with the ancestral sources of wisdom. The adoption of such a totem is a powerful link with the Otherworld, conveying not only the virtues and qualities of that beast to the person under its aegis, but also contact with ancestral levels. The totem beast is not the same as an animal of the same species which can be hunted or eaten for food; it is a beast of otherworldly reality. The appearance of talking beasts in folk story denotes a shift of emphasis to a deeper level of awareness; such beasts are not anthropomorphic animals, but archetypal forms. They may mask enchanted human beings, but more often they are the ancestral resonances or even aliases for the characters within that story.

The freeing of Mabon, told in "Culhwch and Olwen," is brought about by a chain of such totems. Mabon's release may be summarized as follows. Yspaddaden tells Culhwch, "There is no huntsman who can hunt with that dog [Drudwyn, the whelp of Greid ap Eri], but Mabon, son of Modron. He was taken from his mother when three nights old, and it is not known where he is now, nor whether he is living or dead."

Four men are appointed to search for Mabon: Eidoel ap Aer, Mabon's kinsman, who was first to be released from his own imprisonment in the Castle of Glini; Gwrhyr Gwastas Ieithoedd, who knew the language of birds and beasts; Cai; and Bedwyr. They seek first the blackbird of Cilgwri (Gwri's retreat): "Tell me if thou knowest aught of Mabon, the son of Modron, who was taken when three nights old from between his mother and the wall"—this is the ritual request posed to all the beasts by Gwrhyr. The blackbird replies that she has been in that place since a smith's anvil was there, and this she has worn away by the pecking of her beak, but she has never heard of Mabon. She directs them to one of an older race of beasts, to the stag of Rhedynfr (fernbrake hill). He has roamed the plain since a single oak sapling first grew to be an oak of a hundred branches. Now nothing remains but the withered stump, and he has never heard of Mabon. But he directs them to the owl of Cawlwyd (the wood of Caw the Gray).

The owl has flown the wood since a wooded glen had been uprooted twice and grown a third forest, yet has never heard of Mabon. She directs the seekers to the eagle of Gwernabwy (alder swamp), the most widely traveled and eldest bird in the world. The eagle has pecked the stars from a high rock every night, but now the rock is a span high. In seeking food he attacked a salmon, which then drew him to the deep. After a long contention they made peace, but he has never heard of Mabon. He directs the seekers to the salmon of Llyn Llyw (lake of the leader.) The salmon has heard cries coming from the walls of the castle at Gloucester, and takes Cai and Gwrhyr on his shoulders. Gwrhyr asks, "Who is it who laments in this house of stone?' He is answered: "It is Mabon, son of Modron, who is imprisoned; and no imprisonment was ever so grievous as mine, neither that of Lludd Llaw Ereint, nor that of Greid ap Eri." (See chapter 9.)

Mabon cannot be released with the payment of ransom, but only by fighting. Accordingly, the company returns to fetch Arthur and his warriors, who attack the castle. Cai, while carried on the salmon's back, breaks through the dungeon walls, and the salmon carries Cai and

Mabon out again. Mabon subsequently leads the hunt for Twrch Trwyth and obtains the razor from between the boar's ears.

Throughout the story, no one, neither man nor beast, can tell where Mabon is, or whether he is indeed still alive. The reason for this is clear from the context of the story: No one is old enough to remember. It follows that Mabon is the eldest, the firstborn of his mother, Modron, but because he was stolen as a newborn child, he is also the youngest. Only the salmon is able to locate Mabon, although the chain of totems inexorably leads the seekers to him. As we have seen, the Salmon of Wisdom is one of the totemic identities of the inner guardian on the Poet's Wheel.

The loss of Mabon dates from such an early time that even the most ancient memory is out of its reckoning. Here we may perceive the Celtic and native pre-Celtic legend of paradise—not a myth concerned with lust for power, but one where knowledge is immortality, based on reverence for memory. In this paradise, beasts have understanding, memory, and knowledge; and the sweet singer of dawn—Mabon, son of Light, by whatever name he is known in every age—sings in the garden very early. Before humankind, there were animals; before animals, there were trees and rocks. The reckoning of time's continuity is by means of generations of successive men, animals, and elements.

We have already seen that the totems represent successively deeper levels of understanding in the story of Taliesin. This can be seen more clearly if we look at some of the methods of reckoning time. One of the earliest of these is recorded in Plutarch's *Moralia*:

> *Nine generations long is the life of the crow and*
>    *his cawing,*
> *Nine generations of vigorous men. Lives of four*
>    *crows together*
> *Equal the life of a stag, and three stags the old*
>    *age of a raven.*
> *Nine of the lives of the raven the life of the*
>    *Phoenix doth equal:*

*Ten of the Phoenix we Nymphs, fair daughters of*
*Zeus of the aegis.*[84]

Within native tradition, a similar pattern is found:

*Three ages of a horse, the age of a man.*
*Three ages of man, the age of a deer.*
*Three ages of a deer, the age of an eagle.*
*Three ages of an eagle, the age of an oak tree.*[36]

This Scottish Gaelic saying takes us back at least 2,800 years. But closest to the totems of the Mabon sequence is this reckoning from the Irish *Book of Lismore:*

*Three life-times of the Stag for the Blackbird;*
*three life-times of the Blackbird for the Eagle;*
*three life-times of the Eagle for the Salmon;*
*three life-times of the Salmon for the Yew.*[50]

Interestingly, in folk tradition Christ is crucified on the yew tree, thus aligning himself with the guardian who has passed beyond the totems, as both Mabon and Taliesin do.

Triad 92 relates that the three elders of the world are the owl of Cwm Cowlwyd, the eagle of Gwernabwy, and the blackbird of Celli Gardarn (strong wood). This omits both the stag and the salmon of Mabon's liberation, but it is clear to see that the totem beasts have a unique place in ancestral memory.

What is the significance of these ages of time? They predate numeracy on one level; on another, they connect us with the roots of memory. The reckoning of successive ages had little to do with linear time as we understand it. If a person was not immortalized in story or song, then he or she was forgotten after three generations, which must have been the extent of human memory—hence, the importance for learning genealogies. Poets boasted that their praise songs kept memory alive, for "no man can be famous without an *ollamh* (poet)."[54]

Beyond human memory lay ages uncounted. The longest-living animals drew their memory from their own kind, and within them, genetically encoded, were even older species. The remembrance of times past could be garnered from some part of creation. The earth remembers, even if we do not.

The proto-story which relates the great memory of the oldest animals is found in an Irish folk story, "The Hawk of Achill," numerous variants of which are found across the Celtic world: The coldest night in the history of the world was one Beltane Eve. Hundreds of years later there came another severe night when the hawk of Achill took shelter in an eagle's nest, killing the fledging within it. The mother eagle returned, and thinking that the hawk was her chick, she fed it. She complained about the night's coldness. The hawk replied that he remembered a yet colder night. "How is that possible, for you were only hatched from the egg a month ago?" The hawk then bade her go to the blackbird of the forge for confirmation. The blackbird (ghobha-dhu, also Irish for "blacksmith") had rubbed an iron bar nearly in two, but couldn't remember a colder night. The eagle flew on to the bull or stag who had lived four thousand years and whose horns/antlers had gone to make a fence for a one-acre field. He sent the eagle to the blind salmon of Assaroe, who remembered a colder night. He had been frozen into the ice of the pool and the hawk of Achill had pecked out his eye. The salmon told the eagle, "By which reckoning that fledgling of yours is none other than the hawk of Achill itself." The eagle flew back to her nest, but the hawk was gone.[33]

In another variant it is said that this salmon was none other than Fintan, the great ancestor who had lived through all the ages of Ireland. Yet another tells that the hawk and salmon are younger still than the cailleach Beare, to whom they award the branch of victory because she is as old "as the old grandmother long ago who ate the apples."[50] Whatever the variant, each story pushes back memory to the beginning of time, when time was not.

These ancient stories form part of the native mystery tradition, giving us keys to deeper levels of the Otherworld and its knowledge. Taliesin's own transformations bring him through the turning of the totems, through successive ages where wisdom is stored until he emerges, apprised of ultimate knowledge. As a seer-poet he stands in unique relation to the source of life. Mabon's case is slightly different in that he stands at the end of a chain of totems by whose memory he is found and liberated. He is, in fact, in the position of the inner guardian, unable to leave the Otherworld and assume his position of Wondrous Youth and champion to the Pendragons.

His association with the animals is a very subtle one: He is guarded by them, and yet he is also their guardian and brother. This will be clearer in the next chapter where the Mabon theme is shown to parallel that of other *Mabinogion* heroes whose birth and death days are shared with totem beasts.

Yet the initiate who has passed through the totems is enabled to become initiator and instructor in his turn, for he or she has the power of the totems and the knowledge of every age. This power is granted only to one who is willing to acknowledge the totems, as we can witness in folk stories worldwide in which, for instance, the two elder brothers or sisters who will not aid animals in distress are rejected by the animals in their hour of need. Only the youngest sibling is successful on his quest because he has given his last crust or sip of water to an animal in need. There is nothing anthropomorphic or Disney-like in this revelation. It is a fundamental law of the Otherworld that when a mortal helps a totem beast, that totem is obligated in turn to aid the mortal. To find and associate with one's ancestral totem is therefore of great importance[71]—it is one step on a personal ladder of successive totems which lead to the initiator, the great ancestor, either male or female, who acts as the guardian of the totems.

The role of ancestors both in traditional lore and in modern life has been discussed at length by R. J. Stewart,[98] and for those who attempt any practical work with them, his seminal texts should be consulted. Each living person has many thousands of ancestors, among whom may be persons famous and infamous, as well as those who are forgotten. The great ancestor we speak of here is the inner guardian from whom we learn—the one who lives within the Otherworld but whose teachings are available to us by means of meditative resonance. This guardian will be one who has passed through the turning of the totems and is willing to instruct others. It is possible to find your own access guardian by means of active meditation or shamanic journey, or through the agency of a traditional teacher.[145] One such teacher is Merlin, as we can see from T. H. White's novel *The Once and Future King,* which draws on this teaching. Here, Merlin turns the youthful Arthur into many different kinds of animal in order to help him understand the nature of the kingdom he is to govern and gain a deeper knowledge than the mere acquaintance of mankind can give him.[128] Arthur learns the nature of the beasts and the foolishness of man-made rules and boundaries, and finds the resources of courage, caution, and love which he will need to survive. The only defense he does not learn is how to cope with betrayal by his own kind. Nevertheless, for the young Arthur this is a real initiation into the totems conducted at the hands of Merlin, a master behind whom stands an array of mighty ancestral powers who are themselves guardians of the totems.

## Guardian of the Beasts

Within the *Mabinogion* we are given a clear picture of this guardian in both "Culhwch and Olwen" and in the later romance "The Lady of the Fountain." We have already met Custennin, the monstrous herdsman who sits outside Yspaddaden's fort and warns all comers of imminent danger. But his role is not very clearly defined within the context of the story; we need to look at the romance to understand just what he represents.

In "The Lady of the Fountain," Owain and Cynan each make a journey to the Otherworld in search of adventures beyond the ordinary. On their journey, each man is directed to a crossroads within a wood:

Thou wilt see a black man of great stature on the top of the mound. He is not smaller in size than two of the men of this world. He has but one foot; and one eye in the middle of his forehead. And he has a club of iron . . . he is the woodward [guardian] of that wood.[4]

Each man in turn finds this Wild Herdsman and is dumbfounded at his stature and strength. The Herdsman will speak only in answer to questions, and so Cynan inquires what power he has over the thousands of animals grazing near him. He replies:

"I will show thee, little man." And he took his club in his hand, and with it he struck a stag a great blow so that he brayed vehemently, and at his braying the animals came together, as numerous as the stars in the sky. . . . There were serpents, and dragons, and divers sorts of animals. And he looked at them, and bade them go and feed; and they bowed their heads, and they did homage as vassals to their lord. Then the black man said to me, "Seest thou now, little man, what power I hold over these animals?"[4]

He is the guardian of the totems, a powerful figure who instructs adventurers which paths to follow, urging them on to more daring feats and dangerous enterprises. Because he is rough and primitive in appearance, he is a figure many might pass with a shudder, yet he holds many important keys to initiation within the Otherworld.

The Wild Herdsman is indeed an ancient archetype. He can be seen depicted on the Gundestrup cauldron in Denmark as Cernunnos, the antlered god with the torc of sovereignty in his left hand and a serpent in his right. Nearby sport many animals, including the stag and the boar. He is likewise identifiable as the Irish Dagda, who carries a club and wears a grotesquely short tunic which reveals his genitals, and is also discernible as Custennin, the herdsman of Yspaddaden. Last, Merlin is a representative of this archetype.

While popular imagination has retained Merlin as an aged sorcerer, forgotten is Merlin Emrys, the Wondrous Youth who refutes

Vortigern's wizards; and barely heard of is the poet-seer who runs mad into the lonely forest of Celyddon after a catastrophic battle. The Merlin of Celtic tradition is a man of the woods, a shaman nearer in type to the medieval legend of the wild man, an Adamic guardian of beasts and trees. Merlin's association with the Wild Herdsman can be seen in the *Vita Merlini,* the complexities of which have been untangled by R. J. Stewart.[96] In this presentation, because he is deranged, his former wife is going to remarry. When he hears the news, Merlin "went all about the woods and groves and collected a herd of stags in a single line, and the deer and she-goats likewise, and he himself mounted a stag."[104] Driving the other animals before him, he rides to his former wife and her suitor, whereupon he wrenches the antlers from his mount and flings them at the suitor, killing him.

The role of Wild Herdsman is often associated with temporary madness and displacement from society and is a state which many heroes undergo. Merlin's madness is related to that of Lailokan of Scottish tradition and Suibhne Gelt of Irish story.[103] Even Lancelot in the Arthurian legend undergoes a temporary madness after the shock of sleeping with Elaine, whom he believes to be Guinevere. Custennin's own herdsmanship is onerously placed upon him after Yspaddaden has stripped him of his property; displaced from his former rank, he falls to a low-caste position. We are forcibly reminded of the role of the powerful swineherd assumed by Pryderi and Tristan (see Triad 26 and here, chapters 4 and 6). But what seems to be a phase of madness or temporary servitude is in fact an initiation in which the candidate is forced to face the wilderness and become responsible for himself by acknowledging his relationship and kinship with the totems. This removal from the world of men is a sabbatical for the purpose of intense tuition in otherworldly ways. Only such a sequestration is able to heal trauma inflicted by the world. It is seldom a gentle healing, but is wholesome and invigorating.

The role of Wild Herdsman is held only by one who has passed through the totems and, as a result, has great knowledge, which is why this figure is one of the great ancestors. His role of instructor is more clearly seen in the story "Fintan mac Bochra." This extraordinarily rich tale relates an entire sequence of ages, shows the relationship between the worlds, and hints at the relationship between oldest man and the oldest animals.

Bith, the granddaughter of Noah, flees to Ireland before the Deluge, but she and all her companions are drowned except her son, Fintan. He survives alone in many animal shapes until he finally becomes a salmon. He is known as Goll of Assaroe (the blind one) because the hawk of Achill plucked out his eye one night when he was stuck in the ice during the coldest winter since the beginning of the world. In the times of men, when he is once more in human shape, he is called upon to judge how Ireland should be divided. He begins to relate his own history until someone casts doubt upon his memory. In order to show the length of his life, he tells this story: He had once picked up a yew berry, which he then planted. It grew into a tree big enough to shelter a hundred warriors under its branches. Yew trees live for several thousand years, but when this tree at last grew old, he made vessels and barrels from its wood until at length the iron hoops fell off the aged and rotted wood. Of the remaining wood he made smaller and smaller vessels until there was nothing left of the original tree.

Over the great abyss of time, Fintan's memory stretches to this present point of arbitration. He is asked how he has acquired his great wisdom and memory and tells how he had once been present at a great assembly at which an otherworldly being appeared:

[H]e was high as wood . . . the sky and the sun visible between his legs . . . a shining crystal veil about him, sandals upon his feet . . . golden-yellow hair . . . falling to the level of his thighs. . . . Stone tablets in his left hand, a branch with three fruits in his right hand . . . nuts, apples and acorns.[142]

This being's name was Trefuilngid Tre-eochair (triple support of the three keys), and his role was to cause the rising and setting of the sun. Because the sun had not risen that day over the Paradise of Adam (the East), he had traveled as far West as was possible to find out what kept it from rising. It had been revealed to him that on that day a man had been tortured and crucified. Tre-eochair wished to know about the antecedents and ancestors of the assembly and demanded that chroniclers be brought. And those assembled answered, "We have no old *seanachies* . . . to whom we could entrust the chronicles till thou didst come to us." Tre-eochair undertook to instruct them, "for I am a learned witness who explains to all everything unknown." Fintan was entrusted with remembering and was given some berries from Tre-eochair's branch. From these, the greatest trees of Ireland were sprung, including the yew tree.

When this answer satisfies his questioners, Fintan is allowed to relate all the stories of Ireland to the people of his race until the trees themselves decay. He ends his life with the affirmation:

> *I am Fintan, I have lived long,*
> *I am an ancient seanachie of the noble hosts.*
> *Neither wisdom nor brilliant deeds repressed me*
> *until age came upon me and decay.*[142]

It was asserted that his mortal body was taken to await the resurrection of the world with Elijah and Enoch in the secret paradise.

Here is a complete cycle of one of the oldest ancestors whose wisdom comes from his own passing through the totems, and from an otherworldly instructor who gives him a branch of the great tree of tradition, the axial tree, which interpenetrates both the ancestral wisdom and that of the stars. After instructing others in his wisdom, Fintan is withdrawn to the "secret paradise" of the Otherworld. He does not die or suffer further translation.

Logically, Fintan's prime totem is the salmon, for he is the receptacle of memory and knowledge. He has undergone the transformations and, like Odin, he loses an eye in his search for wisdom. He joins the Wild Herdsman in his guardianship of deep native memory.

What, then, is the nature and function of the Wild Herdsman? This is sometimes hard to discern, for whenever this archetype appears in later stories he is classed with devils, demons, and ancestral horrors who have power to scathe good Christian souls. In "Peredur" he appears under many guises, but chiefly as the black man; in "The Lady of the Fountain" he turns up as the Black Oppressor; in later Arthurian story he appears frequently as the ubiquitous Black Knight at the ford. But although he has black skin and an uncouth appearance, his aid is wholesome and real at the deepest levels. He is one of the original beings who hold all beasts in their stewardship. He is the guardian of the totems and the repository of memory.

We have already remarked on his role as obstructor of the seeker. But "hostility . . . is often a camouflage for really goodwill on the part of supernatural beings."[63] This is not an evil function, but a helpful one. We must view it as we would that of a master-class teacher who elicits all that the apprentice knows in order to push him to greater heights. He throws back criticism which is not intended to be destructive, but which roots out bad habits and mental apathy obstructing the path of progress. He cannot be avoided, only challenged. This is clear from every text in which the archetype appears, for he answers all questions put to him in a clear and unambiguous manner. Those who are afraid to ask come to know nothing.

This ancient druidic teaching model can be observed in many stories and songs. "The False Knight Upon the Road"[26] is a typical challenge song in which a child responds with quick-witted answers to the challenges of the knight. It is the dialogue of master and apprentice. The dialogue between Custennin and the seekers for Olwen is of this nature, and on one level it can be seen that Custennin actually initiates Culhwch into the correct course of action to gain Olwen, as well as enabling Goreu to avenge his brothers and his father's disgrace. In this regard, the Wild Herdsman is also the knight of the riddles,[24] the master enchanter with all the answers whose delight is, at the last, to be bested by his pupil. The meaning is clear: The seeker cannot succeed on his or her quest without a worthy challenger. Because the quest is a serious one requiring professional knowledge and precise technique, the guardian of the beasts is remorseless in his challenges and in his manipulation of the totems which the seeker encounters on his way.

This has led to the Wild Herdsman's reputation as the Black Oppressor, a saturnine guardian with horns whom later cultures have incorporated into their dark pantheons of fear. But his real nature is not uncompassionate. He may be the Wild Herdsman, but he is also a *buachaill,* a herder of flocks, one whose first thought is for his beasts. His nature is to draw out the seeker's ability to be truthful, courageous, and resourceful in the face of challenge, to become one who will respond with the instinctive senses of an animal. After all, he is always looking among his apprentices for his successor, for one who will surpass him.

In the oral Irish tale "Spioras na H-Aoise,"[82] a boy sets out to serve an old man who has caused the disappearance of his sister and brothers. After his term of service is over and the boy has visited the many regions of the Otherworld without shrinking from his duty of herding the old man's vigorous cow, he demands that the old man release his siblings from enchantment. The old man, who is none other than a guardian of great power, replies:

> Under enchantment! What is enchantment? The cunning device of the crafty, the foolish excuse of the timorous. What is enchantment?—the bugbear of fools, a cause of dread to the fainthearted—a thing that was not and that is not and shall not be. Against the dutiful and the upright there is no magic nor device.

The boy is sent home with his sister, but his worthless brothers, who have failed to serve the old man, are made to roam the world as wanderers. The boy asks the old man curiously who he is. "I am the Oldest," he replies. "The blessing of age be on your journeying and on your going."

The Wild Herdsman is, after all, the chieftain of the totems who will not deceive the determined seeker, but who will lead the way with his herdsman's staff.

## The Initiation of the Totems

When totem beasts make their appearance in the *Mabinogion,* they usually signify a shift from everyday to otherworldly reality. If we have been alert to these changes while reading the stories, we will have discovered many such instances.

In native shamanic lore, the path to deep memory is via the oldest animals. In order to learn that lore, to meet those animals, it is necessary to find the personal animal spirit, to enter into the unspoken, pre-verbal understanding of the animal and to bypass human intellect, reasoning, and analysis.

Within the *Mabinogion* we see that every being, mortal or otherworldly, has its transmigratory form, its spirit double or *riocht* or co-*immuimeadh* (co-walker): Rhiannon's otherworldly persona is a mare; her son Gwri turns into hay or into a foal; Bran is alder-strong; Lleu soars as an eagle; Gwion Bach is a salmon before he beaches as Taliesin; only his barber knows that King March has horse's ears; and Merlin's life and prophecy are symbiotically linked with dragons.

The oldest animals exist on the other side of the worlds and have access to the timeless realms. It is only we who are time-bound. When something beyond ordinary knowledge or capability is asked of us, it is shamanically essential to seek out the oldest animals to find the solution. The answer rises from the shamanic soul-flight, from communion with our own guardian animals down the pre-verbal pathways of deep song.

Animal lore is sophisticated yet immediate. Animal spirits and totems are trustworthy and true in both folk story and shamanic literature; they invariably act as messengers, bridges, and helpers in daimonic ways. This sense of true alliance guides us surely to the source of Mabon. The druidic transmigration, or *tuirgen,* of the soul involves the soul passing from one form into another—though not necessarily into a human one. The passage into animal form leads the soul from life to life, form to form. The knowledge that we gain in this way is different from the knowledge that we have through evolutionary means: Each of us reads in his or her body the signs which tell us that human beings are also animals—in the scales of our skin, the horn of our nails, the remains of the animal pelt upon our heads and bodies.

The chain of animal lives leads us back to the roots of life, to the sources of the soul. Animals have prior memory and existence in the Otherworlds—before us they have walked the ways between the worlds and so can be our guides and allies. Both animals and ancestors come to us along the paths of blood and memory; the chain of DNA spiraling in our living frames is a ladder by which they walk to us, and by which we can walk to them.[145]

It is precisely in this way that Mabon is discovered—Mabon, son of Modron, son of Mother, a title old as the hills, nameless and numinous in our memory, the preexistent divine child who comes forth from his mother and is then stolen from her when he is only three nights old. The immensity of wonder clutches our heart: This child predates time. We do not know why he is stolen, nor do we know who has stolen him— we are not told. Mabon is that primal innocence and integrity which is our birthright. He is our joy, wonder, delight, and power; he is our wisdom, surety, passion, imagination—all those qualities which are slowly but certainly leached out of us as we grow up. Mabon is whatever is lost and his track can be discovered only through the oldest animals.

The Wild Herdsman is revealed as the Pen Annwfn, lord of the Underworld in "Pwyll, Prince of Dyfed" and in "Manawyddan, Son of Llyr," when he sends his white stag and white boar to fetch Pwyll and Pryderi into the Otherworld. In the course of the chase neither father nor son realizes that they have entered a different state of being until it is too late to retreat. The way through the tangled forest is difficult without the guidance of the totems. Fortunately, the characters within the *Mabinogion* each have their own totemic resonances whereby they can call upon otherworldly aid in times of stress.

Bran's totem is the raven. Although his story is forgotten by visitors to the White Tower of London, his ravens are still there, emblematic of his guardianship of the land. Branwen sends a starling to warn her brother of her treatment, having imbued the bird with her personality by tending and teaching it. Llew becomes an eagle, while his erstwhile wife is condemned to owlhood for her treachery. Only Gwydion—himself a master of the totems—can coax the eagle from its perch because he is a poet who speaks the language of the birds. Traditionally, to speak the language of the birds was to be possessed of prophecy and inner knowledge. The colloquy or battle of the birds is a strong motif in Celtic lore,[24, 50] and we have already seen how the hawk, crow, raven, or eagle was one of the oldest birds.

The oldest and most oracular beast among the totems is the salmon. It is in this guise that both Taliesin and Fintan appear; it is the beast who knows the beginnings of the world, who conveys wisdom, and who, at length, leads the way to Mabon's prison.

Running through the *Mabinogion*, famed for its ferocity, greed, and cunning, is the boar or pig. Although pork was the staple diet of the Celts, this did not make the totem boar any less mysterious. It came from the Underworld and was the gift of Arawn himself. As Twrch Trwyth, it ravages the countryside and sweeps its devastating path across Wales, Ireland, and Cornwall before vanishing into the sea. It was also a chthonic beast, and when it appeared in the shape of a sow, it was a messenger of the dark Earth Mother herself, the feeder-on-carrion: Llew suffers the attentions of a wild sow until released from his totemic shape by Gwydion.

The totem of the parent is sometimes that of the child as well, as is the case with Pryderi, who is foal to his mare-mother, Rhiannon. The appearance of pigs causes Goleuddydd to give birth to her son, who is then called Culhwch (pigsty). Where we are given such direct evidence of personal totems, it is easier to estimate the effect of the Otherworld upon the characters of the *Mabinogion*, for deeper levels of the story are revealed and we are able to glimpse the potency of the native mysteries of Britain.

What, then, is the connection between the totems and the Wild Herdsman, and in what manner are the totems significant of an initiatory pattern? The otherworldly provenance of the totems is our key. As R. J. Stewart has observed, "the Ancestors of the land are at one"; they form a deep matrix of awareness which the totems embody, so that when they make their appearance in a story, the totems "speak with the unified voice of the Ancestors and the land."[98] Whoever encounters the guardian of the beasts meets one of the mighty ancestral guardians of memory and knowledge. In order to have this knowledge, which is the fruit of memory, the initiate—whether poet, hero, or heroine—must suffer the transformation of the totems in his or her own person.

The Wild Herdsman is only one of many possible initiators and instructors. His female counterpart is the Dark Woman of Knowledge, who appears in many guises—as the Loathly Lady or the hag or cailleach—and is, ultimately, the Sovereignty of the Land herself. We are exceedingly fortunate in our possession of "Taliesin," which clearly illustrates the pattern of female initiator and male initiate:

| Taliesin Becomes | Ceridwen Pursues As |
| --- | --- |
| hare | greyhound |
| fish (salmon) | otter |
| bird | hawk |
| wheat | hen |

Here Ceridwen shows herself as the mistress of beasts, like the black Artemis on Ephesian Diana, whose many-breasted shape is attended by numerous animals (she is goddess of the chase and a wise initiator). Ceridwen gives birth to her pupil, after his many transformations through the totems.

We do not have a surviving parallel story which gives the opposite pattern of male initiator and female initiate within the *Mabinogion* itself, but we can reconstruct this from an extant folk song of venerable tradition. "The Two Magicians" is a version of a widely distributed song in which a blacksmith woos a maiden who refuses to give up her maidenhead without a fight. In this song the pattern is as follows:

| Maiden Becomes | Blacksmith Pursues As |
| --- | --- |
| duck | water-dog |
| hare | greyhound |
| eel | trout |
| mare | saddle |
| plaid sheet | green coverlet |

The final pair of transformations sees the maiden's defeat (or assimilation) and the song is roundly enjoyed for its frank sexual connotations. Its title, "The Two Magicians," suggests that the protagonists are indeed seasoned shapeshifters engaged in a totemic initiation. Remnants of this tradition were still apparent in the old religion of Britain, which retained the following song, "The Fith-Fath" or "Shapeshifting Song," in its initiatory rituals:

*I will go as a wren in Spring,*
*With sorrow and sighing on silent wing*
*And I will go in our Lady's name,*
*Aye, till I come home again.*

*We will follow as falcons grey*
*And hunt thee cruelly for our prey.*
*And we will go in the Good God's name,*
*Aye, to fetch thee home again.*

*I will go as a mouse in May,*
*In fields by night, in cellars by day.*
*And I will go in our Lady's name,*
*Aye, till I come home again.*

*We will follow as black tom cats*
*And hunt thee through the corn and vats.*
*And we will go in the Good God's name,*
*Aye, to fetch thee home again.*

*I will go as an Autumn hare,*
*With sorrow and sighing and mickle care.*
*And I will go in our Lady's name,*
*Aye, till I come home again.*

*We will follow as swift greyhounds,*
*And dog thy tracks by leaps and bounds.*
*And we will go in the Good God's name,*
*Aye, to fetch thee home again.*

*I will go as a Winter trout*
*With sorrow and sighing and mickle doubt*
*And I will go in Our Lady's name,*
*Aye, till I come home again.*

*We will follow as otters swift*
*And snare thee fast ere thou canst shift*
*And we will go in the Good God's name,*
*Aye, to fetch thee home again.*

This traditional initiatory song has hidden its true nature by the use of "Our Lady's name" and "the Good God's name." In this instance, the initiate puts him- or herself under the protection of the dark woman of knowledge, the Goddess herself, while the initiators pursue in the name of the Wild Herdsman. The pattern in all instances is remarkably consistent, whether the initiator is male or female.

While both Ceridwen and the blacksmith of "The Two Magicians" appear to modern eyes as predators, in the totemic initiation they are the initiators. Traditionally, the blacksmith was a man of magical powers whose ability to work metals was a godlike skill; it put him in direct contact with otherworldly forces and often enabled him to act in a priestlike capacity. Ceridwen, with her cauldron of herbs which boils for a year and a day, is also an alchemist in the transformational process. They are both fosterers and teachers.

The turning of the totems does not imply a fleshly shapeshifting of the initiate, but a ritual encounter and understanding of the totems whereby animal and human natures are able to meet and meld. The ritual polarity in this scenario is one of dynamic tension, not of mundane sexual congress. Within this alchemical embodiment, one being's power is available to another, but can be assimilated only in a state of grace, which is why the transformation of the initiate renders the subject into one newly born with both innocence and full knowledge, like Mabon and Taliesin. Both have climbed down the tree of tradition, pursuing the totems ever deeper until they find their true selves and oneness with the ancestors. The totems are symbolic of the initiatory changes which are wrought within the subject.

This pattern of initiator and initiate is consistent within the *Mabinogion* as well as within other Celtic texts. The following table gives some of the main correspondences for further study. We have lost Mabon's own initiator from his story, but Apollo, upon whom the Gaulish Maponus was modeled, may supply the deficit. Apollo— hunter, singer, and herdsman—had Cheiron, half man and half horse, for the tutor of his son, Aristaios. We may see Cheiron as a type of Wild Herdsman who shares the nature of the totems in his great power.

| Teacher/Initiator | Initiate Pupil | Totemic Experience |
| --- | --- | --- |
| Cheiron | Aristaios | learns the nature and care of animals |
| Custennin | Culhwch/Goreu | meets the guardian totems of Mabon |
| Math | Gwydion | is changed into stag, sow, and wolf |
| Gwydion | Llew | is changed into an eagle |
| Manawyddan | Pryderi | experiences Otherworld servitude as a foal/horse |

To this list may be added, apocryphally, the transformation of Arthur into many shapes by Merlin, which T. H. White fortuitously stumbled upon.[128] Of these initiate pupils, Aristaios and Pryderi both serve a term as a herdsman, while Culhwch, Llew, and Arthur all marry flower brides in the respective shapes of Olwen, Blodeuwedd, and Gwenhwyfar (Guinevere).

The patterns and characters are converging rapidly into a final pattern and subject. With the help of the totems and the initiator, we may have otherworldly knowledge and skill enough to release Mabon at last.

# 9
# ℳabon, Son of Modron

*The beginning of the Mabinogi of the Maban the*
*Pantocrator, the true and eternal Maponus,*
*and of Rhiannon . . . Matrona of the*
*Calumniations, seven winters at the horse-*
*block telling her own mabinogi of detractions.*

DAVID JONES, *ANATHEMATA*

*Golden, gold-skinned, I shall deck myself in*
*riches, And I shall be in luxury because of the*
*prophecy of Virgil.*

TALIESIN, "CAD GODDEU"

## Perpetual Prisoner and Inner Sovereign

The mystery of Mabon is hard to disentangle and restore. We have
already uncovered much of the background concerning Mabon and
Modron within the *Mabinogion* itself, but it remains to compare our
store of facts. What do we know about Youth, son of the Mother?

The main textual source of Mabon is in "Culhwch and Olwen," as we have seen, yet there are also assorted triads which refer to Mabon, as well as medieval texts from the Arthurian corpus in which he develops into another sort of character. It is also possible to gather more about Mabon from his many aliases who appear as heroes within the *Mabinogion* and related literature, although we must be circumspect when drawing from secondary sources.

Yet texts alone do not give us a full picture. We have only to look at the archaeological evidence to understand that Mabon was a living god among the tribes of Britain. The cult of the Divine Youth, Maponus, was localized in both Gaul and northern Britain. Two significant place-names survive which indicate a connection to this cult: Lochmaben, a village, and Clochmabenstane, a prehistoric stone, both in Dumfriesshire. The stone was a tribal assembly point and stands only one and a half miles from Gretna, where runaway lovers had their marriages solemnized by a blacksmith.[92] The predominant folk theme associated with this place is the story of the harper of Lochmaben who goes to London and steals away King Henry's brown mare. Another place associated with Mabon is Ruabon, the Hill of Mabon, below Wrexham. Significantly, it is on the Severn River that connects this border hill in Wales with Gloucester, or Caer Loyw, the place of Mabon's imprisonment.

The extent of the cult of Maponus cannot be judged prior to the Roman occupation except in the most general terms. After the Roman invasion, it spread swiftly along the length of Hadrian's Wall, where it enjoyed great popularity among the legions stationed on the most northerly frontier of Pax Romana. A great fusion of deities, both Roman and British, occurred at this time so that it is hard to say which gained the upper hand. The Romans swiftly identified many native deities as aspects of their own, but also recognized the *genii loci* of the land in their own right. Maponus was soon identified as a type of Apollo—a Greek aspect which the Romans retained, although they renamed his sister Artemis as Diana.

Apollo had long associations with the British Isles, which, in Pythagorean tradition, were the home of Hyperborean Apollo. Abaris, a priest of these mysteries, had traveled to Greece to meet with Pythagoras, riding on the god's own golden arrow, according to legend. In Greek tradition, the name of Apollo, or Apple-Man, recalled the hidden youth of Britain whose mysteries were celebrated within a circular temple, and whose cult was associated with music and the paradisal Otherworld.[39, 40] The Romans more closely associated Apollo with the sun, while retaining his functions as god of healing and prophecy. To the legionaries stationed on the Wall, men drawn from as far away as North Africa, Bulgaria, and the Rhine, the cold, gloomy northern winter must have seemed intolerable. As a god of the sun, of music, and of hunting, it is not hard to understand the popularity of Maponus/Apollo. For those legionaries, he must have represented the restoration of the light after winter's darkness, and liberation from interminable watches along the Wall.

Several Romano-Celtic stone heads, identified as Maponus, have been discovered along the Wall. Although worn and weathered, the faces are ritually blank, the face of a youth who has suffered or studied over-long. The formation of the features is comparable to those of the saints and of Christ in the *Book of Kells*. There is also a relief, much worn, showing Maponus in a helmet or cap, flanked by two niches holding statues of Apollo and Diana, who are recognizable from their attributes of sun and moon.[90] Apollo Citharoedus, Apollo the Harper, has been identified closely with Maponus,[92] just as Orpheus has adopted the attributes of Apollo in classical legend.

Although there are no similar dedications to Modron, there are numerous inscriptions and reliefs dedicated to the Matres, the Mothers—a triplicity of goddesses peculiar to the Celts which represents the threefold power and transformatory aspects of the Great Mother herself. We must ever remember that Mabon and Modron are merely titles, not names. They are honorifics, in much the same way that in Greek myth the titles Demeter and Kore merely signify the

Mother and the Maiden. Initiates of a particular cult always spoke of their gods in such a guarded manner, delineating the secret names and inner titles from the profane.

From the archaeological evidence, we can see Maponus as a native god who has acquired classical attributes. But such is the subtle power of Celtic symbolism and magical polarity that though he seems to acquire his musical ability from Apollo, his harp is that of a Celtic poet; and while he seems to be a hunter under the protection of Diana, he is the champion of the Matres, swift and eager to avenge, gentle and loving with animals and women.

The hidden mystery of Mabon, son of Modron, is that of the Youth, son of the Mother—a universal archetype of which all peoples have some knowledge, but which has particular native variants depending on the culture and time scale involved. Within British tradition, "Mabon is not only the great prisoner, he is also the immemorial prisoner, the Great Son who has been lost for aeons and is at last found."[44] And if he is without a personal name, what might that name be?

The great *Mabinogion* scholar W. G. Gruffydd suggested that the Four Branches represent the birth, exploits, imprisonment, and death of Pryderi, son of Rhiannon—that they form, in effect, a "Vita Pryderi." To prove this theory, Gruffydd engaged in some factual contortions which have not proved acceptable to other scholars.[46] While grateful for many of his insights, I cannot follow his thesis to the same conclusions. However, a more exciting realization arises from consideration of his argument: that there is an archetypal mystery pattern underlying the *Mabinogion* in which many of its heroes can be seen as types of Mabon. This theory seems less far-fetched when we consider the evidence presented in the *Mabinogion* itself, especially if this is set side by side with the very important textual evidences of Triad 52:

Three Exalted Prisoners of the Island of Britain:
Llyr Half-Speech, who was imprisoned by Euroswydd,
and second, Mabon son of Modron,
and third, Gwair, son of Geirioedd.

And one [prisoner] who is more exalted than the three of them, was three nights in prison in Caer Oeth and Anoeth, and three nights imprisoned by Gwen Pendragon, and three nights in an enchanted prison under the Stone of Echymeint. This Exalted prisoner was Arthur. And it was the same lad who released him from each of these three prisons—Goreu, son of Custennin, his cousin.[5]

Within the Mabon sequence in "Culhwch and Olwen," Mabon identifies himself as follows: "It is Mabon, son of Modron, who is here imprisoned; and no imprisonment was ever so grievous as mine, neither that of Llydd Llaw Ereint, nor that of Greid the son of Eri." This echoes Triad 52, above.

The first prisoner, Llyr Llediath, is the father of the Irish Mannannan, god of the sea and of the blessed islands to the west (llyr means "sea"). We know nothing about his imprisonment, but if we examine the family tree of Bran (chapter 3, figure 2, page 45), we will see that Euroswydd is the second husband of Penarddun who, with Llyr, is the parent of Bran, Manawyddan, and Branwen. It is possible that there is a lost story about Euroswydd, whose name means "splendid enemy," overcoming Llyr and taking his wife for himself, but not a trace of it has survived.

Rachel Bromwich equates Llyr with Lludd Llaw Ereint, Lludd of the Silver Arm, about whom we know much more. We have already encountered Nuadu of the Silver Arm, his Irish equivalent, who, in "The Second Battle of Mag Tuired," lost his hand in combat and had to resign his kingship until a silver arm was made for him. During his retirement Lugh became his champion and eventually his successor.

Nuadu and Llydd/Lludd are the focus of power behind the Romano-British god Nodens, whose temple at Lydney in Gloucestershire is in tempting proximity both to the site of Mabon's imprisonment at Caer Loyw (Gloucester) and to the place of Pryderi's own boyhood seclusion in Gwent-is-Coed. The totemic symbol of Llydd/Nodens is the salmon, while the temple at Lydney seems to have been used for the purposes of temple sleep, whereby clients slept within the temple precincts in order to have their dreams interpreted under the aegis of the god. Mabon's own liberating totem is, of course, the salmon, it being the totem of wisdom. The method of dream incubation practiced at Lydney seems to have been based on the standard Aesculepian model in which, after prayers, offerings, and preparations, the client would enter an *abaton* or sleeping cubicle to receive the oracular dream of the god, which would subsequently be interpreted by the resident priesthood. It is also in such conditions—in the darkness of an enclosure—that the poets of the ancient Celtic peoples incubated their poetry. Yet there is little of the youth about Llydd/Nodens that encourages us to associate him with Mabon. The silver-handed one is a god nearer in character to Pen Annfwn, albeit a Neptunian interpreter of unconscious states. He is one of the deep guardians from an earlier level of belief.

What of the third prisoner of the triad? We have already seen how Pryderi is closely associated with Mabon's own pattern from the "Preiddeu Annwfn":

> *Predestined was Gweir's captivity in Caer Sidi*
> *According to the tale of Pwyll and Pryderi.*

The myths of Gweir, Pwyll, and Pryderi are not associated accidentally. Pryderi is such a prisoner as Mabon, linked through the name Gweir, one who stands in a long line of prisoners, for his own father had already endured a year in Annwfn before assuming the title of honors of that place.

Who is Gwair son of Geirioedd? This Gweir is the same as Gwair, the prisoner mentioned in the "Preiddeu Annfwn," who is bound by the heavy blue chain in the Underworld. In Welsh, the word *gweir* means "hay," as well as "hoop" or "circle." This is highly reminiscent of the incident in "Manawyddan, Son of Llyr" where Pryderi, son of Rhiannon, is decoyed into an otherworldly castle in which stands a marble slab with a golden bowl upon it. Attached to the bowl are chains that reach to the sky. As soon as Pryderi touches the bowl, his hands become stuck to it. Rhiannon, discovering where he has gone and finding him in the castle, also becomes stuck to the bowl. Both then vanish along with the castle. Manawyddan has to use all of his cunning to restore them to the Middleworld again and ultimately forces their captor to release them from their enchantment. Mother and son then relate where they have been: "Pryderi has had the knockers of the gate of the court about his neck, and Rhiannon has had the collars of the asses, after they have been carrying hay, about her neck. These have been their fetters."

We remember that in "Pwyll, Prince of Dyfed," after Pryderi has been abducted at birth, Rhiannon is forced to tell her story at the gate while, like a horse, she must offer to bear guests into the hall on her own back. We also recall that when Pryderi is rediscovered, it is in a stable that he's found. Both Mother and Son have been translated, acquiring equine functions or associations. But what has this to do with Gweir?

The story of Pryderi and Rhiannon's imprisonment in the Other-world has an alternative title, "Mabinogi Mynnweir a Mynord"—"The Story of the Hay Collars and the Doorknockers," which are the emblems of their imprisonment and servitude. Rhiannon bears the horse collar about her neck after the horses have been bearing the gweir, or hay. Gweir is a kind of mystery name for the one who springs up like grass and is cut down again. This image of grass from deep within the British tradition is paralleled by the eastern Mediterranean mystery cults whose emblem is "a grain of wheat reaped in silence." Gweir is an epithet for the famous prisoner in Annwfn.

Yet, what of Mabon's own words concerning the imprisonment of Greid ap Eri: "No imprisonment was ever so grievous as mine, neither that of Llydd Llaw Ereint, nor that of Greid the son of Eri"? Is there another identification clue here? We will remember that one of the reasons Culhwch needs Mabon is that he is the only one able to handle the hound Drudwyn of Greid ap Eri. This itself suggests that Mabon is merely the latest in a series of prisoners. The site of Gweir's imprisonment is said to be Lundy Island, known in Welsh as Ynys

Weir, the Island of Gweir. In British and Irish myth, the islands off the western seaboard have the reputation of being otherworldly places.

This pattern of imprisonment is not about being held in an ordinary prison for any ordinary crime, but rather seems to be a form of initiatic imprisonment, a mystery that we cannot fully understand. These famous prisoners are remembered as if they had performed some kind of public service on behalf of all people.

As Gware Wallt Euryn, a corruption of his childhood name, Gwri Wallt Euryn, Pryderi is textually linked with Mabon, son of Mellt (lightning). It is also not without significance that the search for Mabon begins with the blackbird of Cilgwri: Gwri is Pryderi's fosterage name, and Cilgwri means "the retreat of Gwri," which is the place of his fostering. And who is the blackbird but one of Rhiannon's own totemic birds that sing the way between the worlds?

Gwri, Gwair, and Gwion: A definite tradition of famous prisoners cross-tracks the Mabon pattern. Yet we are told there is a still more famous prisoner, and are fortunate that the lode-bearing evidence of the Arthurian corpus has such perennial power to move and delight. Whatever is told of lesser heroes becomes lodged in the legend of Arthur so that long-dead traditions live through him. If we look again at Triad 52, we see that Arthur spends three sets of three nights in different captivities. These may be seen as parallel imprisonments to those endured by Taliesin in the prison of Arianrhod. The captivities are:

1.  Within Caer Oeth and Anoeth

2.  By Gwen Pendragon

3.  In an enchanted prison under the Stone of Echymeint.

In "Culhwch and Olwen," we recall, Arthur's porter, Glewlwyd, enumerates the many places to which he has accompanied his king: "I was once in Caer Oeth and Anoeth, in Caer Nefenhir of the Nine Natures." *Anoeth* means both "difficult'" and "a wonder," reminding us of the twin gifts of the blow and wonder of the Mound of Arberth that are so amply meted out to Pwyll and Rhiannon. These Caers have a fabulous air about them and perhaps represent the choice of pathways for those who seek to steer between ease and hardship in their quest, much as the queen of faery invites her protégés to choose among the hard, easy, and middle way to their destination.[98] In this captivity the Pendragon goes down to fetch the wisdom of the ancestors and to become Pen Annwfn in his turn.

No such character as Gwen Pendragon appears anywhere in Arthurian legend. *Gwen,* as an adjective, merely means "white." Some scholars have considered the possibility of Uther as a correspondence because in two Irish Arthurian romances Uther is rendered Uighir Finndraeguin, "the white dragon."[5] This, however, seems an unlikely explanation, for in British symbolism, the white dragon is understood to be emblematic of the Saxons, Britain's enemy.[37, 97] This may suggest a much more likely answer: Arthur, as the Red Pendragon, was at some time imprisoned among the camp of his Saxon counterpart, the White Pendragon. But we cannot go any further down this chesslike road.

Last, there is Arthur's enchanted prison under the Stone of Echymeint. This has never been identified. Immediately parallel, two such imprisoning stones are: the stone under which Lunet is trapped in "The Lady of the Fountain" and the rock or tower which encloses Merlin.

The three prisons of Arthur are a challenge for the serious student of the British mysteries. They represent part of a lost tradition which, like many of the triads and fragmentary poems of Taliesin, remain partially uncovered. We can only pass—with many a backward glance at the clues teasing our understanding. For the purposes of practical research, each captivity may be considered as part of an initiatory cycle of imprisonments within the Otherworld, opportunities for the harrowing of Annfwn by the heroes of their day, the dynamic points of fracture and integration where Arthur joins the succession of the Pendragons, becoming in turn the guardian on the threshold of the worlds.

Let us turn to the final sentence of Triad 52: "and it was the same lad who released him from each of these three prisons—Goreu, son of Custennin." If we turn to the genealogy of Culhwch in chapter 6 (figure 5, page 109), we can see how Goreu, Culhwch, and Arthur are cousins. We will remember that Goreu is hidden in a cupboard by his mother, for fear of Yspaddaden, who has slain twenty-three of her sons, until Cai comes and makes the boy a companion and page. During the attainment of Wrnach's sword, the boy fights his way across three courtyards and gains entrance to the giant's castle. For this feat, the hitherto unnamed boy is called Goreu, or "the best."

Goreu is uniquely suited to act in the role of liberator of Arthur because he combines the qualities of prisoner and champion. To summarize: He is a yellow-haired boy (like Gwri); he is himself imprisoned by his own mother for his own safety (like Peredur); he is the cousin of Arthur and wielder of the sword of light which illuminates the way in Annwfn for Arthur; and he avenges the wrongs endured by his family through slaying the giant who oppresses them (like Lugh). Goreu plays an important part in the succession of the Pendragons in that he cuts through the restrictive layers of custom, releasing all three role-bearers to succeed to their next role, releasing them from former cycles of responsibility and initiating them into the next. We must also consider the name Goreu as a title which is given to the best champion, to the *lleminawc* or "leaping one" who cuts the Gordian knot, bounding over all obstacles to come to the point of the quest.

The path of Goreu is one taken by every champion of the land in every generation, a path that leads through difficulties and across cyclic barriers in order to empower the next Pendragon. We may see, then, that the role of Mabon is a dual one: He bears responsibilities and burdens and releases others from them; he is both prisoner and champion.

The wielder of the sword of light in the "Preiddeu Annwfn" is Lleminawg, whom we have identified with Llew Llaw Gyffes and the Irish Lugh. One of the stanzas of the graves in the poem reveals the correspondence between the prisoner and the champion:

> *The grave in the upland of Nantlleu,*
> *Nobody knows its properties:*
> *It is Mabon's, the swift son of Modron.*[88]

Nantlleu is the place where Llew perched while in his totemic shape as an eagle, the place where Gwydion magically retrieved Llew's soul, conjuring it back into his body. In Welsh folklore it is also traditionally the place named for the mysterious Aurwrychan, or golden-bristled beast that was hunted and killed at this spot.[88] Is this the beast with "seven score links upon his collar" that is guarded for the Mab Darogan, the Son of Destiny who is prefigured in the "Preiddeu Annfwn"?

The grave in Nantlleu may have strange properties—but as a grave for Mabon? Such a consideration is as heretical a prospect as a grave for Arthur, to those who expect his return! Let those who come after us find graves for gods. If Mabon and Arthur should ever leave us, their aerie will be an otherworldly one from which they pass within to become guardians, only to reemerge. All who have negotiated the path of Goreu become immortal and the dust does not claim them. Maponus, the avenging hunter, still rides the northern hills just as Maponus, the harper, still sings under them.

## The Lady's Champion

The Celtic sources for Mabon were sufficiently strong to project the archetype of the prisoner/champion into the Arthurian literature of the Middle Ages where Mabon lived on under other guises, such as Mabuz and Mabonograin. And while Modron is noticeably absent from the early Celtic narratives which survive, her role is more clearly defined in the medieval texts, where she appears in the guise of many otherworldly women, including Arthur's half sister, Morgan.

Mabon reappears as the evil knight, Mabuz, in *Lanzelet,* an Arthurian text written in Middle High German by Ulrich von Zatzikhoven, a Swiss priest who reworked this story from a French original. In this text Lancelot is brought up in seclusion by a water fay on an island, where he is taught skill at arms and where he plays prisoner's base. In all respects, the narrative transfers all the qualities of an imprisoned champion to Lancelot and the role of imprisoner to Mabuz. Mabuz's mother is none other than Lancelot's foster mother. But Mabuz himself is a cowardly knight inhabiting the Castle of Death: "Whoever he captured was led into a vast prison, where lay . . . a hundred knights or more. They were all filled with sorrow, perpetually in fear of death. Whenever Mabuz was angry . . . he ordered a man killed."[105]

It is almost as though the term "Mabon's prison" has suffered a radical misunderstanding. Instead of it meaning "the place where Mabon was imprisoned," it has become "the prison guarded by Mabon." Though our Mabon has suffered alteration in *Lanzelet*, it is interesting to note that the story is still true to its archetypal themes: He is still a species of otherworldly guardian, though nearer to the Pen Annwfn than to the Mabon archetype. From the description of the otherworldly island where Lancelot is fostered, it is clearly a proto-Avalon where Modron rules as queen with her maiden attendants.

But *Lanzelet* is already at a remove of secondary translation and too corrupt to be of much use to us. Is there something nearer home which will serve? Luckily there is, in the shape of the related stories stemming from the British tale "Gereint and Enid." This romance appears in most editions of the *Mabinogion*, though it is much later in date than the four branches and the other tales covered in this book. There has been much dispute as to whether "Gereint and Enid" or Chrétien de Troyes's version, "Erec and Enid," was the original. It is evident that both versions come from a common source, whatever the facts of the matter, and that either can be drawn upon confidently as part of the authentic tradition of Mabon's lineage.

In the British story, Gereint, after many adventures, arrives at the castle of Owain and hears about some enchanted games. Knowing nothing about them, Gereint is determined to try his skill, whatever the cost. We take up the story in Chrétien's version, which is fuller. Here Gereint becomes Erec and Owain is Yvain; instead of enchanted games, they are called the Joy of the Court, a strange adventure from which knights do not return. Erec approaches a garden in which this dangerous adventure lies. The garden is bordered solely by air, yet this is impassable save through one narrow entrance. Inside, fruit grows all year round, and he is told that though it is safe to eat the fruit inside the garden, whoever attempts to carry it out becomes at once sealed forever in that place, unable to find the exit. Bewitched by this paradisal garden, Erec strives to recall the mysterious joy which he is seeking to find. He sees a stake, which he is told is intended for his head should he be unsuccessful. (In the British version, the whole garden is surrounded by heads on stakes, in full-blown Celtic fashion.) He sees also the horn which no one has been able to blow. (He who does so will be renowned throughout the land.)

Under a canopy beneath a tree sits a beautiful maiden. When he approaches her, a red knight of great stature challenges him. They fight, and Erec overcomes him. Erec reveals his name to his defeated opponent and demands to know his own name and what the Joy of the Court entails. The Red Knight reveals that he knows Erec's father, King Lac, and was knighted at his court. He has been detained in this garden because of love and service to the maiden under the canopy who made him swear never to leave the garden until a knight should conquer him by force of arms. Being bound by his oath, he has, perforce, defeated and killed many knights who have come to the garden. He continues:

> You have given great joy to the court of my uncle Brandigan and my friends; for now I shall be released from here; and because all those who are at court will have joy of it, therefore those who awaited the joy called it "Joy of the Court." They have awaited it so long that now it will be granted them by you who have won it by your fight. . . . Now it is right that I tell you my name, if you would know it, I am called Mabonograin; but I am not remembered by that name in any land

where I have been, save only in this region; for never, when I was a squire, did I tell or make known my name.[62, 133]

Erec is then asked to blow the horn, which will signal the commencement of the joy. Here is a flowering of Mabon's story! Yet in a German variant text, the amazing similarities among Mabonograin, Mabon, and Pryderi are further reinforced. Mabonograin says:

> Today my troubles are over. . . . Your coming was truly a great blessing for this court, because it lost all its merriment with me and was stripped of its pleasures. There have been no festivals of any kind since I left, because for all my youth and noble birth, I was buried alive—and the Joy of the Court entirely disappeared. But now they shall begin them again, because they have their favourite back. Your brave arm has freed this troubled land from great sorrow and led it back to happiness.[105]

The garden is an otherworldly paradise with its maiden acting as the representative of the Goddess. Yet the Red Knight is trapped there and cannot assume his role as the bringer of joy. He cannot, in fact, succeed to the next appointed role in the cycle. His uncle Brandigan is an echo of Bran, the great Innerworld guardian—the Pen Annwfn who cannot become the Mabon until the Pendragon comes. Just as Mabon's name is unknown, so the red knight's name is unknown and perhaps forgotten. His release can be brought about only by combat with a worthy opponent, just as Mabon can be released only by fighting. And just as Mabon has been imprisoned from the beginning of the world, so Mabonograin has been bound to the garden so long that its paradisal bliss has become a living hell. Only his return can usher in a new reign of joy. The name Mabonograin can be interpreted as "son of the sun" and his enclosure as the place where summer never returns.

Gereint (or Erec) wins great renown for this deed, far beyond the rationale of the story. But if we place him in the line of the great liberators of otherworldly prisoners—with Goreu, Culhwch, and Llew—then this fame seems well earned. Those who take the path of Goreu themselves become candidates in the succession of the Pendragons.

Despite the courtly pleasantries of Chrétien's highly wrought romance, some remarkable features emerge. The impending threat of the stake ready for the loser's head reminds us of Bran's own sacrifice of kingship: It is the action whereby he transfers his power to the Underworld kingdom and becomes a Pen Annwfn. Chrétien's Mabonograin has passed from being a bringer of joy—a role consistent with the Divine Youth, Mabon—into an oppressor of the most restrictive Cronos model. Mabon the youth has become Mabon the titan.

The horn which hangs ready to signal the joy of Mabonograin's return to the world is an important instrument in the lore of recalling the spent Pendragons who use their next cycle to renew their strength through sleep in the Hollow Hills. It is the horn of legend which the shepherd, stumbling into a tumulus, ignores, though he sees Arthur and his court sleeping with a horde of treasure. Disturbed from his otherworldly place of incubation, Arthur berates the unprepared seeker:

> *O woe betide that evil day*
> *On which this witless wight was born.*
> *Who drew the sword—the garter cut,*
> *But never blew the bugle-horn!*[34]

This legend comes from Sewingshields, Northumberland on the Wall, in Mabon's country. The Pendragon can pass from his long rest only when the horn is blown out of the land's need, so that he can walk its hills once more.

Chrétien does not fully understand the role of the lady in the garden; she is a mere cipher of romance, chaining her champion with bonds of love and oaths of loyalty in the way of courtly lovers. Beneath this one-dimensional character stands an otherworldly woman, perhaps Modron herself, in the role of Avalonian queen. The clues to this realization lie in the close association of the hero Owain, under whose aegis these games are held, with Modron. This association is underscored in

"The Lady of the Fountain," one of the late romances from the *Mabinogion*, in which Owain becomes the champion of an otherworldly mistress. But his true relationship with Modron is best understood from a reading of Triad 70, which speaks of "the three fair womb burdens of the Island of Britain," the second of which is "Owain, son of Urien, and Morfudd, his sister, who were carried together *in the womb of Modron, ferch Afallach.*"[5]

Do we have here a vital clue to Mabon's identity? Our long search is almost over, but first we must take ship for the Otherworld and find the lady.

## The Royal Virgin of Avalon

Let us hear a sixteenth-century Welsh story which preserves the bloodline of the mystery:

> In Denbighshire there is a parish which is called Llanferres, and is a Rhyd a Gyfartha [Ford of Barking]. In the old days the hounds of the countryside used to come together to the side of the ford to bark and nobody dared to go to find out what was there until Urien Rheged came. And when he came to the side of the ford he saw nothing there except a woman washing. And then the hounds ceased barking, and Urien seized the woman and had his will of her; and then she said, "God's blessing on the feet which brought thee here." "Why?" "Because I have been fated to wash here until I should conceive a son by a Christian. And I am the daughter of the King of Annwfn, and come thou here at the end of the year and then thou shalt receive the boy." And so he came and he received there a boy and a girl; this is Owein, son of Urien, and Morfudd, daughter of Urien.[5]

The woman washing at the Ford of Barking is none other than Modron—or, we should be careful to note, a woman who bears the title of Modron. After the fashion of women in this role, she bears twins. Owain, like Pryderi, is the child of an otherworldly woman and mortal man; his mother, like Rhiannon, is the daughter of the king of the

Underworld or, according to the Triad 70, the daughter of the king of Avalon.

In Celtic legend the woman who washes at the ford is usually encountered by a hero on the eve of battle: He sees her washing out bloody linen in the waters in an emblematic action that signifies his imminent death. The washer at the ford is invariably a representative of the Dark Goddess or cailleach—the Hecate of Celtic tradition, she whom men fear to encounter, for she usually washes the bloody garments of those destined to fall in battle. In this story Modron appears with her totem hounds at a ford, just as in classical legend Hecate appears at a crossroads with hen dogs who bay at the moon. Her purpose at the ford is solely to conceive a child who will be a savior to her people. In the light of this realization, Rhiannon's appearance at the Mound of Arberth, and her forthright demand of Pwyll that he marry her, can be seen in a more significantly ritual light than before. Both Modron and Rhiannon purposely loiter at the local way-between-the-worlds in order to conceive a son. Modron bears Owain and Morfudd, a twin birth that is a factor which we have already seen as significant to the story of Epona, Rhiannon, and Macha, as well as to the Black Demeter story of Phygalia (see chapter 2).

The story of the Ford of Barking is situated at Llanferres, which is right against Moel Fammau, the Bare Hill of the Mothers. This story tells, perhaps, of a priestess or representative of the Goddess of Sovereignty, Goddess of the Land, or one who lives between the worlds, one who has the sacred blood of the ancestral kindred.

We must not be put off the scent by Triad 70's use of the title Modron as the mother of Urien's children. We know from both Welsh genealogy and Arthurian legend that Owain's mother, Urien's wife, is none other than Morgan, half sister to Arthur, the same Morgan who is elsewhere described as daughter to Rex Avallonis, the king of Avalon.[5] The name Morgan is derived from the same root as the Irish Morrighan, the cailleach aspect of the Goddess, whose totem is a crow. Morgan means "of the sea," and she is associated with Avalon in a very special way. Both Morgan and Modron are affiliated with the aspect of the Goddess that guards the apple orchard of the Otherworld. Modron's realm seems also to be bordered by the sea if we follow the clues supplied by Rhiannon and the water fay of *Lanzelet*. Modron's name is derived from the Celtic Matrona, "great mother," and is the source of the river Marne in France. The cult of the Mothers is attested to all over Britain and Western Europe. There is a Garth Madron, or Madron's garden, in Talgarth in Brecon (west of the Black Mountains, where there is a Ruabon) and a Carn Fadron on the Lleyn peninsula.

The cult of the Mothers, or Matronae, is common to the pan-Celtic countries of Europe. The Museum of London has a relief showing four mothers, though most of the others that have been found depict three. They have bread, cornucopias, fruits, or children on their laps and were central to worship in the Celtic tribes. The expression *bendydd y mamau*, or "blessing of the mothers," remains in the Welsh language as an exclamation or prayer for help. It is also a euphemism for the faery. The blessing of the mothers is still bestowed by Modron, who remains in folk memory as one of the gifting mothers, or the faery godmothers, as we now call them.

We are indeed fortunate that so many texts attest to the role of Modron as she appears in the guise of Morgan, for these help us at last to reconstruct the pattern of female correspondences to the succession of the Pendragons (which are dealt with fully in *King Arthur and the Goddess of the Land*). Morgan is not only the half sister of Arthur but the royal virgin of Avalon, according to both the *Vita Merlini* (c. 1150) and the *Gesta Regnum Britanniae* (c. 1235). She is a mighty queen, attended by her nine maidens, living in an otherworldly state and bliss. Let the *Gesta* tell us about that place:

> This wondrous island is girdled by the ocean; it lacks no good things;
> no thief, reiver nor enemy lurks in ambush there. No snow falls; nei-
> ther summer nor winter rages uncontrollably, but unbroken peace

and harmony and the gentle warmth of eternal spring. Not a flower is lacking, neither lilies, rose nor violet; the apple-tree bears flowers and fruit together on one bough. Youth and maiden live together in that place without blot of shame. Old age is unknown; there is neither sickness nor suffering—everything is full of joy. No one selfishly keeps anything to himself; here everything is shared. A royal virgin is the guardian of this place and everything in it: a nymph of surpassing beauty, attended by the fairest maidens, graceful of feature, sprung of noble ancestors, potent of counsel, renowned for her healing skills.

At the same time when Arthur bequeathed the diadem of royalty and set another king in his place, it was she who brought him over there in the five hundred and forty-second year after the Word became incarnate without the seed of human father. Wounded beyond measure, Arthur took the way to the court of the King of Avalon, where the royal virgin, tending his wound, keeps his healed body for her very own and they live together—if it is lawful to believe this.

Despite that suspicion of doubt from the cleric who transcribed this sequence, we may indeed believe that we have at last found the key which helps turn the cycle of the Pendragons. Morgan, the royal virgin of Avalon, is the Otherworld mistress of Arthur: He goes thither and becomes her consort and champion. Whatever aspect Modron assumes, she remains the Innerworld focus for her hero and champion as he succeeds to the next role, as shown in figure 8 (page 153).

The *Gesta* clearly indicates that Arthur relinquishes his kingship to another voluntarily and "sets another king in his place," but he does not lose the guiding influence of Modron, the Great Goddess. The mother who bore him, the Lady of Sovereignty who upheld his Pendragonship, becomes at last his Otherworld consort and healer. Perhaps now we can see the true nature of Mabon's imprisonment.

Modron, as the Goddess of the Land, is also Fortuna, the turner of the wheel, a figure who can be seen in ancient European iconography

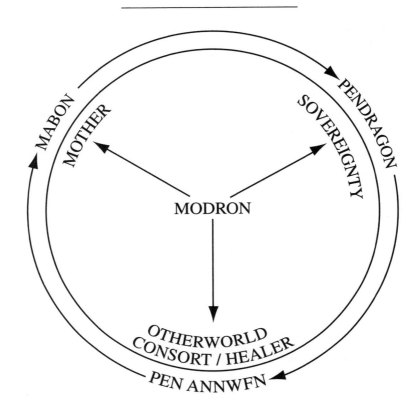

Figure 8. The Goddess of the Wheel

as the goddess of the chariot or cart and in medieval iconography as the Lady Fortuna, whose wheel Arthur dreams about.

In the succession of the Pendragons, the hero who descends to the Underworld becomes the guardian of the otherworldly hallows in the paradise of Avalon. Those who have eaten of the fruit of the apple which grows there can only return as the reborn Mabon, the son of Modron, because that fruit bestows eternal youth with potent restoration of spent strength. Cronos is chained in the middle of his island paradise as Gweir is chained in Annwfn; Merlin does not return from the embraces of Niniane in *Le Val sans retour* of Breton legend; Mabonograin is bound to serve his mistress; Mabon is hidden by his mother in a secret place, as is Goreu; Gwion is assimilated by Ceridwen.

Endlessly the imprisonment theme is retold, and always the storytellers miss the cause: They blame a beguiling woman, an enchantress, or a hag. And even though Taliesin boasts of his initiatory service with the Goddess ("I have been three periods in the prison of Arianrhod"), they still cannot see the pattern.

The farther back we penetrate into the roots of the native mysteries, the clearer it becomes that the hero's imprisonment is a willing one. Merlin is not beguiled by Nimue but goes willingly with her to the abode of bliss at the end of his appointed cycle to become the arbiter and master of wisdom at the side of the Lady of the Hollow Hills, who is the queen of Faeryland, the Dark Woman of Knowledge herself.

In the succession of the Pendragons, the series of captivities becomes clear to us:

| Nature of Captivity | Position | Exemplified By |
| --- | --- | --- |
| initiatory | Mabon | Goreu and Mabon |
| sacrificial | Pendragon | Arthur and Bran |
| redemptive | Pen Annwfn | Bran and Merlin |

Set against this is the pattern of Modron, the Great Goddess:

| Aspects | Exemplified By |
| --- | --- |
| Initiating Mother | Ceridwen; Rhiannon |
| Lady of Sovereignty | Branwen; the Flower Bride in all her guises |
| Otherworld Consort | Arianrhod, Morgan |

Modron is the enabling and empowering goddess who controls the cycle, but, because she is the daughter of Pen Annwfn or Rex Avallonis, she must fight in order to keep the cycle revolving. Whoever becomes her consort automatically defeats her father; and if her consort fails, then she uses him to engender a son who will grow up and defeat his grandfather. The Goddess of the Land requires that her current champion and consort keep the dynamic vitality of the land's life. As soon

as it becomes static or unmoving, restrictive and unyielding, she spins
the wheel.

Modron must use all her power to unseat the titanic strength of
her father, which is why she has to resort to mortal men who are likely
to be worthy champions. Nowhere is there a clearer template for this
theme than in the story of Cronos, Rhea, and Zeus (see chapter 3).
Beside the orthodox legend let us set this Akkadian story, recorded by
Pausanius:

> When Rhea gave birth to Poseidon, she left him in a sheepfold to live
> with the lambs. She told Cronos her baby was a horse and gave him
> a foal to swallow instead of her son, just as later on she gave him a
> stone to swallow wrapped in baby clothes in place of Zeus.[40]

And so Zeus defeats Cronos, as Gwri, the son of another Modron,
defeats his father's ancient enemy from Annwfn. Mabon defeats the
Pen Annwfn and there is an exchange of attributes. But Pen Annwfn
grows even younger in the Otherworld and is again reborn as Mabon,
just as Cronos puts away his oppressive rule to become the king of the
paradisal island.

Modron, whether she is Rhea or Rhiannon, triumphs through her
sons, who are as countless as the blossoms blowing from the bough in
Avalon, ever fruiting and flowering into eternity.

## The Lost Fifth Branch

The patient reader may well wonder whether there is indeed a lost Fifth
Branch to discover, for this tree has more branches than can be count-
ed at one blink, not to speak of innumerable roots to be tripped over.
We have discovered the mythic continuum of the themes linking the
four branches with "Culhwch and Olwen" and "Taliesin"; we have
descended with Arthur to Annwfn; we have met the totems and their
guardian and have sailed to Avalon to meet the Goddess. Where else
can we go but home?

An amalgamation or conflation of the stories in which Mabon's mysteries can be found would make for a very confusing narrative. All that is possible is to establish a pattern, applicable on many levels of storytelling to many protagonists who stand in the place of Mabon. Mabon is "the birth that has never been born, and never will be"[30]; his titles and names are many, but he is recognizably the same, just as the color blue is universally understood no matter what language we speak.

The following table of correspondences, showing the different examples of Mabon and Modron, is in no way a full list; other names will also occur to the reader, drawn from other traditions. It demonstrates the manner in which the mythic pattern reasserts itself throughout the *Mabinogion* as it does within other traditions.

The "father in flesh" of the child in the Mabon position below may find himself out of the picture early in the story, while the "father in spirit" is the most formative influence, sometimes revealed as a foster father, sometimes in the role of the child's grandfather. The women in the Modron role are always liminal; they are mediators between the earthly and otherworldly conditions who have their own location between the worlds.

| Modron | Mabon | Father in Flesh | Father in Spirit |
|---|---|---|---|
| Rhiannon | Gwri/Pryderi | Pwyll | Arawn |
| Custennin's wife | Goreu | Custennin | Yspaddaden |
| Arianrhod | Llew | ? | Gwydion/Math |
| Morgan | Owain | Urien | Rex Avallonis |
| Igrayne | Arthur | Uther | Merlin |
| Eithne | Lugh | Cian | Balor |
| Mary | Jesus | Joseph | Holy Spirit |

The inclusion of the last triplicity of names is not intended blasphemously, but only to show the true universality of this salvific story which has not despised the vehicle of folk story, mythology, or scripture. If the mystery of Mabon and Modron is truly the lost Fifth

Branch, then it is a remarkably ill-hidden mystery, for it lodges in any likely crevice of traditional story. The kernel of the mystery story always follows this pattern: The boy is conceived by a virgin, of an unknown father, or is fathered by a mortal man upon an otherworldly virgin. The virgin's father or tribe rejects her because of a prophecy which will endanger the tribal order of things if she bears a son. She gives birth to her child in great difficulty, friendless but for beasts or servants. The child is in great danger and is hidden among animals or poor people, who also rear and foster him. The qualities of the child soon bring him to the notice of a person of wisdom who agrees to foster the child and teach him his knowledge or skills. The boy is then brought to court, among his own kindred, where he astounds royalty and wise men with his precocity. His mother, who has lost her child or put him from her for safety, receives him again secretly and gives him a name and destiny, arming him with weapons or magical powers.

He becomes either a great hero of deep wisdom and daring or a visionary. He changes the old order of things, brings fresh vigor to the land, and overturns evil customs. His opponents challenge him, but are unable to overcome him, for this can be achieved only when he voluntarily accepts his destiny. Before the final test he has, in the order of things, slept with a virgin unknown to him, who will give birth to the next Mabon in the new cosmic sequence.

He accepts his destiny, encountering all his geis at once. If his life-pattern has been as an earthly ruler or Pendragon, then he submits to his destiny as Pen Annwfn, a withdrawn or Underworld guardian. If he has been a seer-poet, he passes within to become an otherworldly guardian and mentor to future seekers.

Modron's theme is similar. She is a virgin of the royal or holy bloodline serving the land, who will act as the vehicle for Mabon's manifestation. She suffers disgrace and exile from her tribe to give birth to her son. She prepares suitable foster parents for his early rearing, and later supplies a tutor of her choosing. She then prepares a suitable mate for her son, instructing her in the rites of engendering a

Mabon. Last, she oversees and conducts him through the final change of the passing within.

The succession of the Pendragons is continuously occurring and recurring at the thresholds of the worlds, when conditions in generation after generation so dictate. There is always an imminent Mabon, and there is always an appointed guardian. If there is only one story at the heart of the mystery, then this is it. Ultimately it is for you, the reader, to discover the living qualities of Mabon and Modron, remembering the promise that resounds to succeeding generations:

> *For Modron's son they do me call*
> *And Mabon is my name.*
> *Who does me find shall blessing have,*
> *Who frees me shall have fame.*

# $A$fterword:
# The Song of Remaking

*Time is already big by sacred commerce with
the Timeless courses. Fore-chose and lode-
bright, here is the maiden, Equity! The chthonic Old Sower restores the wastelands. The
First-Begotten, of the caer of heaven . . . would
bring his new orient down for our alignment.*

DAVID JONES, ANATHEMATA

$T$he stories of the *Mabinogion* bear their own wisdom into our
hearts, sparking inspiration and longing, but the timeless traditions
preserved here need new storytellers to bring their enchantment so
that the song of remaking can be sung. Mabon and Modron are not
just characters in a Welsh story, but the living exemplars of change and
becoming. Truth and justice are timeless concepts which need human
exemplars.

There is a mystery question: "Who shall be Pendragon in the time
when Saturn shall descend from his sphere?" In other words, how shall
these mysteries find their continuance in our own times?[120] This question is one which Merlin asks Ransom in C. S. Lewis's novel *That
Hideous Strength,* but it is a crucial one which all who work with the
*Mabinogion* must attempt to answer. It underscores the great work of
remaking, which concerns every generation. The prophecy of Saturn's

return to earth and the reinstitution of a Golden Age also concerns the return of the goddess Justice to earth.

We must be cautious in attempting to realize these prophecies within our lives in a literal or political light, and still less should we view the present millennium in an apocalyptic manner. In primal, Otherworld tradition, the Golden Age has long been recognized as the metaphorical glyph of the blessed Otherworld, wherein the sacred harmonies are maintained in balance. It is a condition, not a political reality that can be established anymore than the Holy City of Jerusalem depicted in the biblical Book of Revelation can be imposed upon the terrestrial Jerusalem. In primordial lore, however, the Golden Age is understood to restore the earth rather than to erase its memories.

In classical times the king of the Golden Age was Saturn or Cronos who, as we have read, is imprisoned on the Blessed Isles by his son Zeus, there to rule over the heroes at the westernmost edge of the world.[85] The reign of Saturn/Cronos is called the Saturnia Regna, analogous to the timeless period which Bran and his company enjoyed on the Island of Gwales. It is also the reign of Pen Annwfn, Bran, and Afallach, who, as lord of the Underworld, guardian of the land, and king of Avalon, respectively, are actively present on each level of the Otherworld. When Saturn/Cronos descends from his sphere, his post is vacant, necessitating a new officeholder. When he descends, the Golden Age begins because time no longer runs. An instance of this timeless joy is foreshadowed by the celebration of Saturnalia, when the gateway of the gods is opened at the solstitial gate of midwinter. It is a time of rest in order to celebrate the incarnation of a god who comes to earth, according to the neo-Platonist writings of Macrobius.[71]

This understanding is inextricably tied up with the prophetic writings of Virgil, particularly with his "Fourth Eclogue," wherein we hear about the return of the Golden Age in connection with a Wondrous Child:

> *Now has the last great age begun,*
> *by Cumae's seer foretold;*

*new born the mighty cycles run*
*their course, and quit the old.*

5    *Now too, the Virgin reappears,*
*and Saturn re-controls the spheres.*

*Now is a new race on the way*
*from heaven; do thou befriend*
*the Infant, all but born, whose day*

10    *the iron brood shall end*
*and with the golden fill the earth.*
*O chaste Lucina, speed his birth.*

*Thy own Apollo now is king.*[102]

Line 2 refers to the oracle at Cumae whose Sibyl was under the aegis of Apollo; she was the compiler of the *Sibylline Books,* which were consulted by the Roman augurs at times of national calamity. Line 5 refers to the return to the earth of the goddess Justice, also called Dicte or Astraea. Astraea left the earth for the stars at the end of the Golden Age, becoming associated with the constellation of Virgo.[10, 132] Lucina, line 12, is one of Juno's titles in her role as goddess of childbirth. Her festival, the Matronalia, was celebrated in March, corresponding to the British Lady Day, March 25. We remember that Matrona was also one of the titles of Modron.

The prophesied child of this poem is described in terms of Apollo, although many early Christian commentators excitedly read it as a reference to the messianic coming of Christ. This poem accorded Virgil the status of a wise pagan in Christian eyes, and for the medieval world he had the acclaim of a magician. Both the return of the goddess and the reign of an Apollonian child are indicated in this poem. The myth of the Golden Age exercised the classical imagination a good deal: It was the otherworldly reality made manifest for them, analogous to the Celtic vision of Avalon, complete with Arthur and his court, returning to the earth. This theme, translated into the Kingdom of Heaven, was also a potent hope for successive ages in the West.

If we trace the descent of Saturn through the traditions of the West, we notice that, like T. H. White's Merlin, he "youthens."[128]

> Saturn/Cronos, he whom his own son, Zeus, dethroned by throwing him off his chariot, and banished in chains to a blissful island, where he dwells in sleep. Being immortal, Saturn cannot die, but is thought to live a life-in-death, wrapped in funerary linen, until his time, say some, shall come to awaken again, and he will be reborn to us as a child.[31]

The child is Mabon, the transformed Pen Annwfn, whose star rises once again. What kind of imprisonment and release can be endured and effected by a mere child? To answer this question we must broaden our vision beyond the particularities of one native tradition, and embrace a more cosmic pattern of archetypal occurrence. Mabon's story is a template for other stories; he shows forth the archetype of the Puer Eternus whose youth and strength are polarized against the titan of age and rigidity. Or, to look at this from a spiritual standpoint, it is the battle to release into a new cycle of enlightened strength all prisoners of the planet from the sterility of outworn tradition in which they lie bound.

Each mystery tradition, from pre-classical times onwards, has worked from this central premise: A young and vital savior is, of his or her own free will, made prisoner of an older cycle of spiritual bondage. Through breaking the cycle—usually by means of a simple affirmation of belief or by a redemptive offering—he or she establishes a new pattern of responsibility, which can then be taught to initiates of that cult. This process of redemption is unfortunately often misunderstood by those who have experienced its application only in a narrow religious context. To revalue the process of redemption—a term which means "to buy back" or "to ransom from prison" or "to realign what has been warped or diverted from its prime purpose"—we need to observe the recurrent patterns of cyclic renewal in many traditions. The one who ransoms, either male or female, stands in the place of Mabon, whose task is to share the common lot of the prisoner for the sole purpose of ending all imprisonment in order to realign all beings with their primal directive.

The task of ransoming occurs on all levels of existence, not only in cosmic or Innerworld alignment. Anyone who has succeeded to a post of responsibility is aware of the challenge to maintain the pure archetype of service, whether it be to promote justice, peace, beauty, or wholeness. A welter of lethargy, stale custom, and corruption of practice stands between the maintenance of duty and its actual performance. This is why many positions of public power are formally conferred by the administration of a solemn oath binding the individual to uphold only the purest ideals.

Within the native British tradition, the model of service is the Pendragon and his court. An examination of the Arthurian legends will reveal that this is an ideal not always successfully maintained, for even at the center of the Round Table lurk all the human failings to which flesh is heir. Arthur's reign begins with the scouring of the land of evil custom and the restraint of unchecked forces. Once peace and order are established and complacency settles in, the Pax Arturus begins to wither and the Round Table fellowship is dispersed. And yet it is possible to see how "the old story of the breeding and birth of the infant, his seclusion and foster training, and his final claim to the rightful throne, may be successfully applied as an analogy of the inner development of any man or woman."[98]

The most crucial oath which the Pendragon makes is that by which the sovereign is wedded to the land, a promise which is both literal and figurative. In order to rule a land, the monarch must first of all respect the land. On an inner level, the king joins with Lady Sovereignty, who personifies the land itself. Further to his coronation oath, the king must guard the treasures and traditions of the land—often represented by the hallows, which are the regalia bestowing Innerworld power. These are neither freely given nor thoughtlessly bestowed. Because these hallows reside in the possession of the ancestral guardians, the

Pendragon must venture into the Underworld in order to fetch them. And here the king makes a contract with the Otherworld as well, for whoever ventures thither to fetch the hallows becomes the candidate for guardianship in his turn.[133]

R. J. Stewart has given ample evidence of such figures who have passed within, or who have attuned to an otherworldly resonance in order to become guardians of tradition.[98] Their names are familiar to us from folk story and history alike: The Reverend Robert Kirk, Michael Scot, and Thomas the Rhymer all entered Faery, as the Otherworld was latterly perceived. Some say they strayed there, others that their going had a purpose. Such people pass within the Otherworld in order to exemplify the Son of Destiny, the Redeemer, or Mabon.

We must remember that just as some notable visionary human beings may enter the Otherworld and become effective therein, so also do otherworldly beings enter our world and become manifest here. It is our duty to perceive and cooperate with the harmonics of any new Mabon cycle, which is usually heralded by times of great repatterning and deep changes sending a vibratory ripple through every being. These harmonics and sometimes disturbing vibrational ripples are perceived through means of symbols, archetypes, and cosmic patterns by those who are attuned to their music. Outer events are merely symptomatic of greater changes as Otherworld affects Outerworld. At the intersection of linear time and cosmic time, where Outerworld and Otherworld meet, we must carefully listen and attend.

The descent of Saturn implies the epiphany of Mabon, whose coming accesses primordial energy that resonates with the foundations of the earth as he utters the note of remaking. In order to effect such a change, Mabon is a virgin—that is, one of unadulterated power and purpose in all his phases. As child, youth, or sage, he brings the gift of creation intact from the wells of life. He is Blake's Albion, the glad day breaking on the hillside; he is Apollo, the singer of morning; he is Merlin appearing in Arthur's dream as a young child. Deep dreams bring creation's weave into our hands; we are bespelled and quieted, forgetful of our mundane problems as we listen to the song of creation which Mabon sings.

As Merlin Emrys was sought by Vortigern, who wished to entomb him in the foundations of his tower, so too is Mabon destined to become the prisoner of the planet for the false purposes of our will, unless we discern our motives. For he comes as a virgin to reconcile differences, to bestow the peace of the shepherd upon the flocks of the perplexed who wander into the self-made toils of the world. He comes into manifestation by means of the rainbow bridge of light—a bridge between the worlds which is opened to all seekers of reconciliation. He himself is a ray of sunlight across the waters, down which the influence of the Otherworld is shed and by which we may cross over. "Who would be chief, let him be a bridge."

The answer to the mystery question is a mystery answer: Mabon shall be Pendragon, he who is child of the Modron, daughter of Afallach, ruler of the Blessed Isles. New times need new guardians. The insights of native spirituality combine with those of classical and Christian modes to form a full-voiced choir of response in us. None of these otherworldly visions may be jettisoned or spurned without loss of harmony, for each has been grafted onto our traditional mysteries.

The role of mystery guardian today is open to any who are willing to take up the story of the loss and finding, of the helping animals, of the royal succession of Mabon. It is a story which can be told anywhere to anyone, using the most appropriate names and exemplars of that tradition. It is a story which you can tell. But remember: Those who go in search of the treasures of tradition become candidates for the role of Innerworld guardian. And if that is so, how then shall the mystery question be answered in our own age? Mabon comes in many guises, through many exemplars.

Those who have heard Mabon's lyre become enchanted and inspired; they become rememberers and guardians of the notes which sang the worlds awake. When these notes are sounded harmoniously throughout the world, the otherworldly gates open and many are enabled to pass to and fro between the worlds once more, inspiring and reenchanting our desacralized world. Those with no experience or belief in any other reality than that of their senses rarely access the revitalizing renewal that comes from communion with the deep primordial life that we share between the worlds. Otherworld and our world are two sides of a unitive reality which we all shuttle between in dream and in the creative processes. If these things move you, then the chances are you have already found the door between the worlds. These threshold points of communion have become appropriated by formalized religions who appoint their own priests as custodians, refusing entry to those who come. But the reality is that no one can forbid entry to the birthright that all beings share. No special permission is needed; only a desire to serve and the faculty to perceive are requirements within the indigenous mysteries of the earth.

The *Mabinogion* is but one means of revitalizing the native mysteries of the West, but it is a very effective one because its ancient resonances are couched in the form of myth and story which are the universal language of human creatures. The prime movers in this valuable work realize that for such a revitalization to be effective, it must spring from the very source of the Otherworld tradition, which is timelessly current. Only in this way will it be regenerated. Any attempt to live in the past or indulge in obsessive nationalism renders the transformation powerless, for the primordial mysteries must be accessed at the threshold of universal truth, not drawn from a vein of atavistic homesickness or divisive racism. The work must go forward under the aegis of Mabon, not under the restrictive Cronos aspect.

Who are these people who are rediscovering the ancient mysteries? They are those successors of the seer-poet, the shaman and storyteller who retell the old stories, setting them into relevant contexts for today; those who reenact the mysteries as a sacred anamnesis; those who mediate the life-giving strength of the Otherworld through to our own world. Drawing on many different traditions, they nevertheless have a family likeness. At the deepest levels, the initiates of all mysteries drink from the primal wells of the Otherworld. As artists, singers, and writers their work is imbued with an archetypal force and beauty. As mystics, prophets, and rememberers, their sayings are wise and profoundly moving. As ordinary people who dream extraordinary dreams, their eyes are bright and their hearts compassionate, but their feet are firmly upon the ground.

How is their work accomplished? They turn their faces to the Otherworld, profoundly meditating on its living stories and symbols to find their meaning for our world. They then synthesize their realizations into their own lives. If the mysteries cannot be applied in such a way, then they are redundant and deserve to be forgotten indeed.

The times are at their end and their beginning. The horn is already blowing. Like a titan, imprisoned and encrusted within the carapace of old glories, this world must become young and fresh again. The succession of the Pendragons awaits our capable and daring initiates, and only those who know the inner name of the land may set out on this quest—not only the name of our own land, but of its mother, the Earth herself.

Our collective vocation is to look for the places where the justice of Modron is most needed upon the earth and to invoke Mabon's influence in the darkest of prisons.

> *Dark is the night, far is the dawning,*
> *Sing for the shining of light on the way.*
> *Hearken, be ready, attend to my calling,*
> *Sing all you guardians who wait at the door.*

> Chorus:
> *Sing, sing, sing for the dawning,*
> *Sing for the midnight, the noon and the day.*
> *Sing, sing, sing for the morning,*
> *Sing for the dawning of this glorious day.*

## The Song of Remaking

*Some say that wisdom is born of believing,*
  *Sing for the shining of light on the way.*
*Some say that wisdom is born of deceiving:*
*But wisdom shines bright in the night or the day.*

*Stones they were standing when starlight was*
      *breaking,*
  *Sing for the shining of light on the way.*
*The seas and the rivers attend to their courses,*
*When sunlight and moonlight upon them do play.*

*The old times returning, the new times restoring,*
  *Sing for the shining of light on the way.*
*From the beginning the old ones are singing*
*The song of the making that welcomes this day.*

CAITLÍN MATTHEWS

# Appendix:
# Three Mystery Songs
# to Mabon

### *The Song of Mabon*
#### A mystery sequence for voice and harp

Chorus:
*Oh do you know, or have you heard*
*Of Mabon, Modron's son?*
*Who from his mother's womb was reived*
*When time was first begun?*

Verse:
*Go ask the ousel on the green if beast or bird on earth*
*Knows aught of Mabon, Modron's son, who vanished at his birth.*

(Sung by Blackbird)
*When first I came into this place, a mighty anvil stood;*
*But I have pecked it all away, right down unto the wood.*

*A race of beasts more ancient yet there lives upon the earth.*
*Go ask the stag upon the plain if he can help you search.*

THREE MYSTERY SONGS TO MABON

Chorus

(Sung by Stag)
*When first I came into the plain, a lone oak sapling grew,*
*Became a tree of many tines, now branches it has few.*

*Though I have roved the plains so wide, of Mabon I've seen none;*
*Go ask the owl of the wood, if he knows Modron's son.*

Chorus

(Sung by Owl)
*When first I came, a valley bare raised upon a wooded glen,*
*But twice it was uprooted by hordes of greedy men.*

*Though I have flown this valley wide, since day was birthed with*
    *dawn,*
*I never met with Modron's son, though thin my wings have worn.*

*A race of birds more ancient yet still wings upon the air,*
*Go ask the eagle of the heights if he knows Mabon's lair.*

Chorus

(Sung by Eagle)
*When first I came I pecked the stars each evening from this height;*
*But now it is a bare span tall, and hungry is the night.*

*I stuck my talons in a fish: he drew me to the deep;*
*We made a peace the two between—go see the salmon leap.*

Chorus

(Sung by Salmon)
*With every tide I heard a cry, in every stream a moan;*
*I swam to Gloucester's walls so high, and found a wicked wrong.*

*Upon my back I shall you bear, upon my shoulders strong,*
*And we shall find who is it groans within these walls alone.*

## THREE MYSTERY SONGS TO MABON

*Oh tell us who is it laments within a house of stone:*
*But Mabon, born of Modron's womb, within these walls alone.*

(Mabon)
*Now I have dwelt within this house before the birth of time;*
*Three hours from my mother's womb, and what was then my*
  *crime?*

*Go back beyond the birth of time and see the giant stand.*
*He swallowed me up and snatched me from my own sweet mother's*
  *hand.*
*For Modron's son they do me call and Mabon is my name;*
*Who does me find shall blessing have, who frees me shall have fame.*

CAITLÍN MATTHEWS

## Mabon's Hunt
### To be chanted with drum and horse brasses

*Seek for the Mabon;*
*He shall be found.*
*Son of the Modron,*
*Lord of the Hound.*

*Seek for the Modron,*
*Under the hill.*
*Seek for the salmon,*
*Swimming there still.*

*Seek for the Modron*
*In the wood;*
*There she sorrowed*
*And there she stood.*

*Animals come*
*At break of day,*
*To wash the stain*
*Of the blood away.*

*Seek for the Mabon;*
*He shall be found*
*Near the smithy,*
*Beneath the ground.*

*Seek for the Mabon,*
*Under the hill.*
*There he waits*
*Till she eats her fill.*

*Seek for the Modron*
*Cantering by;*

*The hill her manger,*
*Her stall the sky*

*Animals bow*
*As she rides past;*
*Modron first*
*And Modron last.*

*Seek for the Mabon;*
*Call his name.*
*He shall enter*
*And join our game.*

*Mabon dances*
*Like the sun;*
*Mabon's hounds*
*And hunters run.*

*How they canter*
*And how they cry:*
*Modron's daughters*
*Stand on high.*

*Seven bright shiners*
*Hold the glass,*
*Watching their brother*
*Hurrying past.*

*When sun and moon*
*Stand in one sky:*
*Mabon and Modron!*
*We shall cry.*

CAITLÍN MATTHEWS

## Mabon's Journey
### Song for two voices

Modron: *Where are you going to, Mabon, my son?*
*Where are you going to, my pretty one?*

Mabon: *I'm bound on a journey, Mother, he said,*
*To the lands of the living, the lands of the dead.*

Modron: *Where is that country, Mabon, my son?*
*Who is its ruler, my pretty one?*

Mabon: *Where the cold winds cease blowing, where snows*
*never fall,*
*To the place where the Sleeping Lord sits in his*
*hall.*

Modron: *How will you journey, Mabon, my son?*
*What will you fetch there, my pretty one?*

Mabon: *On the ship that is silent, by the cold river deep,*
*And I'll bring back the cauldron from the Lord*
*locked in sleep.*

Modron: *When will I see you, Mabon, my son?*
*When will I kiss you, my pretty one?*

Mabon: *When the ages turn round at the brink of the sun,*
*When the birds at the wellhead have ended their*
*song.*

Modron: *How shall I find you, Mabon, my son?*
*How shall I know you, my pretty one?*

Mabon: *By leaf, flower and feather, by ways high and low.*
*By the brand of the cauldron, the radiant brow.*

CAITLÍN MATTHEWS

# Bibliography

## Textual Sources in Translation

1. Ellis, T. P. and J. Lloyd, trans. *Mabinogion*. London: Oxford University Press, 1929.

2. Ford, P. K., trans. *The* Mabinogi *and Other Medieval Welsh Tales*. Berkeley: University of California Press, 1977.

3. Gantz, J., trans. *Mabinogion*. Harmondsworth: Penguin, 1976.

4. Guest, Lady C., trans. *Mabinogion*. London: Ballantyne Press, 1910.

5. Bromwich, R., trans. *Trioedd Ynys Prydein*. Cardiff: University of Wales Press, 1961.

## General References

6. Allen, R. H. *Star Names: Their Lore and Meaning*. New York, Dover Publications, 1963.

7. Anwyl, E. *Value of the* Mabinogion *for the Study of Celtic Religion*. Vol. 2 of Transactions of the Third International Congress for History of Religion. London: Oxford University Press, 1908.

8. Apollodorus. *The Library*. Vols. 1 and 2. London: Heinemann, 1963, 1976.

9. Apuleius. *The Golden Ass*. Harmondsworth: Penguin, 1950.

10. Aratus. *Phaenomena*. London: Heinemann, 1921.

11. Ashe, G. *Camelot and the Vision of Albion*. London: Heinemann, 1971.

12. Bailey, A. *Treatise on White Magic*. London: Lucis Trust, 1934.

13. Barber, C. *Mysterious Wales*. London: Paladin, 1982.

14. Best, R. I. "Settling of the Manor of Tara." In *Eriu*. Vol. 4, part 2. N.p., n.d.

219

BIBLIOGRAPHY

15. Birley, E. *Maponus: The Epigraphical Evidence.* Vol. 31. Dumfriesshire and Galloway National History and Antiquarian Society Transactions, 1954.

16. Blake, W. *Poetry and Prose.* London: Nonesuch Press, 1975.

17. Brewer, E. *From Cuchulainn to Gawain.* Cambridge: D. S. Brewer, 1973.

18. Brown, A. C. L. "Barinthus." *Revue Celtique* 22 (n.d.): 339–44.

19. ———. *The Origin of the Grail Legend.* Cambridge, Mass.: Harvard University Press, 1943.

20. Bryant, N. *High Book of the Grail (Perlesvaus).* Cambridge: D. S. Brewer, 1978.

21. Byrne, F. J. *The Irish Kings and High Kings.* London: Batsford, 1973.

22. Calder, G. *Auraicept na N'Éces (Scholar's Primer).* Edinburgh: John Grant, 1917.

23. Callimachus. *Hymns and Epigrams.* London: Heinemann, 1921.

24. Campbell, J. F. *Popular Tales of the West Highlands.* 4 vols. London: Wildwood Press, 1983, 1984.

25. Chadwick, N. K. *Poetry and Prophecy.* Cambridge: n.p., 1942.

26. Child, F. J. *English and Scottish Popular Ballads.* 5 vols. New York: Dover Publications, 1963.

27. Cornford, F. M. *Principium Sapientiae.* Cambridge: Cambridge University Press, 1952.

28. Cross, T. P. and C. H. Slover. *Ancient Irish Tales.* Dublin: Figgis, 1936.

29. Crossley-Holland, K. *Norse Myths.* London: Andre Deutsch, 1980.

30. Curtin, J. *Hero Tales of Ireland.* London: Macmillan, 1894.

31. De Santillana, G. and H. Von Dechend. *Hamlet's Mill.* London: Macmillan, 1969.

32. Dillon, M. *Cycles of the Irish Kings.* London: Oxford University Press, Geoffrey Cumberlage, 1946.

33. Dorson, R. M. *Folk Tales Told Round the World.* Chicago: University of Chicago Press, 1975.

34. Embleton, R. *Hadrian's Wall.* Newcastle-upon-Tyne: Frank Graham, 1984.

35. Fontenrose, J. *Python: A Study of the Delphic Myth and Its Origins.* Berkeley: University of California Press, 1959.

36. Forbes, A. R. *Gaelic Names of Beasts, Birds, Fishes, Insects, Reptiles, etc.* Edinburgh: Oliver and Boyd, 1905.

37. Geoffrey of Monmouth. *History of the Kings of Britain.* Harmondsworth: Penguin, 1966.

38. Glob, P. V. *The Bog People.* London: Paladin, 1971.

39. Gorman, P. *Pythagoras.* London: Routledge and Kegan Paul, 1979.

40. Graves, R. *The Greek Myths.* London: Cassell, 1958.

41. ———. *The White Goddess.* London: Faber, 1961.

42. Green, M. J. *The Gods of Roman Britain.* Aylesbury: Shire Archaeology, 1983.

43. Gruffydd, W. J. *Folklore and Myth in the* Mabinogion. Cardiff: University of Wales Press, 1955.

44. ———. *Mabon and Modron.* Cardiff: University of Wales, W. J. Gruffydd Collection, n.d.

45. ———. *Math vab Mathonwy.* London: Oxford University Press, Humphrey Milford, 1928.

46. ———. *Rhiannon.* Cardiff: University of Wales Press, 1953.

47. Hall, L. B. *Knightly Tales of Sir Gawain.* Chicago: Nelson-Hall, 1976.

48. Hayward, R. *Border Foray.* London: Arthur Barker, 1957.

49. Hill, J. *The Tristan Legend.* Leeds: University of Leeds Press, 1977.

50. Hull, E. "The Hawk of Achill." In *Folklore.* Vol. 43. N.p., 1932.

51. Humphrey, E. *The Taliesin Tradition.* London: Black Raven Press, 1983.

52. Hyde, D. "Adventures of Leithin." In *Celtic Review* 10 (1914–16): 116–43.

53. Jackson, K. H. *International Popular Tale and Early Welsh Tradition.* Cardiff: University of Wales Press, 1961.

54. Jarman, A. O. H. *A Guide to Welsh Literature.* Vol. 1. Swansea: Christopher Davis, 1976.

55. John, I. B. *The Mabinogion.* London: David Nutt, 1901.

56. Jones, G. Kings, *Beasts and Heroes.* London: Oxford University Press, 1972.

57. Kerenyi, C. *Gods of the Greeks.* London: Thames and Hudson, 1951.

58. Kitteridge, G. L. *A Study of Gawain and the Green Knight.* Gloucester, Mass.: Peter Smith, 1960.

59. Lethbridge, T. C. *Witches.* London: Routledge and Kegan Paul, 1962.

60. Levi, P. *A History of Greek Literature.* London: Viking, 1985.

61. Lewis, C. B. *Classical Mythology and Arthurian Romance*. London: Oxford University Press, 1932.

62. Loomis, R. S. *Arthurian Tradition and Chrétien de Troyes*. New York: Columbia University Press, 1949.

63. ———. *Celtic Myth and Arthurian Legend*. New York: Haskell House, 1967.

64. ———. *Wales and the Arthurian Legend*. London: Folcroft Library Editions, 1977.

65. MacCana, P. *Branwen, Daughter of Llyr*. Cardiff: University of Wales Press, 1958.

66. ———. *The Mabinogi*. Cardiff: University of Wales Press, 1977.

67. MacQueen, J. "Maponus in Medieval Tradition." In Dumfriesshire and Galloway Natural History and Antiquarian Society Transactions. Vol. 31. N.p., 1954.

68. Magnen, R. *Epona: Déesse Gauloise des Chevaux*. Paris: Delmas, 1953.

69. Matthews, C. "The Rosicrucian Vault as Sepulchre and Wedding Chamber." In *Underworld Initiation*, edited by Bob Stewart. Wellingborough: Aquarian Press, 1985.

70. ———. "Sophia as Companion on the Quest." In *At the Table of the Grail*, edited by J. Matthews. Routledge and Kegan Paul, 1981.

71. Matthews, C. and J. Matthews. *The Western Way*. Vols. 1 and 2. London: Arkana, 1985.

72. Matthews, J. *The Grail: Quest for the Eternal*. London: Thames and Hudson, 1981.

73. Matthews, J. and B. Stewart. *Warriors of Arthur*. Poole: Blandford Press, 1987.

74. Morris, J. *The Matter of Wales*. London: Oxford University Press, 1985.

75. Newstead, H. *Bran the Blessed*. New York: Columbia University Press, 1939.

76. North, F. J. *Sunken Cities*. Cardiff: University of Wales Press, 1957.

77. Nutt, A. "Branwen, Daughter of Llyr." In *Folklore Record*. Vol. 5. N.p., 1882.

78. O'Flaherty, W. D. *Women, Androgynes and Other Mythical Beasts*. Chicago: University of Chicago Press, 1980.

79. Oosten, J. G. *War of the Gods*. London: Routledge and Kegan Paul, 1985.

80. O'Rahilly, T. F. *Early Irish History and Mythology.* Dublin: Dublin Institute for Advanced Studies, 1976.

81. Ovazza, M. "D'Apollon Maponos à Mabonograin." In *Actes du 14ième Congrès International Arthurian.* Rennes: Presses Universitaires, 1984.

82. Parker, W. *Gaelic Fairy Tales.* Glasgow: Archibald Sinclair, 1908.

83. Pearce, S. M. "Cornish Elements in the Arthurian Tradition." In *Folklore.* Vol. 85. N.p..

84. Plutarch. *Moralia.* Vol. 5. London: Heinemann, 1947.

85. ———. *Moralia.* Vol. 12. London: Heinemann, 1958.

86. Powys, J. C., *Obstinate Cymric.* London: Village Press, 1973.

87. Rees, A. and B. Rees. *Celtic Heritage.* London: Thames and Hudson, 1961.

88. Rhys, J. *The Hibbert Lectures.* London: Williams and Norgate, 1888.

89. ———. *Studies in the Arthurian Legend.* London: Oxford at the Clarendon Press, 1891.

90. Richmond, I. A. "Two Celtic Heads in Stone from Corbridge, Northumberland." In *Dark Age Britain,* edited by D. B. Harden. London: Methuen, 1956.

91. Ross, A. *Pagan Celtic Britain.* London: Routledge and Kegan Paul, 1967.

92. ———. *A Traveller's Guide to Celtic Britain.* London: Routledge and Kegan Paul, 1985.

93. Scott, R. D. *Thumb of Knowledge.* New York: Columbia University Press, 1930.

94. Senior, M. *Myths of Britain.* London: Orbis, 1979.

95. Skeels, D. *Romance of Perceval in Prose (Didot Perceval).* Seattle: University of Washington Press, 1966.

96. Stewart, R. J. *Mystic Life of Merlin.* London: Arkana, 1986.

97. ———. *The Prophetic Vision of Merlin.* London: Arkana, 1985.

98. ———. *The Underworld Initiation.* Wellingborough: Aquarian, 1985.

99. ———. *The Waters of the Gap.* Bath: Bath City Council, 1981.

100. Sutherland, E. *Ravens and Black Rain.* London: Constable, 1983.

101. Kinsella, T., trans. *Tain Bo Cuailnge.* Dublin: Dolmen Press, 1970.

102. Todd, J. and J. M. Todd. *Voices from the Past.* London: Reader's Union, 1956.

103. Tolstoy, N. *The Quest for Merlin*. London: Hamish Hamilton, 1985.

104. Parry, J. J., ed. and trans. *Vita Merlini*. Champaign and Urbana: University of Illinois Press, 1925.

105. von Zatzikhovan, U. *Lanzelet*. New York: Columbia University Press, 1951.

106. Williams, G. A. *When Was Wales?* Harmondsworth: Penguin, 1985.

107. Wood, J. "The Elphin Section of the Hanes Taliesin." *Etudes Celtiques* 18 (1981): 229–44.

## The *Mabinogion* and the Mysteries of Britain in Literature

Please note that F = Fiction, D = Drama, P = Poetry

108. Arden, J. and M. D'Arcy. *The Island of the Mighty*. London: Eyre Methuen, 1973. (D)

109. Ashe, G. *The Finger and the Moon*. London: Heinemann, 1973. (F)

110. Garner, A. *The Owl Service*. London: Collins, 1967. (F)

111. Herbert, K. *The Ghost in the Sunlight*. London: Bodley Head, 1986. (F)

112. ———. *Lady of the Fountain*. Frome: Bran's Head Books, 1982. (F)

113. ———. *Queen of the Lightning*. London: Bodley Head, 1984. (F)

114. James, J. *Not for All the Gold in Ireland*. London: Cassell, 1968. (F)

115. Jones, A. R. *Presenting Saunders Lewis*. Cardiff: University of Wales Press, 1973. (D)

116. Jones, D. *Anathemata*. London: Faber, 1952. (P)

117. ———. *In Parenthesis*. London: Faber, 1937. (P)

118. ———. *The Sleeping Lord*. London: Faber, 1974. (P)

119. Kipling, R. *Puck of Pook's Hill*. London: Macmillan, 1983. (F)

120. Lewis, C. S. *That Hideous Strength*. London: Bodley Head, 1945. (F)

121. Morris, K. *The Fates of the Princes of Dyfed*. North Hollywood: Newcastle Publishing Company, 1978. (F)

122. Powys, J. C. *Porius*. London: Village Press, 1974. (F)

123. Walton, E. *Children of Llyr*. New York: Ballantyne, 1971. (F)

124. ———. *Island of the Mighty*. New York: Ballantyne, 1964. (F)

125. ———. *Prince of Annwfn.* New York: Ballantyne, 1974. (F) (126)

126. ———. *The Song of Rhiannon.* New York: Ballantyne, 1982. (F)

127. Watkins, V. *Ballad of the Mani Lwyd.* London: Faber, 1946. (P)

128. White, T. H. *The Once and Future King.* London: Collins, 1952. (F)

## Other Publications

129. Garner A. *The Voice That Thunders.* London: Harville, 1997.

130. Haycock, M. "Preiddeu Annwfn and the Figure of Taliesin." In *Studia Celtica,* 18/19 (1983).

131. Hayton, S. *The Last Flight.* Edinburgh: Polygon, 1993. (F)

132. MacKillop, J. *Dictionary of Celtic Mythology.* Oxford: Oxford University Press, 1998.

133. Matthews, C. *King Arthur and the Goddess of the Land.* Rochester, Vt.: Inner Traditions, 2002.

134. ———. *Celtic Book of the Dead.* London: Connections, 1999.

135. ———. *Celtic Love.* San Francisco, HarperSanFrancisco, 1999.

136. ———. *Celtic Spirit.* San Francisco, HarperSanFrancisco, 1998.

137. ———. *Celtic Wisdom Sticks.* London: Connections, 2001.

138. ———. "Princess Diana: Flower Bride and Queen of Hearts." In *Mythological Europe Revisited,* edited by Fons Elders. Brussels: VUB University Press, 2000.

139. ———. *Sophia: Goddess of Wisdom, Bride of God.* Wheaton: Quest Books, 2000.

140. ———. "The Voices of the Wells: Celtic Oral Themes in Grail Literature." In *At the Table of the Grail,* edited by John Matthews. N.p.: Watkins Publications, 2002.

141. Matthews, C., and John Matthews. *The Arthurian Tarot.* London: Harper Collins, 1990.

142. ———. *The Encyclopedia of Celtic Wisdom.* London: Rider, 2001.

143. ———. *Ladies of the Lake.* London: Harper Collins, 1994.

144. Matthews, J. *Celtic Shaman.* London: Rider, 2001.

145. ———. *Celtic Totem Animals.* Glastonbury: Gothic Image, 2002.

146. ———. *Song of Taliesin.* Wheaton: Quest Books, 2001.

BIBLIOGRAPHY

147. ———. *Taliesin: The Last Celtic Shaman*. Rochester, Vt.: Inner Traditions, 2002.

148. Matthews, J. and Caitlín Matthews. *The Encyclopedia of Celtic Myth and Legend*. London: Rider, 2002.

149. Stephens, M. *The Oxford Companion to the Literature of Wales*. Oxford: Oxford University Press, 1986.

150. Stewart, R. J. *The Power Within the Land*. Shaftesbury: Element Books, 1994.

For more details about courses, events, and books by the author, visit www.hallowquest.org.uk. Or write, enclosing a self-addressed envelope and three paid international reply coupons, available from post offices, to Caitlín Matthews, BCM Hallowquest, London WC1N 3XX, U.K.

# Index

226

227

# Books of Related Interest

**KING ARTHUR AND THE GODDESS OF THE LAND**
The Divine Feminine in the *Mabinogion*
*by Caitlín Matthews*

**TALIESIN**
The Last Celtic Shaman
*by John Matthews with additional material by Caitlín Matthews*

**KING OF THE CELTS**
Arthurian Legends and Celtic Tradition
*by Jean Markale*

**THE MAKING OF A DRUID**
Hidden Teachings from *The Colloquy of Two Sages*
*by Christian J. Guyonvarc'h*

**THE CELTS**
Uncovering the Mythic and Historic Origins of Western Culture
*by Jean Markale*

**WOMEN OF THE CELTS**
*by Jean Markale*

**THE CELTIC WISDOM TAROT**
*by Caitlín Matthews*
*Illustrated by Olivia Rayner*

**THE CELTIC BOOK OF DAYS**
A Guide to Celtic Spirituality and Wisdom
*by Caitlín Matthews*

Inner Traditions • Bear & Company
P.O. Box 388
Rochester, VT  05767
1-800-246-8648
www.InnerTraditions.com

Or contact your local bookseller